Rhetoric
for
Exposition

Rhetoric for Exposition

ROGER D. CHITTICK
Fresno State College

ROBERT D. STEVICK
University College of the West Indies

New York
APPLETON-CENTURY-CROFTS, INC.

691-2

Library of Congress Card Number: 61-8390

PRINTED IN THE UNITED STATES OF AMERICA

Preface

FOR some time we have felt the need for a rhetoric textbook essentially descriptive in procedure rather than prescriptive, or one that would at least derive its prescriptions by means of descriptive analysis of writings notable for rhetorical excellence. Present rhetoric texts are ineffective, or not so effective as they ought to be, because they reverse what seems to us to be the more successful pedagogical procedure. That is, they begin by saying, in effect, "this is what definition (or argument, or whatever) ought to do" and then point out examples of definitions and arguments which fit their prescriptions. It seems to us sounder pedagogy to begin with a skilled definition or argument, then to describe how it is constructed, and from the description to derive some principles of rhetoric.

A second weakness in current rhetoric texts is that they are generally slanted toward a literary point of view. They have chapters on narration, description, and the like; even their discussions of argument, diction, and definition have a strong literary bias, appropriate only if college courses in composition are to be introductory courses in creative writing. But the kind of writing skill most college students actually need as students and citizens is more modest. In short, for the first two years in college English, they need a rhetoric that concentrates on the practical, everyday use of written English.

Thirdly, although almost all current rhetoric texts deal with logic to some extent, none of them provides adequate treatment of logic as it occurs in the ordinary language of serious exposition and argument—in newspaper editorials, textbooks, and magazine articles. In most, only the categorical syllogism is discussed, and it is presented only through such examples as "All men are mortal/Socrates is a man/therefore . . ."; "All fish are vertebrates/A cod is a fish"; and so on. This has, of course, some value to the average student, but he is rather put upon to find it. Syllogisms are indeed basic to a large portion of our written discourse, but hypothetical and disjunctive syllogisms (*if-then* and *either-or*) are more frequent in ordinary discourse than categorical syllogisms. Yet only a handful of texts consider reasoning other than categorical, and these few consider it only casually—in two pages or less. In order to provide an extended piece of expository discourse built around the syllogism, a teacher must carefully select a companion volume of readings. Moreover, no available rhetoric text even hints at the logical basis of explanation.

Rhetoric for Exposition, on the other hand, is calculated to draw the student, inductively, into an understanding of the conventional forms of expression used in the written discourse of educated Americans. The book's organization, assumptions, and technique are novel in three ways: in the ultratraditional divisions of the discipline of rhetoric; in the assumption that individual responsibility, not a book or a class or a set of rules, enables a student to write and read effectively; and in the technique of close textual analysis—as important to expository prose as it is to literary criticism.

Through examples of good writing on important as well as interesting topics, the student is encouraged to discover and observe principles of rhetoric. Thus, prefaced to most chapters is an essay that the chapter itself analyzes in terms of its principal rhetorical interest. The subject matter of these essays varies widely: philosophic method, history, linguistics, ethics, literary criticism, religious belief, and social economics. Other chapters include short passages from published sources with analysis and comment upon them. Our principal tactic is always to present the student with examples from which he can learn the principles of rhetoric inductively, by close textual analysis.

The assumption that individual responsibility is imperative to both reading and writing underlies the book. This assumption is evident in the exclusion of rules, discussion of the mechanics of writing (spelling, grammar, and punctuation), and any index to usage. Because students have already completed, more or less successfully, several courses in English in high school, they may reasonably be held to competence in the mechanics and common distinctions of written English. Should their competence prove faulty, any of a number of recognized handbooks of English may be urged upon them.

Individual responsibility for rhetoric is also assumed because it is an essential condition of effective writing; expression is improved chiefly by the exercise of choice among alternatives of statement and the individual must explore on his own these alternate choices of words, sentence structure, or total organization.

The major divisions of this book are elemental and of long tradition: definition, classification, procedures of logical inference, explanation, and some nonlogical patterns for the structuring of discourse. The introductory chapter defines the language—a formal written American English—in which skillful use of rhetorical forms will be an asset to all students. Two chapters are devoted to definition. Together with their illustrative essay they present traditional forms of definition—material, formal, functional or final, and historical—and examples varying in length from a sentence to a full-length essay. In another chapter, the principles of classification are analyzed in terms of both the process and the forms of classification. Three chapters consider problems and forms of logic as they are related to rhetoric. A chapter is devoted to each of the logical forms—the categorical, the hypothetical, and the disjunctive; each chapter analyzes a separate essay embodying a logical form. All three deal with deduction in terms of its principal methods and rules, its fallacies, and its implications, as a logical method, for the forms of discourse. Use of the forms of deduction is extended into another chapter in the treatment of explanation. This discussion of the logic of explanation constitutes, we believe, the first treatment of explanation in a rhetoric textbook to include discoveries in scientific philosophy made over the past thirty years. Inductive reasoning is considered as an adjunct of explanation. In the four chapters on logic and explanation, the student can learn as much logic as is relevant to writing without concerning himself with technical problems appropriate only to a logic course proper. Finally, two chapters consider specifically some nonlogical forms for writing, including paradox and thematic structure.

As is apparent, the book deals mainly with the basic traditional forms of expression. There are no chapters devoted specifically to other kinds of rhetorical concepts—to tone, style, metaphor, denotation and connotation, or persuasion. The authors do not believe that these concepts can be dealt with effectively apart from specific contexts, and certainly would not offer a set of rules or abstract discussion of them. In this book, these concepts are dealt with when the context makes them significant, just as in the classroom, where they are most effectively taught in comment on and discussion of student writing.

Exercises, intended to extend the interest of the chapters and to make the student aware of the degree and implications of his new knowledge, are provided at the end of each major division. Because experience shows their necessity, brief sections on outlining, the nature of the report, and the problems of correct acknowledgment —footnotes, bibliography, quotation, plagiarism, and the like—are included as appendices.

To form the habit of critical reading for rhetorical principles is to begin that lifetime of improvement in reading and writing which a college course in composition should initiate.

R. D. C.
R. D. S.

Contents

Rhetoric
for
Exposition

CHAPTER ONE

The Language and the Responsibility

OF the several varieties of usage within the English language, there is one which all educated persons may be expected to master. This is the written language commonly used for the significant communication of matters of public interest—in economics, literary criticism, physical and social sciences, business, politics, and government. The college student, among others, has the responsibility for using this language effectively for both his writing and his reading.

We may identify this kind of English, which we may call *formal written American English*, by distinguishing it from other varieties of the language, by recognizing its uses, and by tracing its origins.

By calling it *American* English, we recognize that there are some usages that are peculiarly American. An Englishman, an American, a Jamaican, and an Australian will each use certain words and phrases that will have to be translated to be understood by the others. For example, Britishers say *petrol*, *tube*, *lift*, and *hadn't got;* Americans say *gas*, *subway*, *elevator*, and *didn't have*. By specifying *written* English, we make a further distinction. Ordinarily, written English is more economical and careful than spoken English because it requires planning. It must achieve its effects without the help of voice, facial expression, or gesture. When we speak we can shout, glare, or wave our hands; but a piece of paper has no hands. Formal English is not, of course, the language Americans use every time they write. Personal letters employ an informal usage that would not be appropriate to an article in an economics journal or even to a business letter. *Formal* indicates that it follows a generally accepted grammar, mechanics, and word usage.

We see, then, that formal written American English is only one of the varieties of English and that it represents a specialized selection from the total of English language characteristics. Its specialization results from, or reflects, its function. It is the language appropriately used by Americans to communicate publicly, in the medium of writing, on matters of public concern.

To use this specialized language effectively, one must understand its nature and assume responsibility for using it competently. The most obvious fact about the nature of this language is that it follows certain conventions in mechanics—in spelling, punctuation, grammar, and syntax. Since these conventions are the result of heterogeneous, even fortuitous, historical forces, they are anything but neat, logical, and predictable. They are, in fact, the products of custom and caprice. Some conventions accepted today were unfamiliar a century or two ago: as common a verb form as the passive progressive (the bridge *is being built*) was deplored by grammarians and teachers a century ago, and was first recorded in 1769; the use of contractions, while frequent in the eighteenth century, is largely avoided today. However, some forms have been accepted as good usage for a very long time: it is natural (as this clause demonstrates) to begin a sentence with a "false" subject in the form of a pronoun that has no real (or semantic) referent. Moreover, spelling was finally standardized about two hundred years ago by arbitrary means —standard orthography retains old spellings which reflect obsolete pronunciation (*k*nig*h*t and dau*gh*ter), spellings which do not reflect English pronunciation either current or past (de*b*t), un-English spellings of early printers (g*h*ost), and spellings which clarify etymologies (*neighbor*).

English punctuation resembles spelling in its apparent irregularity. As its basis it has had two principles which were not always consistent. One was elocutionary punctuation, the practice of punctuating written language according to the pauses and inflections in speaking. Writing, when punctuated in this way, is an imitation of words, pauses, and inflections of the spoken language. Grammatical punctuation, on the other hand, follows the principle of punctuating words and word-groups consistently with the formulated (standard) rules of grammar. Writing, when punctuated in this way, is a method of representing words and their logical (that is, grammatical or syntactical) relations. Because it is now generally accepted, grammatical punctuation enables us to distinguish readily the three meanings in "She was my girl; however, I left her," "She was my girl, however; I left her," and "She was my girl, however I left her." The distinction would be clear in speech; but elocutionary punctuation, because it punctuates by ear, so to speak, might not make the necessary distinction. Grammatical punctuation, the more recently developed of the two, has had support of two hundred years of schoolroom instruction and thus has largely displaced elocutionary punctuation in those areas where schools have had a great effect on language. Grammatical punctuation has become the dominant principle in formal written American English, whereas elocutionary punctuation is the dominant principle of unschooled—hence nonstandard—writing.

Thus although a great number of irregularities are crystallized in the conventions of formal written American English they are nevertheless well established, and anyone who assumes responsibility for communicating with this type of English can consult handbooks and dictionaries for conventions he is unsure of. English spelling is the most irregular of all alphabetical systems, but a dictionary will list standard spellings. These conventions should not be discounted despite their arbitrary and irregular nature. Consider the following sentence: "From the writtings in Emersons Journals Ripley might resonably have expected an afermative answer." Nonstandard spelling distracts our attention and, in addition to the nonstandard syntax (dangling modifier), probably obscures *on first reading* the fact that it is the writer (not Ripley) who has read Emerson's Journals and is making an inference about the relationship between the two men. Or take this example: "Ripley also said that if they do not get the financial support necessary the project will be retarded and may even injure the enterprise." It is annoying to have to spend attention and energy straightening out the writer's nonstandard syntax. When we read something which follows conventional patterns, we can absorb concepts without distractions of this kind and hence read more efficiently. Only so long as standard mechanics and structure are used in reading and writing—habits of spelling, of sentence patterns, of punctuation, of meaning, and so on—can we proceed without interruption or distraction in the process of communication.

Certain conventions also hold for the vocabulary used in formal written American English. Handbooks usually list only the vocabulary distinctions which students frequently miss; but dictionaries, especially those listing synonyms and related words, show the full range of vocabulary distinctions needed for precise written expression. The vocabulary of this variety of English is also limited. Because formal written American English is public, its vocabulary is restrained, impersonal, and conservative; it seldom uses slang, clichés, and special meanings that only a limited number of people will understand. Even informal or intimate expressions are omitted except for special effect.

Since this language is specialized and *written*, it is possible to concentrate information to a greater degree than in spoken English. Written form enables one to refer at any time to what has been, or will subsequently be, mentioned. Use of the written form assumes complete attention—interruptions do not have to be allowed for. Visible punctuation, which includes division into paragraphs, assists concentration, since it graphically shows relations of word-groups. The written language develops and uses precise ways of showing subordination by syntactic and graphic means rather than the impractical methods of circumlocution and gesture.

It is possible, however, to follow conventional mechanics without clearly communicating the idea one intended to express. Consider the following illustration:

(1) I shall attempt to prove that if it is impossible to control the real thoughts and ideas of people, then the policy of repression, which is based on the control of the thoughts and ideas of people, is impossible. (2) The two most important words in my syllogism are the words *control* and *repression.* (3) In the discussion of these two terms I hope to prove that it is impossible to control the real thoughts and ideas of people through repression.

(4) The first of the two words I shall discuss is the word *repression.* (5) Discovered by Freud in his work with neurotic patients, *repression* was defined as the reaction in which a person "rejects from consciousness impulses or thoughts that produce anxiety." (6) This is, in reality, a type of "temporary forgetting" and applies not only to memories but also to any thoughts or motives.

(7) Repression as a psychological term has many methods of achieving this "temporary forgetting" and they are discussed in *Introduction to Psychology*, by Clifford T. Morgan. (8) In each method of repression, it is clearly stated that the methods of repression are not successful to

any degree. (9) The repression either goes so far as to lead to a form of mental disorder or the problem is dealt with and the need for repression is dissolved. (10) This, I believe, shows that there is no such thing as true repression.

(11) The second term I shall discuss is the word *control*. . . .

Because our eye has caught no mistakes in proofreading—all the punctuation is right, spelling is correct, titles are italicized and so on—we may suppose *on first reading* that we have successful communication. An attempt to restate the meaning—the "idea" communicated—shows us, however, the failure of communication.

In sentences 1-3 the writer is concerned with "the policy of repression"—apparently a kind of thought-control imposed from the outside; but he defines the word *repression* (sentence 5) and uses it subsequently as meaning the individual's own rejection of thoughts producing anxiety—a defensive thought-control imposed from the inside. Sentence 7 says that the term *repression* "has methods"—but we know that no *term* (or word) has methods, and to state that the term "has methods of achieving 'temporary forgetting' " is nonsense, if taken literally. In sentence 8 we are told that "the methods of repression" are stated "*in* each method of repression." Then (sentence 9) we read that repression leads to other things and, for this reason, there is no such thing as repression (sentence 10). Thus confused, we are reluctant to venture into a discussion of the second term, *control*.

Responsible use of formal written American English requires knowledge of those mechanical conventions already mentioned: correct spelling, and the punctuation, grammar, word order, vocabulary, and types of sentence customary for this language. This knowledge is basic. But it is not enough. In dealing with materials as complex as those to be expected in college courses, one needs to know general techniques for presenting complex materials: among these are some forms and methods of definition, some methods of classification, some elements of logical form, and some aspects of nonlogical forms. Although these techniques are conventionalized to some extent, they cannot be codified and listed conveniently in reference books, as can the mechanical conventions. They are, however, considered essential to the writing of an educated person because they facilitate clear thinking and accurate communication, and for this reason they are demanded by college courses. Having mastered them, one can begin his understanding of intentional and individual aspects of rhetoric, an understanding which will develop only through long and sensitive experience as both writer and reader of written formal English.

The readings that follow, therefore, illustrate the formal written English as it has been used importantly and well, and the chapters analyze those readings in order to demonstrate some of the conventional methods and forms by which, when we assume responsibility for what we say, we can use it well ourselves. Responsibility is the individual's obligation.

EXERCISES

1. After consulting one or more collegiate dictionaries (and checking etymologies) for the less familiar words in this chapter, write a paragraph of not more than 100 words in which you *restate* the substance of the sentence in which each word first occurs. The following words are suggested:

obsolete	syntax
etymology	orthography
heterogeneous	fortuitous
semantic	referent
circumlocution	cliché

2. Understanding of what a special language is ultimately depends on recognizing specific examples of that language. From general observation supply illustrations of "English language" usage which are ordinarily (a) not American, (b) not written, (c) not formal.

3. In so far as it is possible, determine the intended meaning in the four-paragraph illustration which deals with *repression*. Then rewrite this material so that *your* writing leaves no question about the meaning intended, and so that the reader does not have to revise (mentally) as he reads.

4. Whenever we "watch our language" we are aware of varying levels of language usage. We notice that we speak differently with a teacher, a clergyman, or an employer, than we do with close friends. The problem in writing, so far as level of language is concerned, is mainly one of maintaining consistency of level. Examine what you have written for the preceding exercises: check closely each word and phrase to determine whether the level is consistently maintained, testing each

questionable case with synonyms or alternate expressions from other levels, from the most casual to the most formal.

5. There are many types of public, written communication in English which share the characteristics of formal English. A chemist writes in one way when he reports his finding in a research project to other chemists, but in another way when he writes a textbook or lecture. A person writes differently when taking sides in a public controversy than he does in his routine correspondence. Military regulations employ one manner of writing, "how-to-do" directions another, a sermon another, a letter of consolation, a tribute, an analysis of a poem yet others.

Describe actual examples of several distinct types of writing. Point out such things as the differences in the order in which material is presented, how much illustration is used and what kinds, the degree of restraint or specialization in vocabulary, and the degree of complication in sentence forms. Point out also those aspects of formal written English which all of them share.

6. Even two individuals writing on the same topic, using the same resources, and pursuing the same purpose will not write in exactly the same way. Compare two encyclopedia articles on the same subject and of approximately the same date and length, in order to show individual differences in writing. (The same kind of comparison may be made with exercises and theme assignments written for this course.)

WILLIAM JAMES

*What Pragmatism Means**

SOME years ago, being with a camping party in the mountains, I returned from a solitary ramble to find every one engaged in a ferocious metaphysical dispute. The *corpus* of the dispute was a squirrel—a live squirrel supposed to be clinging to one side of a tree-trunk; while over against the tree's opposite side a human being was imagined to stand. This human witness tries to get sight of the squirrel by moving rapidly round the tree, but no matter how fast he goes, the squirrel moves as fast in the opposite direction, and always keeps the tree between himself and the man, so that never a glimpse of him is caught. The resultant metaphysical problem now is this: *Does the man go round the squirrel or not*? He goes round the tree, sure enough, and the squirrel is on the tree; but does he go round the squirrel? In the unlimited leisure of the wilderness, discussion had been worn threadbare. Every one had taken sides and was obstinate; and the numbers on both sides were even. Each side, when I appeared, therefore appealed to me to make it a majority. Mindful of the scholastic adage that whenever you meet a contradiction you must make a distinction, I immediately sought and found one, as follows: "Which party is right," I said, "depends on what you *practically mean* by 'going round' the squirrel. If you mean passing from the north of him to the east, then to the south, then to the west, and then to the north of him again, obviously the man does go round him, for he occupies these successive positions. But if on the contrary you mean being first in front of him, then on the right of him, then behind him, then on his left, and finally in front again, it is quite obvious that the man fails to go round him, for by compensating

* From *Pragmatism and Other Essays*. Copyright 1907 by Longmans, Green and Co. Reprinted by permission of Paul R. Reynolds and Son, 599 Fifth Avenue, New York 17, N. Y.

movements the squirrel makes, he keeps his belly turned towards the man all the time, and his back turned away. Make the distinction, and there is no occasion for any further dispute. You are both right and both wrong, according as you conceive the verb 'to go round' in one practical fashion or the other."

2. Although one or two of the hotter disputants called my speech a shuffling evasion, saying they wanted no quibbling or scholastic hair-splitting, but meant just plain honest English "round," the majority seemed to think that the distinction had assuaged the dispute.

3. I tell this trivial anecdote because it is a peculiarly simple example of what I wish now to speak of as *the pragmatic method.* The pragmatic method is primarily a method of settling metaphysical disputes that otherwise might be interminable. Is the world one or many?—fated or free?—material or spiritual?—here are notions either of which may or may not hold good of the world; and disputes over such notions are unending. The pragmatic method in such cases is to try to interpret each notion by tracing its respective practical consequences. What difference would it practically make to any one if this notion rather than that notion were true? If no practical difference whatever can be traced, then the alternatives mean practically the same thing, and all dispute is idle. Whenever a dispute is serious, we ought to be able to show some practical difference that must follow from one side or the other's being right.

4. A glance at the history of the idea will show you still better what pragmatism means. The term is derived from the same Greek word *pragma,* meaning action, from which our words "practice" and "practical" come. It was first introduced into philosophy by Mr. Charles Peirce in 1878. In an article entitled "How to Make Our Ideas Clear," in the *Popular Science Monthly* for January of that year, Mr. Peirce, after pointing out that our beliefs are really rules for action, said that, to develop a thought's meaning, we need only determine what conduct it is fitted to produce: that conduct is for us its sole significance. And the tangible fact at the root of all our thought-distinctions, however subtle, is that there is no one of them so fine as to consist in anything but a possible difference of practice. To attain perfect clearness in our thoughts of an object, then, we need only consider what conceivable effects of a practical kind the object may involve—what sensations we are to expect from it, and what reactions we must prepare. Our conception of these effects

whether immediate or remote, is then for us the whole of our conception of the object, so far as that conception has positive significance at all.

5. This is the principle of Peirce, the principle of pragmatism. It lay entirely unnoticed by any one for twenty years, until I, in an address before Professor Howison's philosophical union at the University of California, brought it forward again and made a special application of it to religion. By that date (1898) the times seemed ripe for its reception. The word "pragmatism" spread, and at present it fairly spots the pages of the philosophic journals. On all hands we find the "pragmatic movement" spoken of, sometimes with respect, sometimes with contumely, seldom with clear understanding. It is evident that the term applies itself conveniently to a number of tendencies that hitherto have lacked a collective name, and that it has "come to stay."

6. To take in the importance of Peirce's principle, one must get accustomed to applying it to concrete cases. I found a few years ago that Ostwald, the illustrious Leipzig chemist, had been making perfectly distinct use of the principle of pragmatism in his lectures on the philosophy of science, though he had not called it by that name.

7. "All realities influence our practice," he wrote me, "and that influence is their meaning for us. I am accustomed to put questions to my classes in this way: In what respects would the world be different if this alternative or that were true? If I can find nothing that would become different, then the alternative has no sense."

8. That is, the rival views mean practically the same thing, and meaning, other than practical, there is for us none. Ostwald in a published lecture gives this example of what he means. Chemists have long wrangled over the inner constitution of certain bodies called "tautomerous." Their properties seemed equally consistent with the notion that an instable hydrogen atom oscillates inside of them, or that they are instable mixtures of two bodies. Controversy raged, but never was decided. "It would never have begun," says Ostwald, "if the combatants had asked themselves what particular experimental fact could have been made different by one or the other view being correct. For it would then have appeared that no difference of fact could possibly ensue; and the quarrel was as unreal as if, theorising in primitive times about the raising of dough

by yeast, one party should have invoked a 'brownie,' while another insisted on an 'elf' as the true cause of the phenomenon."

9. It is astonishing to see how many philosophical disputes collapse into insignificance the moment you subject them to this simple test of tracing a concrete consequence. There can *be* no difference anywhere that doesn't *make* a difference elsewhere—no difference in abstract truth that doesn't express itself in a difference in concrete fact and in conduct consequent upon that fact, imposed on somebody, somehow, somewhere, and somewhen. The whole function of philosophy ought to be to find out what definite difference it will make to you and me, at definite instants of our life, if this world-formula or that world-formula be the true one.

10. There is absolutely nothing new in the pragmatic method. Socrates was an adept at it. Aristotle used it methodically. Locke, Berkeley, and Hume made momentous contributions to truth by its means. Shadworth Hodgson keeps insisting that realities are only what they are "known as." But these forerunners of pragmatism used it in fragments: they were a prelude only. Not until in our time has it generalized itself, become conscious of a universal mission, pretended to a conquering destiny. I believe in that destiny, and I hope I may end by inspiring you with my belief.

11. Pragmatism represents a perfectly familiar attitude in philosophy, the empiricist attitude, but it represents it, as it seems to me, both in a more radical and in a less objectionable form than it has ever yet assumed. A pragmatist turns his back resolutely and once for all upon a lot of inveterate habits dear to professional philosophers. He turns away from abstraction and insufficiency, from verbal solutions, from bad *a priori* reasons, from fixed principles, closed systems, and pretended absolutes and origins. He turns towards concreteness and adequacy, towards facts, towards action and towards power. That means the empiricist temper regnant and the rationalist temper sincerely given up. It means the open air and possibilities of nature, as against dogma, artificiality, and the pretence of finality in truth.

12. At the same time it does not stand for any special results. It is a method only. But the general triumph of that method would mean an enormous change in what I called in my last lecture the "temperament" of philosophy. Teachers of the ultra-rationalistic type would be frozen out, much as the courtier type is frozen out in republics,

as the ultra-montane type of priest is frozen out in protestant lands. Science and metaphysics would come much nearer together, would in fact work absolutely hand in hand.

13. Metaphysics has usually followed a very primitive kind of quest. You know how men have always hankered after unlawful magic, and you know what a great part in magic *words* have always played. If you have his name, or the formula of incantation that binds him, you can control the spirit, genie, afrite, or whatever the power may be. Solomon knew the names of all the spirits, and having their names, he held them subject to his will. So the universe has always appeared to the natural mind as a kind of enigma, of which the key must be sought in the shape of some illuminating or power-bringing word or name. That word names the universe's *principle*, and to possess it is after a fashion to possess the universe itself. "God," "Matter," "Reason," "the Absolute," "Energy," are so many solving names. You can rest when you have them. You are at the end of your metaphysical quest.

14. But if you follow the pragmatic method you cannot look on any such word as closing your quest. You must bring out of each word its practical cash-value, set it at work within the stream of your experience. It appears less as a solution, then, than as a programme for more work, and more particularly as an indication of the ways in which existing realities may be *changed*.

15. *Theories thus become instruments, not answers to enigmas, in which we can rest.* We don't lie back upon them, we move forward, and, on occasion, make nature over again by their aid. Pragmatism unstiffens all our theories, limbers them up and sets each one at work. Being nothing essentially new, it harmonizes with many ancient philosophic tendencies. It agrees with nominalism, for instance, in always appealing to particulars; with utilitarianism in emphasizing practical aspects; with positivism in its disdain for verbal solutions, useless questions, and metaphysical abstractions.

16. All these, you see, are *anti-intellectualist* tendencies. Against rationalism as a pretension and a method pragmatism is fully armed and militant. But, at the outset, at least, it stands for no particular results. It has no dogmas, and no doctrines save its method. As the young Italian pragmatist Papini has well said, it lies in the midst of our theories like a corridor in a hotel. Innumerable chambers open

out of it. In one you may find a man writing an atheistic volume; in the next some one on his knees praying for faith and strength; in a third a chemist investigating a body's properties; in a fourth a system of idealistic metaphysics is being excogitated; in a fifth the impossibility of metaphysics is being shown. But they all own the corridor, and all must pass through it if they want a practicable way of getting into or out of their respective rooms.

17. No particular results then, so far, but only an attitude of orientation, is what the pragmatic method means. *The attitude of looking away from first things, principles, "categories," supposed necessities; and of looking towards last things, fruits, consequences, facts.*

18. So much for the pragmatic method! You may say that I have been praising it rather than explaining it to you, but I shall presently explain it abundantly enough by showing how it works on some familiar problems. Meanwhile the word pragmatism has come to be used in a still wider sense, as meaning also a certain *theory of truth.* I mean to give a whole lecture to the statement of that theory, after first paving the way, . . . so I ask for your redoubled attention for a quarter of an hour. If much remains obscure, I hope to make it clearer in the later lectures.

19. One of the most successfully cultivated branches of philosophy in our time is what is called inductive logic, the study of the conditions under which our sciences have evolved. Writers on this subject have begun to show a singular unanimity as to what the laws of nature and elements of fact mean when formulated by mathematicians, physicists, and chemists. When the first mathematical, logical, and natural uniformities, the first *laws*, were discovered, men were so carried away by the clearness, beauty, and simplification that resulted that they believed themselves to have deciphered authentically the eternal thoughts of the Almighty. His mind also thundered and reverberated in syllogisms. He also thought in conic sections, squares, and roots and ratios, and geometrized like Euclid. He made Kepler's laws for the planets to follow; he made velocity increase proportionally to the time in falling bodies; he made the law of the sines for light to obey when refracted; he established the classes, orders, families, and genera of plants and animals, and fixed the distances between them. He thought the archetypes of all things,

and devised their variations; and when we rediscover any one of these his wondrous institutions, we seize his mind in its very literal intention.

20. But as the sciences have developed farther, the notion has gained ground that most, perhaps all, of our laws are only approximations. The laws themselves, moreover, have grown so numerous that there is no counting them; and so many rival formulations are proposed in all the branches of science that investigators have become accustomed to the notion that no theory is absolutely a transcript of reality, but that any one of them may from some point of view be useful. Their great use is to summarize old facts and to lead to new ones. They are only a man-made language, a conceptual shorthand, as some one calls them, in which we write our reports of nature; and languages, as is well known, tolerate much choice of expression and many dialects.

21. Thus human arbitrariness has driven divine necessity from scientific logic. If I mention the names of Sigwart, Mach, Ostwald, Pearson, Milhaud, Poincaré, Duhem, Heymans, those of you who are students will easily identify the tendency I speak of, and will think of additional names.

22. Riding now on the front of this wave of scientific logic, Messrs. Schiller and Dewey appear with their pragmatistic account of what truth everywhere signifies. Everywhere, these teachers say, "truth" in our ideas and beliefs means the same thing that it means in science. It means, they say, nothing but this, *that ideas (which themselves are but parts of our experience) become true just in so far as they help us to get into satisfactory relation with other parts of our experience*, to summarize them and get about among them by conceptual shortcuts instead of following the interminable succession of particular phenomena. Any idea upon which we can ride, so to speak; any idea that will carry us prosperously from any one part of of our experience to any other part, linking things satisfactorily, working securely, simplifying, saving labour—is true for just so much, true in so far forth, true *instrumentally*. This is the "instrumental" view of truth taught so successfully at Chicago, the view that truth in our ideas means their power to "work," promulgated so brilliantly at Oxford.

23. Messrs. Dewey, Schiller, and their allies, in reaching this general conception of all truth, have only followed the example of

geologists, biologists, and philologists. In the establishment of these other sciences, the successful stroke was always to take some simple process actually observable in operation—as denudation by weather, say, or variation from parental type, or change of dialect by incorporation of new words and pronunciations—and then to generalize it, making it apply to all times, and produce great results by summating its effect through the ages.

24. The observable process which Schiller and Dewey particularly singled out for generalization is the familiar one by which any individual settles into *new opinions*. The process here is always the same. The individual has a stock of old opinions already, but he meets a new experience that puts them to a strain. Somebody contradicts them; or in a reflective moment he discovers that they contradict each other; or he hears of facts with which they are incompatible; or desires arise in him which they cease to satisfy. The result is an inward trouble to which his mind till then had been a stranger, and from which he seeks to escape by modifying his previous mass of opinions. He saves as much of it as he can, for in this matter of belief we are all extreme conservatives. So he tries to change first this opinion, and then that (for they resist change very variously), until at last some new idea comes up which he can graft upon the ancient stock with a minimum of disturbance of the latter, some idea that mediates between the stock and the new experience and runs them into one another most felicitously and expediently . . . .

25. A new opinion counts as "true" just in proportion as it gratifies the individual's desire to assimilate the novel in his experience to his beliefs in stock. It must both lean on old truth and grasp new fact; and its success (as I said a moment ago) in doing this, is a matter for the individual's appreciation. When old truth grows, then, by new truth's addition, it is for subjective reasons. We are in the process and obey the reasons. That new idea is truest which performs most felicitously its function of satisfying our double urgency. It makes itself true, gets itself classed as true, by the way it works; grafting itself then upon the ancient body of truth, which thus grows much as a tree grows by the activity of a new layer of cambium.

26. Now Dewey and Schiller proceed to generalize this observation and to apply it to the most ancient parts of truth. They also once were plastic. They also were called true for human reasons.

They also mediated between still earlier truths and what in those days were novel observations. Purely subjective truth, in whose establishment the function of giving human satisfaction in marrying previous parts of experience with newer parts played no role whatever, is nowhere to be found. The reasons why we call things true is the reason why they *are* true, for 'to be true' *means* only to perform this marriage-function. . . .

27. Such then would be the scope of pragmatism—first, a method; and second, a genetic theory of what is meant by truth.

CHAPTER TWO

The Method and Form of Definition

JAMES' essay defines pragmatism. James, like any writer of a definition, assumes that his readers do not know what the word means and believes that they ought to know. He therefore describes what things are referred to by the word *pragmatism.* A definition, then, establishes the meaning or meanings of a word by describing what the word refers to. It is a description which follows a specific method and makes use of certain characteristic forms. Analysis of James' essay, which is an important and successful definition, will make his method clear and show the properties of the forms it uses.

In the course of his definition James answers three basic questions about pragmatism: What is it? Where does it come from? What is it good for? These are questions we all ask about anything we don't understand. The answers to these questions may be presented in various ways; but however they are presented, an adequate definition must answer them as fully as possible in order to make meaning clear.

James answers the question "What is it?" in two ways. He first suggests that the problem of meaning, illustrated by the anecdote of the squirrel, may be solved by using the pragmatic method. "The pragmatic method [of determining meaning] is . . . to interpret each notion by tracing its respective practical consequences." A statement of this sort and others like it is called a FORMAL definition. "Pragmatic method" is the *term*-to-be-defined, and the phrase "to interpret each notion by tracing its respective practical consequences" is the *definer.* Pragmatism is shown to be a part of a class of things—methods—and is distinguished from all other things in that class by the defining term. The formal definition is a characteristic form of description used to answer the question "What is it?" But because the formal definition is a one-sentence definition we often need more information before we can fully understand what a word means.

The pragmatic method, James says, implies a theory of meaning and a theory of truth. As a theory of meaning it holds that meaning is determined by consequences. For illustration James cites the argument about the two theories of the inner constitution of tautomerous bodies. From this he concludes that from the pragmatic point of view, the argument is meaningless, for no experimental difference could have resulted from one or the other being correct. And any dispute which does not result in a practical (experimental) difference is meaningless. "There can *be* no meaningful difference anywhere which doesn't *make* a difference elsewhere—no difference in abstract truth that doesn't express itself in a difference in concrete fact and in conduct consequent upon that fact." The pragmatic method puts theories to work. It appeals to particulars. It emphasizes consequences. It disdains verbal solutions. It does not stand for particular results, but for an attitude, an attitude which looks away from "first things" and looks toward "last things, fruits, consequences, facts."

As a theory of truth the pragmatic method holds that ideas become true only insofar as they work satisfactorily in a given situation, insofar as "They help us get into a satisfactory relation with other parts of experience." There is no such thing as Truth as a principle apart from consequences. If we want to find out what is "true" in a given situation (and we can know truth only in terms of particular situations), we discover the alternatives possible, find out what the practical consequences of each would be, and conclude that that alternative which gives us the consequences we want is true. Thus the truth of a proposition varies with the circumstances and is judged in terms of the consequences.

James' analysis of the pragmatic method as a theory of meaning and a theory of truth constitutes a MATERIAL definition. The material definition completes the answer to the question "What is it?" In his material definition James amplifies the implications of his formal definition by analyzing the materials and their arrangement and the varieties of the thing defined.

James answers the question "Where does it come from?" in three ways. First he gives us the derivation of the word itself. He tells us that the word *pragmatism* is derived from the Greek word *pragma*, meaning action, and that our words *practice* and *practical* come from the same source. He also notes that *pragmatism* was first used by the American philosopher Charles Peirce in his essay "How to Make Our Ideas Clear." Peirce used the word to express his belief that the meaning of an idea can be determined only by the conduct it is fitted to produce. Although the word was unused and unnoticed for about twenty years, James points out that it is at present (1907) very popular, and that it is frequently misunderstood.

In addition to giving us the etymology (derivation) of the word, James traces the antecedents of the method of pragmatism—both as a theory of meaning and as a theory of truth. As a theory of meaning it derives from Socrates, Aristotle, Locke, Berkeley, Hume, and many others, who, when they used it, used it methodically and made momentous contributions to truth by means of it. But these men used it only in fragments. They all believed, to some extent, in the magic of names; they were all concerned, more or less, to discover the "principle" of the universe and to possess it. Pragmatism denies that in finding names, such as God, Matter, Reason, Energy, and so on, one finds anything of value; it denies that there is a "principle" to be possessed. Pragmatism has "no dogmas, and no doctrine save its method." Thus, the pragmatic theory of meaning, representing an application of the empiricist attitude, is both more radical and less objectionable than its antecedents.

As a theory of truth the pragmatic method derives from modern science and inductive logic. Early scientists, James notes, believed that physical laws expressed the eternal thoughts of God as revealed in His creation. But as science developed, scientists came to believe that perhaps these physical "laws" were only approximations; perhaps these "laws" were merely summarizations of old observations which could most profitably be used to lead us to new observations —not eternal laws of God but simply arbitrary human ones. Schiller and Dewey are the leaders of this new attitude. They teach us that "truth" in our beliefs means the same thing that "truth" means in science. There are no absolute Truths revealing God's eternal thoughts in time; there are only local, arbitrary, and approximate truths based on old observations which may be changed as new observations are made. "Messrs. Dewey, Schiller, and their allies," James suggests, "have only followed the example of geologists, biologists, and philologists."

James' discussion of the derivation of the word *pragmatism* and of the antecedents of the pragmatic method as a theory of meaning and a theory of truth constitutes an HISTORICAL definition. It answers the question "Where does it come from?" by giving the origin of the *word*, both linguistically and historically, and by giving the origin of the *idea* by tracing its historical development.

The goal of pragmatism, James contends, will be to eliminate absolutes and fixed principles. The rationalist and absolutist philosophers try to create the universe by thinking it, and by inventing words to name what they think. But they never deduce a single actual particular from their notions. The real world, James says, is wide open, constantly changing, never showing the same face twice; but the rationalists make systems which are absolute and closed. Pragmatism does away with systems. It does this by substituting a method for a system and by changing our concept of truth. Everything must be set within the ever-changing "stream of experience"; and this is good. It is good because: (1) It eliminates "word magic" by refusing to consider that differences of opinion which do not have practical consequences can be meaningful; thus it eliminates futile and profitless disputes. (2) It supplies a program for further investigation by concentrating on consequences rather than causes. (3) It helps us to see that all laws are only approximations—useful in summarizing old and leading to new facts. (4) It promulgates a workable and practical theory of truth. (5) It allows plasticity of opinion. (6) It harmonizes empirical ways of thinking (the truth of science) with the religious demands of human beings (the truth of belief); for if theological ideas prove to have a practical value for human life, they will be true in the pragmatic sense of helping us "to get into a satisfactory relationship with other parts of our experience." As James states elsewhere, "The true is the name of whatever proves itself to be useful in the way of belief, and useful, too, for definite, assignable reasons."

Thus James answers the question "What is it good for?" This kind of answer, called a FINAL OR FUNCTIONAL definition, describes the end or purpose of the thing defined. It analyzes the function or describes our method of using the thing defined to attain the end or accomplish the purpose stated. And, finally, it suggests the value of the thing defined, measured by the efficiency with which it attains its end or serves its purpose: the purpose of pragmatism is to eliminate absolutes and fixed principles. It does this by means of a theory of meaning and a theory of truth. And it is valuable because it succeeds in accomplishing its purpose in the ways enumerated.

A definition is successful when the person for whom it is intended is able to understand what the writer means by the term he is defining. James' definition assumes a vocabulary and an intellectual background which might reasonably be expected of a college freshman. His definition would be useless to a fifth grader. A reader who has the knowledge James assumes might be unaware of what pragmatism is, but he would be perfectly qualified to understand a definition of it if he were willing to assume the responsibility of careful reading. Such a reader ought to be interested in assuming this responsibility and mastering, for his own use, a word which is frequently used and frequently misunderstood.

James' definition, then, is a successful definition. Its success depends largely upon the method and the forms James uses. His method is to answer the three questions essential to an establishment of meaning. It is a method which utilizes certain characteristic forms but which does not employ a set order. In the course of his description he uses the forms of the formal, material, historical, and final definitions. These, in turn, constitute the form of his essay as a whole.

The method and forms James uses may be presented in any order the author deems most useful to his purpose. For example, an adequate definition need not begin, as James' does, with historical description, though such a beginning has a chronological priority and is frequently employed. It is also important to note that the forms which James uses are not mutually exclusive, that they tend to blend into one another, and that it is frequently impossible to answer one question without implying the answer to another. James himself suggests this when he notes that the reader may say that pragmatism has been "praised" rather than "explained." In this essay, to describe is to praise: the material and final definitions tend to combine. For purposes of study, however, we can take the essay apart and see how the various parts work, as long as we remember that the part is not the whole and that a complete definition does not function properly without all of its parts.

In this chapter we have done just that, because analysis of this sort is useful to the student both as reader and as writer. As a reader, it gives him understanding of the essay and of the nature of definition itself. As a writer, it gives him the means to make his ideas clear if he assumes responsibility for what he says.

The following outline suggests points to be considered by the student who wishes to write a definition:

I. An adequate definition should answer as fully as needed three questions about the term-to-be-defined. These are:
What is it?
Where does it come from?
What is it good for?

II. These queries are answered by:
What is it?
A. FORMAL definition in the form of:
"It is something which . . . (give characteristic attribute)."
B. MATERIAL definition stating:
1. substance,
2. arrangement, and
3. varieties of the thing defined.
Where does it come from?
C. HISTORICAL definition giving:
1. development of the *word*,
2. origin of the *thing* in race or in individual, and
3. evolution, extent, cause, and so on, of the thing defined.
What is it good for?
D. FUNCTIONAL definition giving:
1. purpose of the thing defined,
2. method of using it to accomplish this purpose, and
3. value, measured by the desire for the thing itself or by the efficiency with which it attains its end.
EXAMPLE: The purpose of a clock is timekeeping and its value depends upon the efficiency with which it keeps time.

III. These questions and answers can be arranged in a multitude of ways.

CHAPTER THREE

Types and Tests of Definition

A DEFINITION, as we have seen, establishes meaning or meanings for a word by describing what the word refers to. Any type of description which enables the person for whom it is intended to understand the meaning of a term is a successful definition. For example, when we point to a narrow cylindrical object on our desk and say "pencil," we indicate what the word refers to; when we move our bodies in a certain fashion in the water, to show the backstroke, we demonstrate the meaning of our term; when we draw a map showing the location of the Rio Grande, we have a kind of definition. This sort of description, called OSTENSIVE definition, is an effective method of establishing meaning whenever we have objects or diagrams at hand to describe a term's reference. In the study of rhetoric, however, we will be concerned only with those types of definition which make use of verbal description—with methods of description that operate entirely within the medium of words.

Some verbal means of definition do not require extensive rhetorical consideration. When we offer a synonym for the term to be defined, we have only the problem of substituting another term for the one to be defined. Tests for definition by synonym are social, not formal; if the synonym is familiar to the person for whom it is intended and if the term refers conventionally to the same thing, the definition is successful. Or, when we offer a phrase longer than the term to be defined but referring to the same thing, we have definition: "chemical substances secreted by ductless glands" defines *hormones;* "Southeast Asia Treaty Organization" defines

SEATO; "Apes, monkeys, men, and lemurs" defines *primates.* Since matters of form of expression are not involved, these types of definition, called NOMINAL definition, pose no serious rhetorical problems.

On the other hand, the FORMAL definition (also called the ARISTOTELIAN) is governed by tests which are at the same time logical and rhetorical, as well as social. *It is subject to formal tests.* Formal tests provide advantages similar to standardization in spelling, punctuation, and grammar, for they provide common ground on which both reader and writer can meet. A formal pattern of definition can be of great help in compensating for lack of personal presence and the give-and-take of conversation. We cannot see (or hear) whether our written description is understood, so we rely on the common ground of standard patterns of definition.

The formal definition is thus a somewhat rigid method of defining, a method usually useful to the degree it is kept rigid. For example:

A *diameter* (in plane geometry) is a straight line which contains the center of a circle and extends from one side of the circle to the other.
A *diameter* is a straight line which bisects a circle and is contained by it.
A *diameter* is a straight line composed of two radii of the same circle.
A *meniscus* (in physics) is the curved upper surface of a column of liquid, when the curve is the result of capillarity; the curve is concave when the walls of the container are wet, convex when they are dry.
A *function F* (in mathematics) is a rule which associates with each member of a certain set of objects *D* (called the domain of the function) a unique member of a set of objects *R* (called the range of the function).[1]
Cubism is a movement in modern art marked by distortion of represented objects in the direction of simplified geometrical forms, especially angular planes.[2]
A *motive* (in psychology) is a conscious experience or subconscious condition which serves as a factor in determining an individual's behavior or social conduct in a given situation.[3]
The *Idea of Progress* is the belief that mankind, by making use of science and invention, can progressively emancipate itself from plagues, famines,

[1] From Roy Dubisch, *Trigonometry* (Copyright 1955, The Ronald Press Company).
[2] *Collier's Encyclopedia* (1959), Vol. 6, p. 155. Used with permission of the publisher.
[3] Howard C. Warren, ed., *Dictionary of Psychology* (Boston, Houghton Mifflin Co., 1934).

and social disasters, and subjugate the materials and forces of the earth to the purposes of the good life—here and now.[4]

Each definition consists of *one sentence*. In each case the sentence begins with the TERM-to-be-defined, followed by a form of the verb *be*, and then presents the elements which do the defining, DEFINER. The pattern of the formal definition is this:

Term = *Definer*

(The form of *be* merely indicates equivalence of the two major portions of the definition-equation.)

We can also see that the definer regularly falls into a rigid form. First, it identifies what sort of thing the term names—what more general type of thing it belongs to, what class of things it falls under: "a diameter is a straight line," "a function is a rule," "the Idea of Progress is a belief," and so on. In other words, the definer begins by placing the object named into a larger class of objects. This part of the definer is called the GENUS. The effect of beginning the definer in this way is to associate the unfamiliar particular object with more general and presumably more familiar kinds of objects. When we know what general sort of thing the term names, we have begun to understand the meaning of the term.

The term and the genus are not equivalent, however, since there are obviously many straight lines that are not diameters, many rules that are not functions, many beliefs that are not the Idea of Progress. Thus the remaining (and usually longer) part of the definer must qualify the genus, stipulating the specific thing the term names. In other words, after placing what we are defining within a larger class of things, we must then point out what part of this class is named by the term. The straight lines which we call diameters are those which bisect circles and are contained by them; the only belief we call the Idea of Progress is that one which holds that mankind, by making use of science and invention, can emancipate itself, and so forth. The qualifications of the genus thus differentiate the thing named by the term from the group of things named by the genus. This part of the definer is called the DIFFERENTIAE. Our equation for formal definition can also be written thus:

[4] From Charles A. Beard, "The Idea of Progress," in *A Century of Progress* (New York, Harper & Brothers, 1933). Used with permission of Harper & Brothers.

$$\textit{Term} = \overbrace{\textit{genus} + \textit{differentiae}}^{\textit{Definer}}$$

The definition of *cubism* above shows us an order for the differentiae which is often useful. The following diagram shows how each successive element of the differentiae modifies grammatically the element just preceding it, so that the process of narrowing or limiting the genus ("movement in modern art") is quite apparent:

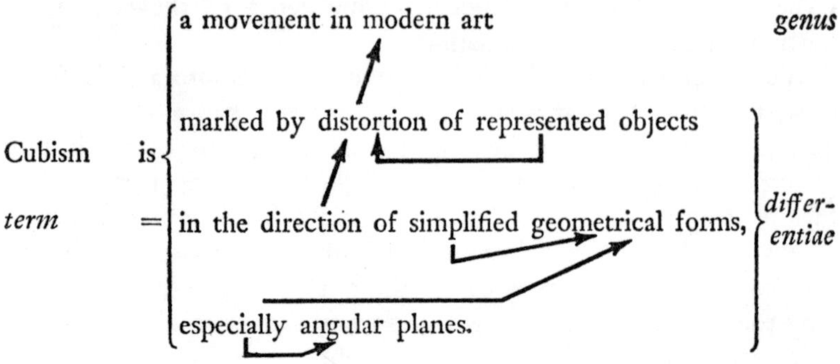

If we attempt now to enumerate formal tests of the formal definition, we find, first, that the formal definition embodies the simple form we have discussed. We may add, second, that the term and the definer should be equal, with the definer neither narrower nor broader than the term. For example, if we define *tautology* as repetition, the definer is misleadingly broad; if we define *marsupial* as an opossum-like animal, the definer is too narrow and too unspecific. Though it is often useful to know what a thing is not, as well as what it is, we can say, third, that the definer of a formal definition should not be dominantly negative (unless the term is negative). To define *lunch* as a meal not eaten in the evening, or to define *paranoia* as a psychosis not to be associated with schizophrenia, does not help us much in understanding the meaning of either term. We can require, fourth, that the term—or even a derivative of it—should not be used in the definer. We do not come any closer to understanding *sublimation* if it is defined as a reaction to frustration in which the frustrated behavior pattern is sublimated by a more complex form of social behavior.

Since to explain the unfamiliar with the unfamiliar will hardly put us on the way to understanding, we need, besides these formal tests, to repeat the tests of vocabulary and intellectual level which govern the appropriateness of the definition to the person for whom it is intended. All the words appearing in the definer, called *primitives*, should be within the vocabulary of the person reading the definition, if he assumes responsibility for careful reading and understanding.

Once we understand the form of the definition, we are ready to recognize another problem in the use of definition and look for ways to solve it. The problem may be put as a question: When do we have the definition we need? How should we define *diameter*—as a straight line composed of two radii within the same circle? a straight line bisecting a circle and contained by it? or a straight line containing the center of a circle and extending from one side of the circle to the other? The tests we apply in solving the problem of choice here are not formal. Rather, they are pragmatic. When we know what our defining needs are—that is, when we know what practical effects we should achieve with our definition—then we can choose among alternate definitions. Because each of the formal definitions of *diameter* will direct our attention to the same thing, we do not ask which one is right, but which one is best. Context, which includes the occasion, the materials at hand, the persons requiring the definition, and our purposes in offering it, will determine our choice. We shall be in a position to examine this problem more fully toward the end of this chapter. But at this point we can see that the use of standard forms for definition corresponds to the use of convention in the mechanics of writing: it is a condition we need to fulfill, but in itself it is never enough.

Another test we must make when writing a definition can also be put as a question: Is the definition complete enough? Does it need to be extended? Do we need to know more? Is a formal definition, regardless of its excellence, simply not adequate? Terms like *diameter* seldom need extensive definition, for usually a formal definition—sometimes supplemented by ostensive definition—is all we require. Etymology would probably help us remember the meaning of *diameter*, but historical and material definition can add little to a determination of its meaning. Functional definitions tell us how to construct or locate a diameter, or they involve geometrical relations familiarly expressed in mathematical formulas like $d = \frac{c}{\pi}$; but although a series of functional definitions may add to our information about the thing named, they add little in the way of establishing meaning. Most terms in a rigorously organized, closed system of scientific or mathematical knowledge—terms such as *meniscus*, *ion*, *acid*, *secant*, *radical*, *vector*, *wave length*, *harmonic*, *specific heat*, *vertebrate*—are of this kind, and formal definition is often sufficient.

Terms like *Cubism*, *motivation*, or *Progress* present a greater problem. Although a formal definition of these terms should have immediate clarity and give genuine help toward establishing meaning, the formal definition *by itself* can provide little more than a good starting-point. We need to extend the definition. Very often, as a matter of fact, the formal definition is used as a starting-point for extending definition through several sentences: its one-sentence form and intrinsic completeness make it valuable, say, as a topic sentence for a paragraph of definition. Cubism, for example, can be defined in paragraph length, beginning with the formal definition given above:

(1) [*Cubism* is] a movement in modern art marked by distortion of represented objects in the direction of simplified geometrical forms, especially angular planes. (2) Certain early Cubist work presented three-dimensional forms, cubical in nature, and from these the movement derived its name; most Cubist work, however, renders objects in terms of flat planes. (3) Although a violent reaction against ordinary realism, Cubism does not resort to complete abstraction. (4) Its shapes are more or less clearly derived from the natural objects represented, even though abstract features are often combined with them. (5) Its period of most intense development lay in the decade from 1910 to 1920, Pablo Picasso, Fernand Leger, Georges Braque, among others, taking part in it.[5]

The paragraph develops from the formal description in terms of material and historical definition. In sentence 2 we have the history of both the *word Cubism* and the *technique* it represents. Sentence 3 provides material definition which clarifies Cubist "distortion of represented objects" by placing it between two familiar types of art (Realism and complete Abstraction) and measuring the distance of Cubism from both, so to speak; and it does this in terms of both historical development and technique of representation. The next sentence (4) expands the material definition by explaining the re-

[5] *Collier's Encyclopedia* (1959), Vol. 6, p. 155. Used with permission of the publisher.

lation of Cubism to Realism and Abstraction. Sentence 5 concludes the paragraph by further historical definition, this time by naming the best-known adherents of Cubism and their period of greatest activity. Perhaps because the purposes of the artists were too vague, too contradictory, or too various to be stated briefly, this paragraph does not include functional definition—that Cubist purposes were to render three sides of an object simultaneously, and so on.

With any less than a paragraph of definition we couldn't expect to recognize very surely a Cubist painting when we saw one. In fact, we might well wish for an accompanying illustration (ostensive definition). Careful reading, however, and responsible use of our own resources should show us the worth of the paragraph defining Cubism; and analysis of its construction provides a good method and test for our own defining needs.

The term *Progress*, as used by the historian to designate a conception of history, requires longer and more complex definition, and here we can never hope for ostensive definition: we will never be able to see Progress in the same way we can see a Cubist painting. Synonymous terms such as *modern doctrine of Progress* or the *Idea of Progress* will hardly help us learn what the term means. Formal definition can give us only a start, as we saw above. A paragraph helps somewhat more:

FORMAL	The Idea of Progress is the belief that humanity is capable by its own efforts of gradually achieving on the earth a state of society free from hunger and disease, as well as from war and other social
HISTORICAL *Historical origin: time and general conditions*	catastrophes. The belief began to develop in Europe when, at the Renaissance, human thought and inspiration turned toward life in this world, after the long medieval orientation toward a destiny beyond life and time. . . .
Causal forces, which created and gave shape to the concept	The main source of its inspiration was the development of modern science and technology, accompanied by a philosophy grounded in natural reason and secular experience, rather than authority and tradition. . . .

FUNCTIONAL	The idea operates as a hypothesis and working belief, rather than an automatic certainty, which maintain that science and technology offer the promise of improving the human lot.
HISTORICAL AND MATERIAL	While it has had opponents from its inception, the Idea of Progress has encountered serious shocks only in the twentieth century, when historical events such as wars and other social disasters seemed to increase, and
Forces that have changed the concept	when historians developed the notion of a plurality of civilizations, some living and some dead. That civilizations can die implies that there is no necessity, and hence no law, of continuous social advance.
Forces that have sustained the concept	It has been the continued existence and success of science and technology that continue to inspire and support the doctrine.
Present shape of the concept	Thus, the Idea of Progress, though once extended to morality and religion, has been forced to return to a narrower premise, that improvement of human conditions through science and technology will continue, but only if they are harnessed to foresight, intelligence, and good will.[6]

Perhaps there is need to extend still further the definition of Progress: when a concept is rather abstract or complex or specialized, a paragraph or two may still leave the term only vaguely defined. If this is the case, it is probably also the case that the more comprehensive we try to make the formal definition, the more awkward and overly long it becomes. In such instances, it is better to release the portions of our formal definition gradually, letting them become the framework for a series of sentences or even of paragraphs. In other words, the elements of a very long formal definition can form the outline of a short essay of definition in which the sentence of formal definition itself never appears. Here is a somewhat longer definition of the Idea of Progress:

[6] Based on "The Idea of Progress," *Collier's Encyclopedia*, Vol. XVI (1959), pp. 372-373. Used with permission of the publisher.

1. The idea of progress is above all a conception of history, an organizing principle for the interpretation and comprehension of the incredibly complicated record of human experience. Progress, as a conception of history, suggests that there is a determinate order in the succession of events in time, that is, a pattern. As Jules Delvaille said, the notion of progress implies that there is a continuity in human experience. The present and the future are conceived to be concatenated to the past without interruption, break, or gap. The sequence of events is believed to have a direction, to follow a given course along an axis of time. This directional sequence may relate to mankind as a whole, to a supposed "life history" of each society, or to a presumed "general" course of change in the several major social institutions.

2. Further, a conception of history, as distinguished from the materials of history, implies that some agency, factor, or group of factors serves as a free or controlling variable to which historical phenomena are in some way bound. There inheres in this view a concept of causality, a suggestion that the directional pattern of change follows from a correspondence between changes in the independent factor and changes exhibited in the data under consideration. . . .

3. An attempt to frame a conception of history, as Professor Kroeber has observed, is an effort to push on beyond the diversity of narrative sequences of events, in order to attain an abstract formulation of a process operating in historical time, or a "metaphenomenal" generalization concerning the particulars of history. Such a generalization rests upon assumptions of a directional order and a controlling causality underlying the course of events. From this point of view, the idea of progress is a generalizing conception of human experience. It is the doctrine that the course of change involves increasing betterment. And in most theories of human progress, the advance of knowledge, which is assumed to be natural and necessary, is postulated as the central controlling variable.

4. The formulation of conceptions of history began, according to Carl Becker, when men first became conscious of themselves, or developed a reflective attitude toward their existence, toward their several schemes of life, and above all toward the labyrinthine mystery of their past and future. Reflective self-consciousness implies, among other things, consciousness of change in time. It leads to an evaluation of human experience, an appraisal of the past and a prognosis of the future. Thus the doctrine of progress involves more than merely a belief that human history follows a determinate natural course. It holds up before mankind in the present the promise of an unlimited increase of well-being in the future. And in this, the doctrine of progress may be distinguished from the idea of social evolution. For though social evolution suggests

that elements of culture necessarily undergo increasing differentiation, it need not be associated with the additional judgment that increasing complexity implies increasing betterment.

5. Taken as a whole, then, the idea of progress includes three principles: first, the belief that history follows a continuous, necessary, and orderly course; second, the belief that this course is the effect of a regularly operating causal law; and, third, the belief that the course of change has brought and will continue to bring improvement in the condition of mankind.

6. The idea, as [J. B.] Bury says, is modern, and stems from the seventeenth century. . . . [It] dominated European thought until the First World War. With the stress of events since 1914 there has occurred a revival of doubt, even granting the persistence of the doctrine of progress in certain theoretical systems and in popular opinion, particularly in the United States.

7. The conception of progress served three purposes. It provided, first, an interpretation of man's past, suggesting steady improvement in a number of ways. It offered, second, a basis for the appraisal of differences in the modes of social life of various peoples of the world, with the proposal that they could be ranked along a common course normal to them all, according to their relative degrees of advancement. It supplied, third, an optimistic vision of human destiny and a faith in the ameliorative power of change.[7]

The formal definition and its simple diagram are inadequate for definition of this scope. The cause of this inadequacy is apparent when we look at the first half of this short essay, where the first three paragraphs and some of the fourth are devoted to expanding the genus *conception of history*. From the point of view of the historian —whose special term we are concerned with—the implications of a conception of history are essential elements of the definition. Without the historian's explanation of *conception of history* the phrase Idea of Progress would, for the average reader, be nearly empty words which could only seem to have meaning. Before he can understand the Idea of Progress he must understand the class of things to which it belongs; the average reader is not expected to be familiar with this special class. For the most part the first four paragraphs, then, provide material definition: Paragraphs 1 and 2 state the conventional implications of the conception; paragraph 3 con-

[7] From George H. Hildebrand's Introduction, "The Idea of Progress: An Historical Analysis," to Frederick J. Teggart, *The Idea of Progress: A Collection of Readings* (Berkeley, University of California Press, 1949), pp. 3-4, 29, 26.

cerns the relation of a conception of history to the psychological domain; paragraph 4 mentions a theoretical origin for a conception of history in the nature of racial development. The fifth paragraph then sums up.

In a definition of this length, using unfamiliar and easily confused materials, it is important in some places to state what the historical conception is not. Thus, in the opening sentence of paragraph 2 we have a conception of history distinguished from the materials of history; in the latter part of paragraph 4 the idea of progress is distinguished from the idea of social evolution.

Paragraph 6 provides historical definition. (Historical definition, in the form of examination of antecedent conceptions of history, forms the greater part of the full version of this essay.) Paragraph 7 adds functional definition in summary form.

The sentence, the paragraph, and the short essay defining the Idea of Progress illustrate three solutions to the crucial problem of how much need be said to establish meaning for a term. To say simply that the one-sentence definition is best because it is shortest is to evade responsibility for judging value or function; from the short definition, the reader may have learned little more than a set of words, without coming any nearer to understanding *Progress*. To say that the short essay is best because it is longest is the same kind of evasion. Besides, even longer definitions of Progress are available.[8] The crucial problem of choosing among definitions of various lengths must ultimately be solved by pragmatic tests. Before we can reach a responsible decision we must both analyze fully the practical effects we wish to achieve by our definition and explore the range of possibilities for achieving those effects.

The problem of choice may extend even further than this, however. The historian's concept of progress is not the only one. A contractor speaks of the progress in constructing a building; a coach speaks of the progress made by a football team; a doctor speaks of the progress of a disease. These meanings of *progress* are only remotely related to the concept of historical progress we have been

[8] The one-sentence definition above is drawn from a medium-length essay by Charles Beard entitled "The Idea of Progress." The short-essay definition above is drawn from Hildebrand's long-essay introduction to a book of readings; the readings, in turn, constitute historical definition of *Progress*. Besides these, there is a famous book-length study, *The Idea of Progress*, by J. B. Bury.

examining. Clearly, we cannot ask, "Which is the *real* meaning of *progress?*" Nor can we ask simply, "Which is the *best* meaning to establish?" and from that determine which definition is best. Once again we make pragmatic tests of definitions.

Even when a term generally has only one meaning—*diameter*, for example—we need to make a pragmatic test for *when* to define. We may need to define a term like *diameter* only once and briefly even though our audience is encountering the term for the first time; the common dictionary definition may be enough. But with *progress* the decision of when to define requires deliberation. Common dictionary definitions include only general meanings like the following:

Progress is a "movement forward as in time or space; onward course; progression; as, the rapid *progress* of events; the daily *progress* of the sun; the *progress* of a disease."

Progress is "advance to an objective; a going or getting ahead. . . ."

Progress is "the action or process of advancing or improving by marked stages or degrees; gradual betterment. . . ."[9]

These are the meanings familiar to everyone. None of these, however, is *specifically* or *adequately* the meaning used by the historian or physicist. Pragmatically, then, we can often decide when definition is needed, in terms of the degree of specialization of meaning we attach to a term; when we use a term in a sense more specialized than the general meaning familiar to our audience or accessible in ordinary dictionaries, definition is necessary.

When we need to choose among specialized definitions the pragmatic test is more difficult. How shall we define *light* in a scientific sense? Up to 1900, light was traditionally defined by physicists as consisting of waves moving through space. Even now there are certain phenomena involving light that can be explained only if light is defined in terms of the wave theory. For example, a beam of light passing through a round aperture projects a sharply defined disk upon a screen; but if the aperture is reduced to the size of a pinhole, the disk becomes ribbed with alternating concentric bands of light and darkness. This phenomenon is known as diffraction. If two

[9] By permission. From *Webster's New International Dictionary*, Second Edition, copyright 1959 by G. & C. Merriam Co., publishers of the Merriam-Webster Dictionaries.

pinholes very close together are employed, the diffraction patterns merge in a series of parallel stripes, much like the intermingling of waves when two stones have been thrown into a pool; this phenomenon is known as interference. Diffraction and interference are strictly wave characteristics.

At the same time, however, the wave theory will not explain certain other light phenomena, such as radiation and photoelectric effects. In 1900, Max Planck put forth his Quantum Theory to meet these problems; the Quantum Theory defines light not as a series of unbroken waves, but as a series of discontinuous bits, known as quanta. Einstein's experiments, for which he won the Nobel Prize, resulted in what seems conclusive proof that all photoelectric radiation must be in terms of particles or quanta.

Whether light is waves or particles has never been determined. As one physicist puts it, "On Mondays, Wednesdays, and Fridays the wave theory is true, and on Tuesdays, Thursdays, and Saturdays the Quantum Theory is true."

For some purposes light cannot usefully be considered either as waves or as particles. A biologist, for example, with different needs from the physicist, must define light as "those experiences which we refer to as color, shade, brightness, etc. and through which we gain a conception of spatial depth and relation."[10] Julian Huxley, a contemporary biologist, notes that "For a biologist, [light] should only mean a kind of awareness, a mental experience."[11] It is neither waves nor quanta; it is not something in the outer world at all, but something in the mind—"a mental experience." Light, in this sense, is not something which exists independently of experience, but a kind of experience which has developed over eons of evolutionary time. This is a definition of light which works for the biologist since he is concerned, as the physicist is not, with the relationship between man and his environment. For him, light, like all experience, is a joint product of a complicated transaction—a transaction between photic radiations, sense organs which translate these radiations into nerve impulses, nerves for transmitting these impulses, and certain brain centers for translating these impulses into a particular kind of experience which we call light. In the brain purely quantitative

[10] Julian Huxley, *Evolution in Action* (New York, Harper & Brothers, 1953), p. 74. Used with permission.

[11] *Ibid.*

differences aroused in the nervous system by external radiations are translated into qualities of sensation.

What light "really" is, is a meaningless question. One defines light in terms of what one needs, of what will work in a given situation—in short, pragmatically. All specialized definitions must be approached in this way.

The fact that definitions must be made pragmatically does not mean, however, that we may, like Humpty-Dumpty, make words mean whatever we like. For, in addition to formal and pragmatic tests, definitions used for the written, public language must also pass social tests imposed by general usage. Take, for example, the student who wanted to prove that the Democratic party is socialistic. In his paper he defined as socialistic "any person or group of persons who believes in the Social Security laws . . . ." This is clear enough. It is true that the Democratic Party and most Democrats support the Social Security laws; but so do the Republican Party and most Republicans. The point is not that the above definition is wrong. Rather, this definition defines *socialism* (or *socialistic*) in a way which is not consonant with any established social meaning which the word has. When a word is defined arbitrarily, it loses its usefulness and confuses rather than promotes communication.

When a writer, in order to promote rather than confuse communication, uses a term which needs definition, he has two main responsibilities: (1) To make entirely clear the exact sense in which he is using a term; and (2) To make sure that the meaning of the term remains consistent. Consider the following colloquy:

Student A. I believe in free enterprise. Every manufacturing concern should be allowed to operate as its management thinks best. The anti-trust laws are an attempt on the part of government to restrict the freedom of American business to operate as it pleases; thus they destroy free enterprise.

Student B. I believe in free enterprise, too. Therefore I believe that the government should prohibit combinations in restraint of trade and resultant monopolies in order to allow competition to be really free. This is what the anti-trust laws are designed to do.

A and *B* may think that they disagree about the proper way to secure free enterprise, but the problem in their discussion is that they have not agreed on the meaning of *free enterprise*. For *A* it means the absence of any laws regulating private industry; for *B* it means a condition under which laws make maximum competition in industry possible. Before *A* and *B* can carry on an effective discussion of the way to secure free enterprise, they must first agree on a definition. If they don't, they will merely frustrate each other and confuse their audience.

A recent brochure on modern art contains the following passage:

> People who attack abstraction in modern paintings are blind to the facts of nature. For nature always creates geometrical shapes, though in infinite variety: how could she do otherwise when all shapes are geometrical, strictly speaking? and that is why the non-representational painter fills his canvas with rectangles, triangles, cubes, cones, etc.—for these are the true geometrical shapes.

The problem here is that the writer has used *geometrical* in the second sentence to mean simply "having a shape," for "all shapes are geometrical." But in the last sentence the meaning of "geometrical shape" has shifted to "simple figures studied in plane geometry." Cubism may or may not be justifiable, but it is certain that the shifting meaning of the key term in this paragraph is sufficiently irresponsible to make this particular attempt to justify modern painting a failure.

When the meaning of a term or phrase is unclear or shifting, it is almost certain to confuse the reader—and very often the writer as well. We cannot blame this on the language; words themselves are not tricky or mischievous. In themselves, they are neutral. The responsibility of a writer or speaker is to keep control over the words he uses: first, by seeing that the sense he requires for the purpose at hand, his definition, is clear; and second, by using the word or phrase in only that sense. Clear writing is a matter of control, and control is the responsibility of the writer. In simple, familiar discourse the problem of control is often achieved without difficulty or deliberate thought. If you say to a friend, "I'll meet you at the Hut at eight," it is not likely that any confusion will result; hence no definition is necessary. In relatively more complex and significant language, however, this is often not true. Some very important words like *happiness*, *good*, *fair*, *freedom*, *science*, are almost never safe to use without some clarification of specific meanings.

The most effective sort of control which we can exercise over a word is to define it. The purpose of a definition is to make communication possible where it would break down without it, and to make communication clear where it would otherwise be fuzzy. The responsibility lies with the writer, not with the language.

EXERCISES

1. Apply the tests of formal definition provided in Chapter 3 to the following definitions of *behavior*. Then construct a formal definition of your own for the term.
   a. Behavior is what people do.
   b. Behavior is when an organism responds to changes in its environment.
   c. Behavior is the motivated, deliberate action of an organism for the purpose of attaining a consciously held end or goal.
   d. Behavior is any nonmental action of an organism.
   e. Behavior is ecological equilibration.
   f. Behavior is the adjustment pattern of an organism behavioristically expressed.
   g. Behavior is the observable actions of an organism.
   h. Behavior is how people behave.

2. Using the definition of *behavior* you have constructed as a topic sentence, write a paragraph-length definition of the term, following the Outline for Definition at the end of Chapter 2.

3. After consulting one or more dictionaries for the definitions and etymologies of the less familiar words in Chapters 2 and 3, write a paragraph definition of each of the terms in the sense in which it is used in the chapters. The following words are suggested:

context	nominal
rationalist	empiricist
intrinsic	metaphysical
geometrical	conception
formulation	law
orientation	ameliorative

4. The formal definition of *Progress* in Chapter 3 is drawn from Charles Beard's essay "The Idea of Progress," which appears in the book *A Century of Progress*. Outline this essay. What types of definition does Beard employ? Where does his attitude toward Progress separate itself from his definition of it?

5. Illustrations of paragraph-length definition in Chapter 3 have the formal definition as the opening sentence. It can often serve, as any

other "topic sentence" can, as a concluding sentence for a paragraph, or it can appear elsewhere in the paragraph, so long as it assists clarification of meaning and is in the proper context. Rewrite the paragraph definitions in this chapter, putting the formal definition in another place and adjusting all parts of the paragraph to accommodate this change.

6. We have seen that negative definition–describing what a thing is *not*–is often a pitfall in the path of successful definition. Sometimes, however, definition by elimination may be necessary: "a *scalene triangle* is any triangle which is not isosceles and not equilateral"; "a *snack* is any meal not eaten at conventional meal times." Find other terms which may be adequately defined in this way, and construct definitions for them.

7. Write an essay (approximately 750 words) defining one of the words listed below, as used in the field specified. For information about the meaning of the word, consult the *Oxford English Dictionary*, at least one specialized dictionary for the field, glossaries of relevant textbooks, and at least two encyclopedias (preferably of two dates twenty or more years apart). This information can be gathered and organized most easily with the use of notecards.

motivation (psychology)
atom (physics)
syntax (linguistics or philology)
hypothesis (philosophy)
impressionism (painting)
aristocracy (political science and history)
species (biology)
paradox (literary criticism)
sonata (music)
utilitarianism (social philosophy)

EDWARD SAPIR

*The Types of Languages**

THE languages of the world may be classified either structurally or genetically. An adequate structural analysis is an intricate matter and no classification seems to have been suggested which does justice to the bewildering variety of known forms. [But] it must be obvious to anyone who has thought . . . at all [about the general form of a language] or who has felt something of the spirit of a foreign language that there is such a thing as a basic plan, a certain cut, to each language. This type or plan or structural "genius" of the language is something much more fundamental, much more pervasive, than any single feature of it that we can mention, nor can we gain an adequate idea of its nature by a mere recital of the sundry facts that make up the grammar or the language. When we pass from Latin to Russian, we feel that it is approximately the same horizon that bounds our view, even though the near, familiar landmarks have changed. When we come to English, we seem to notice that the hills have dipped down a little, yet we recognize the general lay of the land. And when we have arrived at Chinese, it is an utterly different sky that is looking down upon us. We can translate these metaphors and say that all languages differ from one another but that certain ones differ far more than others. This is tantamount

* This essay on language classification is a composite of Edward Sapir's writings from two sources: a portion of Chapter VI, "Types of Linguistic Structure," from *Language* (copyright, 1921, by Harcourt, Brace & World, Inc.; copyright, 1949, by Jean V. Sapir. Reprinted by permission of the publishers) and a portion of Edward Sapir's essay, "Language," in *Encyclopedia of the Social Sciences*, Vol. 9 (Copyright 1933 by The Macmillan Company and used with their permission). These two sources are combined as follows: from "Types of Linguistic Structure" is taken the section beginning in paragraph 1, sentence 3, through the end of paragraph 5; the remaining part of the present essay is from "Language," with sentences 3-7 of paragraph 14 transposed from a later portion of the same essay. The title given to the entire essay is supplied by the authors of this textbook.

to saying that it is possible to group them into morphological types.

2. Strictly speaking, we know in advance that it is impossible to set up a limited number of types that would do full justice to the peculiarities of the thousands of languages and dialects spoken on the surface of the earth. Like all human institutions, speech is too variable and too elusive to be quite safely ticketed. Even if we operate with a minutely subdivided scale of types, we may be quite certain that many of our languages will need trimming before they fit. To get them into the scheme at all it will be necessary to overestimate the significance of this or that feature or to ignore, for the time being, certain contradictions in their mechanism. Does the difficulty of classification prove the uselessness of the task? I do not think so. It would be too easy to relieve ourselves of the burden of constructive thinking and to take the standpoint that each language has its unique history, therefore its unique structure. Such a standpoint expresses only a half truth. Just as similar social, economic, and religious institutions have grown up in different parts of the world from distinct historical antecedents, so also languages, traveling along different roads, have tended to converge toward similar forms. Moreover, the historical study of language has proven to us beyond all doubt that a language changes not only gradually but consistently, that it moves unconsciously from one type towards another, and that analogous trends are observable in remote quarters of the globe. From this it follows that broadly similar morphologies must have been reached by unrelated languages independently and frequently. In assuming the existence of comparable types, therefore, we are not gainsaying the individuality of all historical processes; we are merely affirming that back of the face of history are powerful drifts that move language, like other social products, to balanced patterns, in other words, to types. . . .

3. When it comes to the actual task of classification, we find that we have no easy road to travel. Various classifications have been suggested, and they all contain elements of value. Yet none proves satisfactory. They do not so much enfold the known languages in their embrace as force them down into narrow, straight-backed seats. The difficulties have been of various kinds. First and foremost, it has been difficult to choose a point of view. On what basis shall we classify? A language shows us so many facets that we may well

be puzzled. And is one point of view sufficient? Secondly, it is dangerous to generalize from a small number of selected languages. To take, as the sum total of our material, Latin, Arabic, Turkish, Chinese, and perhaps Eskimo or Sioux as an afterthought, is to court disaster. We have no right to assume that a sprinkling of exotic types will do to supplement the few languages nearer home that we are more immediately interested in. Thirdly, the strong craving for a simple formula has been the undoing of linguists. There is something irresistible about a method of classification that starts with two poles, exemplified, say, by Chinese and Latin, clusters what it conveniently can about these poles, and throws everything else into a "transitional type." Hence has arisen the still popular classification of language into an "isolating" group, an "agglutinative" group, and an "inflective" group. Sometimes the languages of the American Indians are made to struggle along as an uncomfortable "polysynthetic" rear-guard to the agglutinative languages. There is justification for the use of all of these terms, though not perhaps in quite the spirit in which they are commonly employed. In any case it is very difficult to assign all the known languages to one or the other of these groups, the more so as they are not mutually exclusive. A language may be both agglutinative and inflective, or inflective and polysynthetic, or even polysynthetic and isolating. . . .

4. There is a fourth reason why the classification of languages has generally proved a fruitless undertaking. It is probably the most powerful deterrent of all to clear thinking. This is the evolutionary prejudice which instilled itself into the social sciences towards the middle of the last century and which is only now beginning to abate its tyrannical hold on our mind. Intermingled with this scientific prejudice and largely anticipating it was another, a more human one. The vast majority of linguistic theorists themselves spoke languages of a certain type, of which the most fully developed varieties were the Latin and Greek that they had learned in their childhood. It was not difficult for them to be persuaded that these familiar languages represented the "highest" development that speech had yet attained and that all other types were but steps on the way to this beloved "inflective" type. Whatever conformed to the pattern of Sanskrit and Greek and Latin and German was accepted as expressive of the "highest," whatever departed from it was frowned

upon as a shortcoming or was at best an interesting aberration.[1] Now any classification that starts with preconceived values or that works up to sentimental satisfactions is self-condemned as unscientific. A linguist that insists on talking about the Latin type of morphology as though it were necessarily the high-water mark of linguistic development is like the zoölogist that sees in the organic world a huge conspiracy to evolve the race-horse or the Jersey cow. Language in its fundamental forms is the symbolic expression of human intuitions. These may shape themselves in a hundred ways, regardless of the material advancement or backwardness of the people that handle the forms, of which, it need hardly be said, they are in the main unconscious. If, therefore, we wish to understand language in its true inwardness we must disabuse our minds of preferred "values" and accustom ourselves to look upon English and Hottentot with the same cool, yet interested, detachment.

5. We come back to our first difficulty. What point of view shall we adopt for our classification? . . . More justifiable [than previous methods for classification*] would be a classification according to the formal processes most typically developed in the language, [to which we may now turn].

6. It is useful to recognize three distinct criteria of classification [by formal processes]: the relative degree of synthesis or elaboration of the words of the language; the degree to which the various parts of a word are welded together; and the extent to which the fundamental relational concepts of the language are directly expressed as such. As regards synthesis, languages range all the way from the isolating type, in which the single word is essentially unanalyzable, to the type represented by many American Indian languages in which the single word is functionally often the equivalent of a sen-

[1] One celebrated American writer on culture and language delivered himself of the dictum that, estimable as the speakers of agglutinative languages might be, it was nevertheless a crime for an inflecting woman to marry an agglutinating man. Tremendous spiritual values were evidently at stake. Champions of the "inflective" languages are wont to glory in the very irrationalities of Latin and Greek, except when it suits them to emphasize their profoundly "logical" character. Yet the sober logic of Turkish or Chinese leaves them cold. The glorious irrationalities and formal complexities of many "savage" languages they have no stomach for. Sentimentalists are difficult people. (Sapir's note)

* Sapir discusses these in a portion of his chapter not reprinted here.

tence with many concrete references that would, in most languages, require the use of a number of words. Four stages of synthesis may be conveniently recognized: the isolating type, the weakly synthetic type, the fully synthetic type, and the polysynthetic type. The classical example of the first is Chinese, which does not allow the words of the language to be modified by internal changes or the addition of prefixed or suffixed elements to express such concepts as those of number, tense, mode, case relation, and the like. . . . The weakly synthetic type of language is best represented by the most familiar modern languages of Europe, such as English, French, Spanish, Italian, German, Dutch, and Danish. Such languages modify words to some extent but have only a moderate formal elaboration of the word. The plural formations of English and French, for instance, are relatively simple and the tense and modal systems of all the languages of this type tend to use analytic methods as supplementary to the older synthetic one. The third group of languages is represented by such languages as Arabic and the earlier Indo-European languages, like Sanskrit, Latin, and Greek. These are all languages of great formal complexity, in which classificatory ideas, such as sex gender, number, case relations, tense, and mood, are expressed with considerable nicety and in a great variety of ways. Because of the rich formal implications of the single word the sentence tends not to be so highly energized and ordered as in the first mentioned types. Lastly, the polysynthetic languages add to the formal complexity of the treatment of fundamental relational ideas the power to arrange a number of logically distinct, concrete ideas into an ordered whole within the confines of a single word. Eskimo and Algonquin are classical examples of this type.

7. From the standpoint of the mechanical cohesiveness with which the elements of words are united, languages may be conveniently grouped into four types. The first of these, in which there is no such process of combination, is the isolating type already referred to. To the second group of languages belong all those in which the word can be adequately analyzed into a mechanical sum of elements, each of which has its more or less clearly established meaning and each of which is regularly used in all other words into which the associated notion enters. These are the so-called agglutinative languages. The majority of languages seem to use the agglutinative technique, which has the great advantage of combining logical analysis with

economy of means. The Altaic languages, of which Turkish is a good example, and the Bantu languages of Africa are agglutinative in form.

8. In the third type, the so-called inflective languages, the degree of union between the radical element or stem of the word and the modifying prefixes or suffixes is greater than in the agglutinative languages, so that it becomes difficult in many cases to isolate the stem and set it off against the accreted elements. More important than this, however, is the fact that there is less of a one-to-one correspondence between the linguistic element and the notion referred to than in the agglutinative languages. In Latin, for instance, the notion of plurality is expressed in a great variety of ways which seem to have little phonetic connection with each other. For example, the final vowel or diphthong of *equi* (horses), *dona* (gifts), *mensae* (tables), and the final vowel and consonant of *hostes* (enemies) are functionally equivalent elements the distribution of which is dependent on purely formal and historical factors which have no logical relevance. Furthermore in the verb the notion of plurality is quite differently expressed, as in the last two consonants of *amant* (they love) . . . .

9. As an offshoot of the inflective languages may be considered a fourth group, those in which the processes of welding, due to the operation of complex phonetic laws, have gone so far as to result in the creation of patterns of internal change of the nuclear elements of speech. Such familiar English examples as the words "sing," "sang," "sung," "song" will serve to give some idea of the nature of these structures, which may be termed "symbolistic." The kinds of internal change which may be recognized are changes in vocalic quality, changes in consonants, changes in quantity, various types of reduplication or repetition, changes in stress accent, and, as in Chinese and many African languages, changes in pitch. The classical example of this type of language is Arabic, in which, as in the other Semitic languages, nuclear meanings are expressed by sequences of consonants which have, however, to be connected by significant vowels whose sequence patterns establish fixed functions independent of the meanings conveyed by the consonantal framework.

10. Elaboration and technique of word analysis are of perhaps less logical and psychological significance than the selection and treatment of fundamental relational concepts for grammatical treat-

ment. It would be very difficult, however, to devise a satisfactory conceptual classification of languages because of the extraordinary diversity of the concepts and classifications of ideas which are illustrated in linguistic form. In the Indo-European and Semitic languages, for instance, noun classification on the basis of gender is a vital principle of structure; but in most of the other languages of the world this principle is absent, although other methods of noun classification are found. Again, tense or case relations may be formally important in one language, for example, Latin, but of relatively little grammatical importance in another, although the logical references implied by such forms must naturally somehow be taken care of in the economy of the language as, for instance, by the use of specific words within the framework of the sentence. Perhaps the most fundamental conceptual basis of classification is that of the expression of fundamental syntactic relations as such versus their expression in necessary combination with notions of a concrete order. In Latin, for example, the notion of the subject of a predicate is never purely expressed in a formal sense, because there is no distinctive symbol for this relation. It is impossible to render it without at the same time defining the number and gender of the subject of the sentence. There are languages, however, in which syntactic relations are expressed purely, without admixture of implications of a nonrelational sort. We may speak therefore of pure relational languages as contrasted with mixed relational languages. Most of the languages with which we are familiar belong to the latter category. It goes without saying that such a conceptual classification has no direct relation to the other two types of classification which we have mentioned.

11. The genetic classification of languages is one which attempts to arrange the languages of the world in groups and subgroups in accordance with the main lines of historical connection, which can be worked out either on the basis of documentary evidence or of a careful comparison of the languages studied. Because of the far-reaching effect of slow phonetic changes and of other causes languages which were originally nothing but dialects of the same form of speech have diverged so widely that it is not apparent that they are but specialized developments of a single prototype. An enormous amount of work has been done in the genetic classification and subclassification of the languages of the world, but very many prob-

lems still await research and solution. At the present time it is known definitely that there are certain very large linguistic groups, or families, as they are often called, the members of which may, roughly speaking, be looked upon as lineally descended from languages which can be theoretically reconstructed in their main phonetic and structural outlines. . . .

12. The technique of establishing linguistic families and of working out the precise relationship of the languages included in these families is too difficult to be gone into here. It suffices to say that random word comparisons are of little importance. Experience shows that very precise phonetic relations can be worked out between the languages of the group and that, on the whole, fundamental morphological features tend to preserve themselves over exceedingly long periods of time. Thus modern Lithuanian is in structure, vocabulary and, to a large extent, even phonemic pattern very much the kind of a language which must be assumed as the prototype for the Indo-European languages as a whole.

13. In spite of the fact that structural classifications are, in theory, unrelated to genetic ones and in spite of the fact that languages can be shown to have influenced each other, not only in phonetics and vocabulary but also to an appreciable extent in structure, it is not often found that the languages of a genetic group exhibit utterly irreconcilable structures. Thus, even English, which is one of the least conservative of the Indo-European languages, has many far-reaching points of structure in common with as remote a language as Sanskrit, in contrast, say, to Basque or Finnish. . . .

14. The complete rationale of linguistic change, involving as it does many of the most complex processes of psychology and sociology, has not yet been satisfactorily worked out, but there are a number of general processes that emerge with sufficient clarity. For practical purposes, inherent changes may be distinguished from changes due to contact with other linguistic communities. Of the linguistic changes due to the more obvious types of contact the one which seems to have played the most important part in the history of language is the "borrowing" of words across linguistic frontiers. This borrowing naturally goes hand in hand with cultural diffusion. An analysis of the provenience of the words of a given language is frequently an important index of the direction of cultural influence. Our English vocabulary, for instance, is very richly stratified in a

cultural sense. The various layers of early Latin, mediaeval French, humanistic Latin and Greek, and modern French borrowings constitute a fairly accurate gauge of the time, extent, and nature of the various foreign cultural influences which have helped to mold the English civilization.

15. [Nevertheless,] the enormous amount of study that has been lavished on the history of particular languages and groups of languages shows very clearly that the most powerful differentiating factors are not outside influences, as ordinarily understood, but rather the very slow but powerful unconscious changes in certain directions which seem to be implicit in the phonemic systems and morphologies of the languages themselves. These "drifts" are powerfully conditioned by unconscious formal feelings and are made necessary by the inability of human beings to actualize ideal patterns in a permanently set fashion.

16. Linguistic changes may be analyzed into phonetic changes, changes in form, and changes in vocabulary. Of these the phonetic changes seem to be the most important and the most removed from direct observation. The factors which lead to these phonetic changes are probably exceedingly complex and no doubt include the operation of obscure symbolisms which define the relation of various age groups to each other. Not all phonetic changes, however, can be explained in terms of social symbolism. It seems that many of them are due to the operation of unconscious economies in actualizing sounds or combinations of sounds. The most impressive thing about internal phonetic change is its high degree of regularity. It is this regularity, whatever its ultimate cause, that is more responsible than any other single factor for the enviable degree of exactness which linguistics has attained as a historical discipline. Changes in grammatical form often follow in the wake of destructive phonetic changes. In many cases it can be seen how irregularities produced by the disintegrating effect of phonetic change are ironed out by the analogical spread of more regular forms. The cumulative effect of these corrective changes is quite sensibly to modify the structure of the language in many details and sometimes even in its fundamental features. Changes in vocabulary are due to a great variety of causes, most of which are of a cultural rather than of a strictly linguistic nature. The too frequent use of a word, for instance, may reduce it to a commonplace term, so that it needs to be replaced by a new

word. On the other hand, changes of attitude may make certain words with their traditional overtones of meaning unacceptable to the younger generation, so that they tend to become obsolete. Probably the most important single source of changes in vocabulary is the creation of new words on analogies which have spread from a few specific words.

CHAPTER FOUR

Systems and Forms of Classification

"The Types of Languages" unites Sapir's discussion of language classification problems and his practical attempt to provide a classification system for the languages of the world. The importance of Sapir's work and the superiority of his writing enable us to learn about classification, about languages, and about writing. The more we learn about any of these the more we will understand of the others.

The first four paragraphs of "The Types of Languages" take up three important aspects of classification: (1) the nature of the classification process, (2) the relation between the *objects* being classified and the *system* within which they are classified, and (3) problems in choosing among classification systems. As soon as we have read the opening sentence of Sapir's essay, we can infer something of the nature of classification. Any set of phenomena which can be identified by the same name—"languages," in this case—is subject to classification; and more than one system of classification can be applied to a single set of phenomena. Sapir classifies languages by their structural and genetic relations. Other systems also suggest themselves: languages may be classified by the number of speakers, the historical period of their use, their geographical location, the form of writing, if any, in which they are customarily transcribed (for example, writing by sounds, by syllables, by ideas), and their social function (for example, religious ritual, familiar speech, law). More fundamental, if less apparent, to the nature of classification is the process by which it takes place. With the phrases "a certain cut," "a basic plan," a "structural 'genius,'" and the more extended metaphor of the familiar and unfamiliar horizons, Sapir suggests that the *process* of classifying is the experience of recognizing some things as more like than different, as having more resemblance to some things, less resemblance to others. When we recognize that walking is more like running than like sitting, we experience this mode of perception. The result of our recognition of similarities and differences is a sorting of these behavior events. In the same manner we can recognize, as Sapir tells us, "morphological types" of languages; it is these types—clusterings of form-aspects of languages which he explains and illustrates later—that he groups languages by, beginning in paragraph 6.

The *process* of classifying is, however, a psychological event. To make it the subject of our writing would require us to describe how a classification system came about, rather than describe the structure of the system itself and the use we wish to make of it. But the *system* of a classification is a logical and rhetorical concern. We can consider it specifically as a mode for achieving form in writing. Ordinarily, we are mainly concerned to communicate the system itself, the reasons for constructing it, and probably some uses of it. To discover a form for writing based on classification, then, our attention must turn to the classification system.

The first aspect of a classification system which Sapir deals with (paragraph 2) is the relation of a *system* of classifying to the *objects* being classified. Languages, he says, usually need trimming before they will fit into any classification system, no matter how minutely divided and subdivided that system is; some characteristics of a language must be emphasized, others minimized or ignored, if, as Sapir puts it, we are to "ticket" languages at all. When we group languages by types we cannot "do full justice to [their] peculiarities." We perceive on the one hand the separate objects, all of them unique. On the other hand, we perceive similarities and differences among the objects which make grouping possible; and this grouping enables us to operate conveniently and economically with the objects, permits "constructive thinking" about them—in short, enables us to have *knowledge about* the objects as well as *experience of* them.

The wider the system the more nearly we satisfy the claims of the objects' uniqueness but the less we satisfy the need for grouping; conversely, the narrower the system of classification the easier it is to use but the less we retain of the concrete and specific nature of the objects. From one point of view this poses a dilemma: we cannot preserve the richness and detail of the full set of objects and at the same time enjoy the clarity and convenience of a neat system. Put in this way, it seems as if we always lose, regardless of the classification system we choose. But to face this matter as a practical problem, we can see that to choose a system of classification—even the narrowest system—is not merely a decision to reject or to ignore the individuality of the objects being classified; it is a decision to attend to something else. Our decision to give our attention to the classes of objects and the system which these classes form is a pragmatic decision in the sense that decisions regarding form and extent-of-definition needs (Chapter 3) are pragmatic. Correlatively, our decisions regarding the proper complexity of a classification system will be pragmatic.

It is with these pragmatic problems that Sapir deals next (paragraphs 3 and 4). When the objects before us present a great variety of characteristics, the first problem is to choose a point of view, to decide on a basis for classifying. It is simple enough to sort out a set of objects and place them in familiar groups when we come to them with a preconceived plan of classification; this is doing a routine job, which requires some ingenuity, but is mainly a mechanical operation. In this way we pack our belongings by size, weight, and fragility, for shipping; we group sports by the objects they use, the number of players, or their national origin; and we arrange our explanations in order of difficulty. When a preconceived classification system is not appropriate to a set of objects, or when we are dissatisfied with existing classifications, we face the problem Sapir is considering: where do we begin our organization of so many different objects? And once we have classified them, does our classification actually serve the needs we had in mind when we undertook it? Instead of doing a routine job, we are in a position to discover new relations and characteristics within the set of objects before us. By trying to classify our friends, as familiar as they are, we can see this. Classification of some sort is not difficult—it seems even inevitable. But to achieve a useful classification may require many trials and frustrations; and only when the proper system has evolved, are we in a position to solve further problems.

The second problem has to do with the completeness of our classification system. If it is to be more than a mere exercise, it must deal with all the facts available. Light, for instance, is easily classified by the color spectrum of the rainbow. But light is not only what human beings see; it is what bees, photographic plates, and certain detection devices "see," and a system for classifying light can be good only to the degree to which it deals with all manifestations of light. Similarly, a classification of dance forms is only as good as the range of dances it classifies, if our intention is to deal with the dance generally. Simplicity in a system is attractive, but simplicity is double-edged—a convenience and a distortion.

Finally, Sapir brings up the problem facing the scientist in particular, but anyone generally, if the objects to be classified are empirical facts. When "cold" facts require classification, we can easily fall into error by adopting "warm" values as the basis for classifying. Categories such as "better," "newer," "more human," and "more desirable" usually reflect subjective values rather than objective criteria. Sapir's example of the zoölogist seeing, through his classification of evolutionary data, "a huge conspiracy to evolve the race-horse or the Jersey cow" is comment enough.

So it is when we attempt to construct and choose among systems of classification. We must be aware of some pitfalls and dead ends, some guideposts and highroads in classifying. Yet ultimately the problem is solved in terms of our needs; the solution is pragmatic.

The first four paragraphs of "The Types of Languages" reveal the careful attention Sapir has paid to the nature and problems of classification method. Besides understanding classification method, anyone undertaking a classification of complex materials must have one other qualification: he must be fully acquainted with the objects to be classified, as well as with other systems by which they have been classified (if any exist). Sapir's qualifications are clearly implicit in the essay. Thus he can proceed to a classification of languages: first, as he tells us in paragraph 5, classification "according to the formal processes most typically developed in [a] language," or *structural classification;* second, classification according to historical connection—historical change—or *genetic classification.*

Sapir begins his structural classification of languages (paragraphs 6-10) by presenting three criteria for classification by formal processes, which will distinguish three groupings of languages:

A. "The relative degree of synthesis or elaboration of the words of the language" (paragraph 6);

B. "The degree to which the various parts of a word are welded together" (paragraphs 7-9); and

C. "The extent to which the fundamental relational concepts of the language are directly expressed as such" (paragraph 10).

Within the first grouping he distinguishes four "stages," which form the bases for four subtypes: (A.1) "the isolating type," (A.2) "the weakly synthetic type," (A.3) "the fully synthetic type," and (A.4) "the polysynthetic type." Sapir describes these subtypes in order to distinguish them. From his descriptions we may supply parallels, or at least approximate illustrations, from our own language. When he speaks of internal change in words we can find in English *freeze-frozen*, *tooth-teeth*, *sing-sang* as examples; prefixed and suffixed elements are of all sorts in English—*un-imaginative*, *a-typical*, *size-d*, *same-ness*, *house-s*, *imagin-able*, and so on. English, because it belongs generally within only one of these subtypes (the weakly synthetic type), cannot provide parallels with the other full classes of languages; but it can provide many illustrations, particularly if we reach into its less ordinary aspects. Modifications of words for the purposes Sapir mentions are listed here:

To express the concept of	*English may use*
number (for example, plurality)	pen-pen*s*, fact-fact*s*, m*a*n-m*e*n
tense	walk-walk*ed*, spen*d*-spen*t*, *e*at-*a*te, wonder-wonder*ed*, g*i*ve-g*a*ve
case relation	stone-stone'*s*, who-whose-whom, she-hers-her
sex gender	actr*ess*, *he*-goat, *she*-wolf, *vixen* (fox)
mood	"If I were he . . ." (hardly a survival of this word modification is to be found in English)

The isolating type of language, Sapir says, employs no modifications of the kinds illustrated; weakly synthetic languages use a few of them—as does English; fully synthetic languages differ from the second group in degree, having a large variety and abundant number of modifications of this sort. Polysynthetic languages, on the other hand, may express by means of word-parts a number of concrete as well as relational concepts. An example is the Santali word, formed on the root *dal* ("strike"), *dal-ocho-akan-taben-tae-tiñ-a-e*, "he, who belongs to him who belongs to me, will continue letting himself be struck"; if, however, the infix *pa* is inserted in the root, *dapal*, the sense is made reciprocal, the person who is struck, striking back.

Sapir's classification by "the degree to which the various parts of a word are welded together," or by their "mechanical cohesiveness" (paragraphs 7-9), produces, similarly, certain subtypes: (B.1) the "isolating," (B.2) the "agglutinative," (B.3) the "inflective," and (B.4) the "symbolistic" groups of language-aspects. All of these are explained sufficiently for our purposes in Sapir's presentation.

The final type of language-grouping depends on "the extent to which fundamental relational concepts of language are directly expressed as such," or classification in terms of the degree to which grammatical relations are expressed separately or in combination with concepts "of a concrete order" (paragraph 10). For instance, the relation of "boy" to the rest of a sentence may be expressed separately if "boy" is the indirect object and if this syntactic relation is expressed by the preposition "to": "He gave eleven marbles *to* the boy." A different word order establishes the same syntactic relation for "boy," without the preposition: "He gave the boy eleven marbles." In the same sentence, however, the syntactic relation of the giver is not expressed separately from the term designating the giver; *he* is the subject of the sentence, and to change the syntactic relation of the giver we would change the form of the word to *him* or *his* (or *whose*, perhaps). Classification by separate ("pure") or implicit ("mixed") expression of relational concepts gives us two main groups of languages, with the latter being the much larger group. We may thus complete our numbering of language groups by structural classification with (C.1) "pure relational languages" and (C.2) "mixed relational languages."

Turning now to genetic classification of languages (paragraphs 11-16), Sapir examines first the problems of establishing "the main lines of historical connection" (paragraphs 11-12) and the relations between genetic and structural classification of languages (paragraph 13). In this essay he does not provide a table or "family tree" of languages. (These are easily found, however, in textbooks for the history of the English language, encyclopedias, and comparative and historical grammars.) Rather, he distinguishes the types of processes by which languages change to produce groups of languages historically (genetically) related. Sapir's first division of linguistic processes of change is a broad one, based on whether the source of change is within a language or outside of it: (A.1) "inherent changes" and (A.2) "changes due to contact with other linguistic communities" (paragraph 14). Under (A.2), for example, is to be considered "borrowing" of words from other languages. Inherent changes, though, operate most powerfully in linguistic change and differentiation. Under (A.1), then, are to be considered three types of change (paragraph 15). First (paragraph 16), drifts in the speech sounds, drifts brought about by a number of causes such as the relation of age groups to each other and economy in articulating sounds in spoken sequences. The sound changes in turn seem to cause the second kind of change—changes in forms of a language. And, third, there are changes in vocabulary to accommodate social, material, and cultural change, to preserve the range and force of vocabulary, and so on.

If we pause now and draw out the headings of Sapir's classification system for languages, perhaps we can see more clearly where we have been and then return to the essay with a fresh orientation. The classification system Sapir laid out for us is as follows:

I. Structural classification: formal processes.

A. "The relative degree of synthesis or elaboration of the words of a language."

1. "The isolating type."
2. "The weakly synthetic type."
3. "The fully synthetic type."
4. "The polysynthetic type."

B. "The degree to which the various parts of a word are welded together."

1. The "isolating" type.
2. The "agglutinative" type.
3. The "inflective" type.
4. The "symbolistic" type.

C. "The extent to which the fundamental relational concepts of the language are expressed as such."

1. "Pure relational languages."
2. "Mixed relational languages."

II. Genetic classification: sources of change and differentiation.
- A. "Inherent changes."
  1. "Phonetic changes."
  2. "Changes in form."
  3. "Changes in vocabulary."
- B. "Changes due to contact with other linguistic communities."
  Example: "borrowing."

In making specific decisions regarding written forms of classification, the classification system we choose is all-important. Other decisions—on extent of the writing, on the scope of each portion of it, on the order and arrangement of the various sections, on the comparison of the system chosen with other systems—depend upon the choice of the system. Let us consider three consequences of this assertion.

Since our concern is first of all to communicate the classification system we have adopted, we need to make entirely clear what the system consists of and our reasons for constructing it. We will present the system, naming and defining the categories which make it up. So obvious a requirement is easily overlooked or mishandled. Sapir is carefully attentive to this matter. At the outset of the essay he names the kinds of classification systems he will deal with: structural and genetic. When he discusses structural classification he states explicitly, at the opening of that section of the essay, what the system consists of by naming and defining its parts. He has stated his topics and intentions so explicitly that we are able to make an outline entirely in his own words. Further, he states specifically what his principles of classification will be (paragraph 6). And he carefully follows the same procedure elsewhere in his essay. At times he even goes a step further and illustrates each part of the system with one or more members (languages) belonging within each part.

These are the things we need to do in presenting a system of classification, and Sapir has done them fully and deliberately. In other cases so full and deliberate a presentation of the system may not be necessary. For instance, if we are presenting a generally familiar system, we can shorten our presentation and perhaps leave some elements of it unstated. Numerical or percentage groupings constitute perhaps the most familiar kinds of classification systems. Regardless of whether we are grouping industrially synthesized molecules, guests at a series of parties, national populations, or the chances of survival, statistical groupings are immediately understood, and the system itself needs no extended description. (The significance of the groupings, of course, may not be obvious.) Other groupings having familiar labels will need little explanation other than that implicit in the names of the classes, supplemented perhaps by a brief statement of the criterion used for establishing the groups. Here is an example from *Collier's Encyclopedia:*

> The modern breeds of dogs are usually classified within six major groupings as defined by the American Kennel Club: Sporting Dogs, Sporting Dogs (Hounds), Working Dogs, Terriers, Toys, and Non-Sporting. This classification is based on the real or fancied use of the several breeds and is in but few particulars a natural or biological classification.[1]

As with definition, the length and detail of each part of the system is determined by the degree of familiarity with it which we may expect in our readers.

Having made sure that the system is identified and adequately defined, we need to put the objects into the system. Here again the extent to which we do this will depend on our needs, on the requirements for informing the reader as fully as we think appropriate. *In this essay* Sapir does not need to place all languages in their appropriate categories. However, the Encyclopedia's presentation of the system for classifying dogs is followed by an extensive list of major breeds of dogs grouped according to the system presented.

At times, the placing of objects into categories may be our primary concern. Our purpose may be to decide into which category an object will be placed or to explain or defend our decision to place something in one subclass rather than another. Shall we classify the duckbilled platypus as a mammal? Shall we classify an act of stealing as theft, burglary, or robbery? Shall we classify jazz as "serious" or "popular" music? Or must we proceed to set up a new system for classifying the objects? The form of our writing will grow out of the system we have chosen and the use we wish to make of it.

The third consequence of our choice of a system may be the need to demonstrate its worth. We shall probably compare other systems to ours, and measure each by its effectiveness and thoroughness.

[1] From *Collier's Encyclopedia* (1959). Used with permission of the publisher.

(This part of Sapir's essay has been omitted.) We can set up certain tests for completeness and accuracy. The completeness of a system may be tested by seeing if the subclasses within any part of the system account for all the objects assigned to that part; the accuracy of a system, by seeing that only one principle of division is used for each classification. A classification of buildings into brick, frame, and business is an inaccurate one. Because more than one principle of division is involved, some buildings would be placed in more than one category. This test of the accuracy of a system provides perhaps the most reliable plan for organizing extended presentation, discussion, and application of a classification system. The principle, the division of objects stemming from that principle, and discussion and application of that division—these elements, in this order, will provide a framework for clear exposition. The whole of Sapir's essay illustrates this method of organizing writing dealing with classification.

By way of postscript, we may consider one more characteristic of classification, best approached, perhaps, through fresh examples.

1. Consider a rainbow or a spectrum from a prism. There is a continuous gradation of color from one end to the other. That is, at any point there is only a small difference in the colors immediately adjacent at either side. Yet an American describing it will list the hues as *red*, *orange*, *yellow*, *green*, *blue*, *purple*, or something of the kind. The continuous gradation of color which exists in nature is represented in language by a series of discrete categories. This is an instance of structuring of content. There is nothing inherent either in the spectrum or the human perception of it which would compel its division this way. The specific method of division is part of the structure of English.

By contrast, speakers of other languages classify colors in much different ways. In the accompanying diagram, a rough indication is given of the way in which the spectral colors are divided by speakers of English, Shona (a language of Rhodesia), and Bassa (a language of Liberia).[2] [See diagram on next page.]

2. If one draws some dozen lines . . . of different shapes, one perceives them as divisible into such categories as "straight," "crooked," "curved," "zigzag" because of the classificatory suggestiveness of the linguistic terms themselves. We see and hear and otherwise experience very

[2] From H. A. Gleason, Jr., *An Introduction to Descriptive Linguistics* (New York, Henry Holt & Co., Inc., 1955). Used with permission.

English:	purple	blue	green	yellow	orange	red

Shona:	cips^{w}uka	citema	cicena	cips^{w}uka

Bassa:	hui	ziza

largely as we do because the language habits of our community predispose certain choices of interpretation.[3]

That the nature of the language a person inherits should impose so heavily not only on his use of that language but on his very mode of experiencing the events of the world is not news to the philosopher and linguist. But it introduces into the study of rhetoric a consideration not ordinarily apparent when we study merely our own language. This consideration, which holds not only for classification but, as we will see, for logic and explanation as well, is that these operations are carried on within the forms of our inherited language, yet purport to concern the world outside of language. Classification uses the words and forms already existing in our language; it is likely to be tyrannical and the habitual forms of writing are likely to be stifling; it is often in danger of being no more than routine practice, done within the stereotype of experience imposed by our language. But the uses—if not the pieces—of a language are flexible; if the procedure in writing about classification is pragmatic, if the form of writing emerges from the classification itself, we may be able to break through some limitations of language. Responsible use of classification systems can emerge from our careful attention to classification method and the forms of writing which embody it.

[3] From Edward Sapir, "The Status of Linguistics as a Science," *Language,* V (1929), p. 210. Used with permission.

EXERCISES

1. After consulting one or more dictionaries for the definitions and etymologies of the less familiar words in this chapter, write a formal definition of each of the terms in the sense in which it is used in this chapter. The following words are suggested:

linguistics	grammatical relations
morphology	genetic
dilemma	color spectrum

2. Write a paragraph definition of each of the terms listed in Exercise 1, developing material definition through a classification of the varieties of the thing defined or of the uses of the term itself. For example, the uses of the term *morphology* can be classified by the sciences in which the term is used. (The paragraph should make clear the principle on which the classification is based.)

3. Classify the objects designated by each of the following terms according to at least three different principles of classification: (Seven different systems were named for classifying languages, p. 50.)

people	sciences
business machines	television programs
paintings	churches
teachers	vegetables

4. By consulting encyclopedias, dictionaries, and textbooks, discover and state in a paragraph (100-150 words) the basis for classifying:
a. a whale as a mammal, as a symbol, as a commodity.
b. a teen-ager as a minor, as a consumer, as a social type.
c. gold as a noble metal, as a dental supply, as a mineral.
d. the word *rotgut* as slang, as a compound word, as a metaphor.
e. Joan of Arc as a saint, as a national hero, as a heretic.
f. books according to the Dewey decimal system, according to their shipping costs, according to their dominant classes of buyers.

5. The following sentences provide a series of notes on the adaptation of organisms to their environment. Organize these notes, adding necessary headings of your own, into an outline for a classification of types of adaptation. In addition, state the principle on which the classification has been made.

a. Succulent leaves enable plants in desert regions to store water.
b. Flatfish can change color within a few minutes.

c. Squids and octopuses change color by expanding or contracting bags of pigment on their outer surfaces.

d. Wild horses have single toes and large hip muscles, enabling them to run with great speed.

e. Many fish and amphibia can change color according to their background.

f. Dogs, monkeys, and human beings are able to scratch or bite every part of the surface of their bodies.

g. Protective coloration is an adaptive characteristic of organisms, both plant and animal.

h. Most animals are lighter below than above, rather than uniformly shaded, and light on most of them comes from above.

i. Horses have teeth and stomachs which enable them to eat only grasses.

j. Intelligence and the capacity to learn produce high versatility in man for adaptation.

k. Some mammals, like pigs and men, are able to eat almost anything.

6. Write a short essay in which you classify at least ten members of one of the following groups:

a. musical instruments
b. musical compositions
c. competitive sports
d. wavelengths of visible light
e. radio wavelengths
f. causes of an historical event (for example, the American Civil War)
g. languages
h. paintings
i. architecture
j. poetry

ALBERT EINSTEIN

*The Laws of Science and the Laws of Ethics**

SCIENCE searches for relations which are thought to exist independently of the searching individual. This includes the case where man himself is the subject; or the subject of scientific statements may be concepts created by ourselves, as in mathematics. Such concepts are not necessarily supposed to correspond to any objects in the outside world. However, all scientific statements and laws have one characteristic in common: they are "true" or "false" (adequate or inadequate). Roughly speaking, our reaction to them is "yes" or "no."

2. The scientific way of thinking has a further characteristic. The concepts which it uses to build up its coherent systems do not express emotions. For the scientist, there is only "being," but no wishing, no valuing, no good, no evil—in short, no goal. As long as we remain within the realm of science proper, we can never encounter a sentence of the type: "Thou shalt not lie." There is something like a Puritan's restraint in the scientist who seeks truth: he keeps away from everything voluntaristic or emotional. Incidentally, this trait is the result of a slow development, peculiar to modern Western thought.

3. From this it might seem as if logical thinking were irrelevant for ethics. Scientific statements of facts and relations, indeed, cannot produce ethical directives. However, ethical directives can be made rational and coherent by logical thinking and empirical knowledge. If we can agree on some fundamental ethical propositions, then

* Albert Einstein, Foreward to Philipp Frank, *Relativity—A Richer Truth* (Boston, The Beacon Press, 1950). Used by permission.

other ethical propositions can be derived from them, provided that the original premises are stated with sufficient precision. Such ethical premises play a similar role in ethics to that played by axioms in mathematics.

4. This is why we do not feel at all that it is meaningless to ask such questions as: "Why should we not lie?" We feel that such questions are meaningful because in all discussions of this kind some ethical premises are tacitly taken for granted. We then feel satisfied when we succeed in tracing back the ethical directive in question to these basic premises. In the case of lying, this might perhaps be done in some way such as this: Lying destroys confidence in the statements of other people. Without such confidence, social co-operation is made impossible or at least difficult. Such co-operation, however, is essential in order to make human life possible and tolerable. This means that the rule "Thou shalt not lie" has been traced back to the demands: "Human life shall be preserved" and "Pain and sorrow shall be lessened as much as possible."

5. But what is the origin of such ethical axioms? Are they arbitrary? Are they based on mere authority? Do they stem from experiences of men and are they conditioned indirectly by such experiences?

6. For pure logic all axioms are arbitrary, including the axioms of ethics. But they are by no means arbitrary from a psychological and genetic point of view. They are derived from our inborn tendencies to avoid pain and annihilation, and from the accumulated emotional reaction of individuals to the behavior of their neighbors.

7. It is the privilege of man's moral genius, expressed by inspired individuals, to advance ethical axioms which are so comprehensive and so well founded that men will accept them as grounded in the vast mass of their individual emotional experiences. Ethical axioms are found and tested not very differently from the axioms of science. *Die Wahrheit liegt in der Bewährung*. Truth is what stands the test of experience.

CHAPTER FIVE

Form and Use of the Categorical Syllogism

AN analysis of the brief essay "The Laws of Science and the Laws of Ethics," by the famous scientist and mathematician Albert Einstein, may be of value in several ways. First, the essay introduces us to the concept of propositions and, by means of a discussion of ethics and science and their relation to logic, to the function of logic in everyday affairs. Second, the essay is itself a logical argument; through analyzing it, therefore, we may discover something of the nature of logical forms. And third, it provides an example of superior writing.

In the first paragraph Einstein notes that "all scientific statements and laws have one characteristic in common: they are 'true' or 'false' (adequate or inadequate). Roughly speaking our reaction to them is 'yes' or 'no.' " Obviously, as he points out in the next paragraph, all statements are not of this sort. "Thou shalt not lie" is a directive; so is "Shut the door." To the sentences "How hot was it yesterday?" or "What is the highest good for man?" we do not respond "yes" or "no"; these sentences are interrogative, calling for information. Other statements are exclamatory: "What a fraud he is!" "Oh, how lovely is the evening." Still others are hortatory: "Let's give it a try"; "Forgive us our trespasses." Some are declarative: "The Harvard University library contains over 2,000,000 volumes"; "The modern horse developed from a five-toed animal not much larger than a rabbit." Of all these illustrations it is only to the last two, the declarative sentences, that we respond "yes" or "no". Only these sentences express something that is either true or false.

That "something" which a declarative sentence declares to be either true or false is called a PROPOSITION. (Einstein introduces the term *proposition* in paragraph 3.) Thus, though sentences are said to express propositions, the proposition is not the same as the sentence which states it. A sentence is *neither* true *nor* false; a proposition, that which the sentence expresses or declares, is *either* true *or* false. This is not to say that we must know whether it is true or it is false. The propositions "There is oil under the White House" and "Cancer is caused by a virus" are either true or false, though we may not know which. A sentence consists of a group of words arranged in a meaningful way; a proposition is distinct from the words that express it. Consider, for example, the following sentences: "Eisenhower was elected president in 1952"; "Eisenhower was victorious in the presidential campaign of 1952"; "In 1952 Eisenhower won the race for the presidency"; "The victor in the 1952 presidential campaign was Eisenhower." In these sentences there are differences in word choice and sentence order which may suggest differing attitudes toward the propositional content and suggest something of the intention of the writer in offering the information. We see these attitudes and intentions in the verbs "was elected" and "won" the race; the words "victor" or "victorious" and "campaign," with their affective military overtones, suggest something different from "was elected." Yet, though the sentences are manifestly different, they express the same proposition.

With these definitions and distinctions we are better equipped to understand the logical structure of Einstein's essay. Logical thinking, as he implies in the third paragraph, is carried on in propositions. Let us return to the beginning of the essay, then, to discover the propositions his sentences express and the pattern or form in which they occur.

In his first paragraph Einstein stipulates that all scientific statements are either true or false. In his second paragraph he stipulates that scientific statements do not express emotions. These two characteristics of scientific statements are assumed. Einstein does not attempt to prove them; he simply states them. He says, in effect, that all scientific statements are either true or false and express concepts which are nonemotive. This is his MAJOR PREMISE. Note that this proposition expresses a relationship between two classes of things: (1) scientific statements and (2) statements which are either true or false and do not express emotions. The relationship expressed is that all of the first class are a part of the second class.

In his second and third paragraphs, Einstein suggests that ethical statements are not true or false in the sense that scientific statements are and that all ethical statements do express emotions. Thus, Einstein's MINOR PREMISE, also assumed, is that all ethical statements are outside the province of those statements which are either true or false and do not express emotions. His CONCLUSION, then, is that no ethical statements are scientific statements. Here again we have propositions that express relationships between two classes of things. In the minor premise and conclusion the relationship expressed is that no member of the first class is a member of the second class. A proposition which states a relationship between two classes of things—called TERMS—is a CATEGORICAL proposition. In categorical propositions something is unconditionally asserted or denied of something else.

Thus we can see that Einstein's first argument consists of three categorical propositions related in such a way that the conclusion follows from exactly two premises. Such an argument is known as a CATEGORICAL ARGUMENT.

Since all categorical propositions express a relationship between only two terms, they can express only four possible relationships, of which Einstein has used two. These four relationships are:

1. *All* of the first class is a part of the second. (All men are mortal.)
2. *None* of the first class is a part of the second. (No men are mortal.)
3. *Some* of the first class is (or are) a part of the second. (Some men are mortal.)
4. *Some* of the first class is (or are) *not* a part of the second. (Some men are not mortal.)

These four sentences express all the possible relationships there may be between two different terms. They may be illustrated as follows:

1. All *X* is *Y*
2. No *X* is *Y*
3. Some *X* is *Y*
4. Some *X* is not *Y*

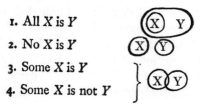

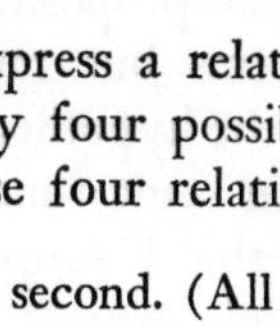

These diagrams illustrate all the possible relationships between *X* and *Y*, or between any two terms whatsoever.

We may show the categorical structure of Einstein's first SYLLOGISM—the formalized statement of an argument—using *S* to symbolize the class of scientific statements, *X* to symbolize the class of statements which are either true or false and do not express emotions, and *E* to symbolize the class of ethical statements:

All *S* are *X*

No *E* are *X*

∴ No *E* are *S*

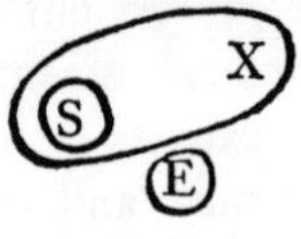

Einstein's purpose in this essay, however, is not merely to show the difference between science and ethics but rather to establish similarities. This he does by means of two further syllogisms. At the end of the third paragraph he states that "If we can agree on some fundamental ethical propositions, then other ethical propositions can be derived from them. . . ." Propositions which take the form "If . . . then . . . " are called HYPOTHETICAL propositions. Unlike categorical propositions, they do not express a relationship between terms but rather between propositions themselves. The if-clause of the hypothetical proposition is itself a proposition—"we can agree on some fundamental propositions"—as is the then-clause—"other ethical propositions can be derived from them." Propositions which express relationships between propositions are called COMPLEX propositions; propositions which express relationships between classes are called SIMPLE propositions. Hypothetical propositions are always complex, as are CONJUNCTIVE (*A* and *B*) and ALTERNATIVE (Either *A* or *B*) propositions.

In his fourth paragraph, Einstein suggests that we can, as a matter of fact, trace ethical directives back to basic premises, or agreed-upon propositions. Since lying destroys our confidence in the statements of other people, and since such confidence is essential to society, the ethical directive "Thou shalt not lie" is seen to derive from the agreed-upon ethical axioms: "Human life shall be preserved" and "Pain and sorrow shall be lessened as much as possible." The if-proposition of his second syllogism is thus affirmed, and the then-proposition—that we may derive our ethical imperatives from axioms about which all may agree—follows.

The above propositional argument sets the stage for Einstein's final, and most significant, argument, which is, once again, categorically formulated. The axioms, he has shown, of both science and ethics are logically arbitrary, and from these arbitrary axioms both science and ethics are able, by reason (deductively) and by experience (inductively), to argue to particular conclusions. Since the method of logic is to begin with arbitrary axioms and proceed from them by reason and experience, all science and all ethics, then, may be considered logical in the widest sense of the word. Thus, though the statements of science and ethics are different, as shown in Einstein's first syllogism, they are also related by the logical method which they hold in common.

Using *S* to stand for scientific statements, *E* for ethical statements, *X* for statements which are logically arbitrary and proceed from reason and experience, and *L* for logical, the above argument may be symbolized as follows:

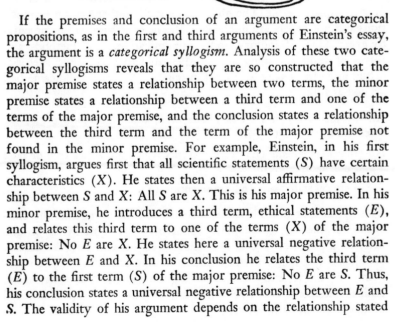

All *S* and *E* are *X*
All *X* are *L*
∴ *S* and *E* are *L*

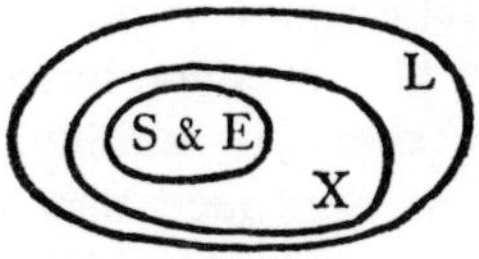

If the premises and conclusion of an argument are categorical propositions, as in the first and third arguments of Einstein's essay, the argument is a *categorical syllogism.* Analysis of these two categorical syllogisms reveals that they are so constructed that the major premise states a relationship between two terms, the minor premise states a relationship between a third term and one of the terms of the major premise, and the conclusion states a relationship between the third term and the term of the major premise not found in the minor premise. For example, Einstein, in his first syllogism, argues first that all scientific statements (*S*) have certain characteristics (*X*). He states then a universal affirmative relationship between *S* and *X*: All *S* are *X*. This is his major premise. In his minor premise, he introduces a third term, ethical statements (*E*), and relates this third term to one of the terms (*X*) of the major premise: No *E* are *X*. He states here a universal negative relationship between *E* and *X*. In his conclusion he relates the third term (*E*) to the first term (*S*) of the major premise: No *E* are *S*. Thus, his conclusion states a universal negative relationship between *E* and *S*. The validity of his argument depends on the relationship stated in the conclusion following necessarily from the relationships stated in the two premises.

The validity of an argument, then, derives from its over-all structure and not from the truth or falsity of the propositions involved. For example, we might substitute the term "ships" for *S*, the term "made of wood" for *X*, and the term "places where people live" for *E*. Thus the syllogism would read:

> All ships are made of wood.
> No places where people live are made of wood.
> ∴ No places where people live are ships.

This is a VALID argument, since the conclusion follows necessarily from the premises, even though all the statements contained in it are false.

Although no valid argument can have its premises true and its conclusion false, there is no necessary relationship between truth and validity. This does not, however, render valid arguments wholly irrelevant to everyday writing. They provide the structures into which our ideas and facts may fit, and from which new facts and new ideas may result. The ability to conclude that certain propositions and not others are implied by the facts at hand is fundamental to every kind of inquiry and communication. The methods and forms of valid reasoning are indispensable to responsible rhetoric.

Suppose, for example, that Einstein, in his first syllogism, had argued as follows:

All statements which are either true or false and nonemotive (*X*) are scientific statements (*S*).

No ethical statements (*E*) are statements which are either true or false and nonemotive (*X*).

∴ No ethical statements (*E*) are scientific (*S*).

This appears, at first glance, to be a reasonable argument; the conclusion is the same, the premises involve the same terms as the original argument. But a moment's thought will suggest certain problems. The major premise does not state that *all* scientific statements (*S*) are *X*, and therefore it is quite possible that some, or all, ethical statements could be non-*X* and still be scientific. This could be diagrammed as follows:

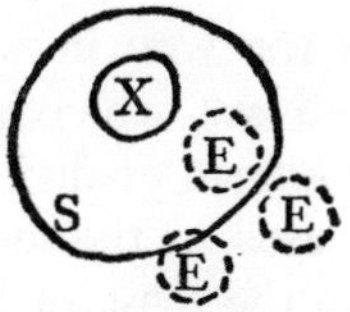

There are three alternatives for *E* here, and any one of them could be true with the given premises. Thus the conclusion of the syllogism does not necessarily follow in all possible cases and the argument is INVALID.

It is precisely in cases of this sort that an ability to distinguish between valid and invalid forms is of value. Invalid arguments often look good at first glance and the unwary reader or writer may be misled by the appearance of validity, especially if the conclusion drawn is one he happens to agree with or the one he is trying to establish. The argument

All dogs are animals.
No cats are dogs.
∴ No cats are animals.

would not likely fool anybody, yet it has precisely the same logical form as the syllogism in the preceding paragraph.

Since the categorical syllogism requires three terms and involves a possible combination of four relationships among these terms, it is impractical to discuss each valid and invalid form. Validity may be tested by diagramming or by a set of rules for validity. The following six rules are necessary and sufficient conditions for validity; every valid syllogism conforms to them and every syllogism conforming to them is valid.

The first rule is: *Each term must be used in the same sense throughout the argument.* Consider the following argument:

All scientists believe in laws which govern the behavior of the whole physical universe.

Any power which can establish laws which govern the behavior of the whole physical universe must be a supernatural power; it must have the attributes of God.

Thus all scientists believe in a supernatural power which has the attributes of God.

The deceptiveness of this argument lies in the dual meaning of the word *law*. There are two kinds of law: natural law, which is descriptive and merely notes the way in which bodies, as a matter of fact, behave, and legislated law, which is prescriptive and must be formulated by some power human or divine. In the first sentence of the above argument *law* is used in the sense of natural law; in the second sentence it is used in the sense of legislated law. The meaning of the term has shifted and thus the syllogism is invalid.

The second rule is: *The middle term must be distributed.* The middle term is that term which occurs in both premises but not in the conclusion. A term is distributed when it is used to apply to all members of the class which it names; it is undistributed when it applies to an indefinite part of those members. The term "dog" is distributed in the sentence "All dogs are animals"; it is not distributed in the sentence "Fido is a dog." The fallacy of the undistributed middle takes the form

$$\text{All } A \text{ is } B$$
$$\text{All } C \text{ is } B$$
$$\therefore C \text{ is } A$$

The fallacy of the undistributed middle is very common and can be extremely convincing. Consider, for example, the following letter received by the parents of a fourteen-year-old boy:

> During the past several years we have administered the Seashore test to thousands of persons of unquestioned musical ability–composers, performers, conductors, etc.–and they have, almost without exception, made scores substantially higher than those of the average untrained layman. Your son recently completed the Seashore test at our testing office and his score placed him in the upper 10% of those taking the test over the last several years. This score shows that he has substantial musical ability, and we would recommend that you take all possible steps to cultivate this talent as soon as possible.

This argument may be summarized as follows:

All persons of unquestioned musical ability make high scores on the Seashore test.

Your son made a high score on the Seashore test.

Therefore your son is a person of unquestioned musical ability.

By this same logic all cats are dogs.

The third rule is closely related to the second: *No term may be distributed in the conclusion if it is undistributed in the premises.* Consider the following argument:

Minority interests can be safeguarded only through legislative action.
The interests of the nation as a whole, however, are not minority interests.
Therefore the interests of the nation as a whole cannot be safeguarded through legislative action.

The second term of the first proposition—legislative action—is undistributed in the major premise and distributed in the conclusion; hence the argument is invalid.

The fourth and fifth rules are: *If both premises are affirmative, the conclusion must be affirmative* and *If one of the premises is negative or limited ("some"), the conclusion must be negative or limited.* Violations of these rules so obviously result in contradictions that they rarely occur in serious arguments.

Violations of the sixth rule, however—*If both premises are negative, no conclusion can be drawn*—cause a good deal of trouble. The following is a good example of a plausible argument which violates this rule.

Nobody would accuse American industry of Communistic tendencies. American business traditionally supports the Republican Party and the interests of investors. On the other hand, American labor traditionally supports the Democratic Party and seeks the welfare of the worker rather than the prosperity of the investor. Clearly, then, labor tends toward Communism.

The implicit syllogism in this argument is as follows:

American business is not Communistic.
American labor is not American business.
Therefore American labor is Communistic.

The fallacy here can best be illustrated by a diagram:

American business (*B*) is not Communistic (*C*)

American labor (*L*) is not American business (*B*)

Therefore American labor (*L*) is Communistic (*C*)

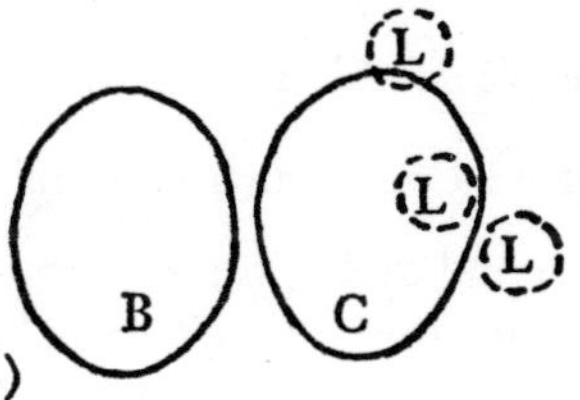

Clearly, on the basis of the two premises no conclusion about American labor can follow. It may be Communistic; it may be partially Communistic; or it may not be Communistic at all.

Though syllogistic arguments are widely used in everyday discourse, in discussions, in debates, and in orations, they are often abbreviated or incompletely stated. For example, if one argues that "nature viewed merely as a cause-and-effect mechanism is a monster which destroys human dignity, for such a view eliminates freedom and the efficacy of the human will," it is clear that the implicit major premise is that "any view which eliminates freedom and the efficacy of the human will destroys human dignity." Whenever any two of the three propositions of a syllogism are given, the third may be inferred in this way, and it is often not necessary to state it explicitly.

Often, on the other hand, a conclusion cannot be reached by using only two premises but requires a series (or chain) of premises. For example, the following:

(1) We know that Communists are people who believe that violent revolution is necessary to bring about the ideal state. (2) People of this sort are willing to sacrifice the means for the end. (3) To sacrifice the means for the end is to be willing to justify any present atrocity in the name of a better future. (4) To be willing to justify any present atrocity in the name of a better future is to acquiesce in present immorality. (5) Thus, Communists are willing to acquiesce in present immorality.

This argument can be broken down into three connected syllogisms which together yield the desired conclusion. The first of these syllogisms consists of the first two sentences together with the implicit conclusion:

All Communists are people who believe that violent revolution is necessary to bring about the ideal state.

All people of this sort are willing to sacrifice the means for the end.

Therefore Communists are willing to sacrifice the means for the end.

The second syllogism consists of the third sentence of the original argument, the implicit conclusion of the first syllogism, and a second implicit conclusion:

All people who are willing to sacrifice the means for the end are willing to justify any present atrocity in the name of a better future.

Communists are willing to sacrifice the means for the end.

Therefore Communists are willing to justify any present atrocity in the name of a better future.

The third syllogism consists of the fourth sentence of the original argument, the implicit conclusion of the second syllogism, and the fifth and concluding sentence of the original argument:

All people who are willing to justify any present atrocity in the name of a better future are willing to acquiesce in present immorality.

Communists are willing to justify any present atrocity in the name of a better future.

Therefore Communists are willing to acquiesce in present immorality.

Obviously it is not always necessary to state explicitly all of the premises and intermediate conclusions by means of which the conclusion is established, but it is important *to be able to do this* in order to demonstrate and test the validity of the argument and in order to organize the exposition of an argument.

An understanding of the logic of the syllogism is not only useful to, but imperative for, an understanding of what we write. It is a prime axiom of composition that we can never write well unless we understand what assumptions we have made and know the rational form of thought which leads us from these assumptions to logical conclusions.

The logical method of both science and ethics, which Einstein elaborates in his essay, is precisely the method called for in composition. If we can agree on some axioms, some assumptions, other propositions can be derived from them and we can reason to the particular propositions we need to establish, always provided, of course, that the assumptions are legitimate to begin with and that the conclusions derived from them really do follow logically. This is the responsibility of the writer.

Einstein's essay suggests various ways in which legitimate assumptions may be derived. In his first syllogism the major premise is, in effect, a definition. He doesn't need to *demonstrate* that scientific statements are either true or false; they are *defined* as such. He doesn't need to prove that scientific statements are nonemotive; the term *scientific* is by definition the opposite of the term *emotive*. In short, we may legitimately assume conventional definitions. Einstein's minor premise in the first syllogism is based on a self-evident truth—that ethical propositions express attitudes or feelings; the scientist, as scientist, does not make value judgments, the moralist does. The hypothetical proposition of Einstein's second syllogism is also a truth to which all men could generally agree. In this syllogism Einstein's minor premise, however, is not assumed; he attempts to establish the truth of the if-clause by means of a factual analysis of the effect of lying on social co-operation. In his third syllogism, Einstein assumes a major premise based on a definition of axioms—"all axioms are arbitrary"—and he uses the factual analysis developed in the minor premise of his second syllogism, as well as a definition of scientific method, to establish his minor premise. An inductive hypothesis may also serve as the major premise of a deductive argument.

The problems of finding a legitimate assumption, of the form of argument to use in a particular circumstance, of whether to use a single syllogism or an interconnected chain argument, of whether to argue deductively at all have no pat solutions. Our approach to any problem must be individual and pragmatic. Einstein might have arrived at the same conclusion with a different set of premises; he might have used different forms of argument.

Whatever methods our particular and individual problems suggest to us, the forms of categorical logic give us some means of reasoning accurately and some tests with which to check our arguments; they demand that we know what our assumptions are and that we be able to state them precisely; and, once our assumptions have been established and our reasoning checked for accuracy, they provide us with a basis for organizing our writing systematically and coherently. By using a set of syllogisms to organize his essay, Einstein has succeeded in putting into an essay of less than 500 words ideas of such importance that the writer ignorant of logic might have spent many pages developing them. Further, the logical tightness of Einstein's essay enables him to make these ideas clear by presenting them in a systematic and disciplined fashion. Logical thought and logical forms of organization are not, of course, the be-all and the end-all of writing. Often our intent is rhetorical rather than logical, and always more than logic is involved. But by understanding the categorical syllogism and its use in writing, we may advance responsible rhetoric at least one step.

EXERCISES

1. Which of the following sentences express propositions?
   a. A man should support his wife and children.
   b. Should a man support his wife and children?
   c. Most men support their wives and children.
   d. Support your wife and children!
   e. All sentences express propositions.
   f. Some sentences express propositions.
   g. Do sentences express propositions?
   h. Propositions are expressed by sentences.
   i. Logical thinking is carried on in propositions.
   j. Logical thinking has nothing to do with propositions.
   k. What is the relationship between logical thinking and propositions?
   l. Think logically!

2. Which of the following sentences express complex propositions?
   a. If ethical laws are derived from axioms they are analogous to the laws of science.
   b. Ethical laws are derived from axioms and they are analogous to the laws of science.
   c. The laws of ethics and the laws of science are both derived from axioms.
   d. Ethical statements express emotions.
   e. Scientific statements are nonemotive.
   f. Ethical statements are neither true nor false, but scientific statements are either true or false.
   g. If ethical statements are neither true nor false then they are not propositions.
   h. Either ethical statements are true or false or they are not propositions.

3. Which of the following sentences express the same proposition?
   a. The laws of ethics may be derived from axioms.
   b. All axioms are the basis for ethical laws.
   c. Ethical laws rest upon axioms.
   d. Ethical laws may be traced back to axioms.

e. All axioms are ethical laws.

f. All ethical laws are axioms.

g. All ethical laws may be traced back to basic premises.

h. The laws of ethics and the laws of science are axiomatic.

4. Demonstrate by diagram or rule the validity or invalidity of each of the following:

a. Only rational persons are responsible for their actions.
Students are responsible for their actions.
∴ Students are rational persons.

b. All advertisements are designed to sell products.
Some devices designed to sell products are misleading.
∴ Some advertisements are misleading.

c. No ethical statements are true or false.
All moral imperatives are ethical statements.
∴ No moral imperatives are true or false.

d. All ethical statements are emotive.
Some statements are not ethical statements.
∴ Some statements are not emotive.

e. Some propositions are untrue.
No ethical statements are untrue.
∴ Some ethical statements are not propositions.

f. All scientific statements are either true or false.
All propositions are either true or false.
∴ All propositions are scientific statements.

g. All scientific statements are either true or false.
All true or false statements are propositions.
∴ All scientific statements are propositions.

h. No scientific truths are absolute truths.
All absolute truths are truths which have not been established by experimental methods.
∴ No truths which have not been established by experimental methods are scientific truths.

i. All men are mortal.
All men are featherless bipeds.
∴ All featherless bipeds are mortal.

j. All propositions are either true or false.
Some sentences are not propositions.
∴ Some sentences are neither true nor false.

k. The test of great poetry is how well it lasts; all truly great poetry becomes richer with successive readings. Milton's poems are of this sort; they reveal something new each time we read them; they become richer with successive readings. This proves that Milton's poems are truly great poetry.

5. Supply the missing premise or conclusion in the following:
   a. Major premise: All propositions are either true or false.
   Minor premise: ______________________.
   ∴ This statement is either true or false.
   b. Major premise: ______________________.
   Minor premise: This statement is an ethical statement.
   ∴ This statement is neither true nor false.
   c. Major premise: All ethical statements are based on axioms.
   Minor premise: This statement is an ethical statement.
   ∴ ______________________.
   d. Major premise: Some propositions are false.
   Minor premise: All false statements are misleading.
   ∴ ______________________.
   e. Major premise: All scientific statements are nonemotive.
   Minor premise: ______________________.
   ∴ This statement is not scientific.

6. Break the following argument down into its component syllogisms: In a democracy the people rule and thus the will of the people prevails. Any state in which the will of the people prevails is a state in which the people get the kind of government they wish. The kind of government the people wish is the kind they deserve. Thus in a democracy the people get the kind of government they deserve.

NOTE: Suggestions for theme assignments appear in the general exercises following Chapter 7.

J. V. CUNNINGHAM

*Logic and Lyric**

IN this essay I shall propose the question: May the principal structure of a poem be of a logical rather than of an alogical sort? For example, to confine ourselves to the Old Logic: May a lyric be solely or predominantly the exposition of a syllogism? and may the propositions of the lyric, one by one, be of the sort to be found in a logical syllogism?

2. The incautious romantic will deny the possibility, and with a repugnance of feeling that would preclude any further discussion. For logic and lyric are generally regarded as opposites, if not as contradictory terms. "It is a commonplace," says a recent writer on logic, "that poetry and logic have nothing to do with each other, that they are even opposed to one another."[1] You will find this explicitly stated, sometimes with the substitution of "science" for "logic," in most of the school handbooks on the study of literature, in most of the introductions to poetry. "The peculiar quality of poetry," we read in one of these, "can be distinguished from that of prose if one thinks of the creative mind as normally expressing itself in a variety of literary forms ranged along a graduated scale between the two contrasted extremes of scientific exposition and lyrical verse." And, a little later, "[Poetry] strives for a conviction begotten of the emotions rather than of the reason." Consequently, we are told, "The approach of poetry is indirect. It proceeds by means of suggestion, implication, reflection. Its method is largely symbolical. It is more interested in connotations than in denotations."[2] This is common doctrine. Poetry is in some way concerned with emotion rather than with reason, and its method is imagina-

* Reprinted from "Logic and Lyric," by J. V. Cunningham, *Modern Philology*, LI (August, 1953), 33-41, by permission of The University of Chicago Press.

[1] Richard von Mises, *Positivism* (Cambridge, Mass., 1951), p. 289.

[2] Harold R. Walley and J. Harold Wilson, *The Anatomy of Literature* (New York, 1934), pp. 143, 144.

tive, indirect, implicit rather than explicit, symbolical rather than discursive, concerned with what its terms suggest rather than with what they state. The kind of poetry which most fully possesses and exhibits these concerns, methods, and qualities is generally thought to be the lyric, and hence the lyric, of all poetry, is regarded as the most antithetical to reason, logic, and science.

3. This was not always the case. In the eighth century, for example, a scholiast of the school of Alcuin regarded not only grammar and rhetoric but dialectic or logic also as the disciplines that nourish and form a poet. In the medieval and Renaissance traditions of commentary on Aristotle's logic, poetic is sometimes regarded as a part, a subdivision, of logic—as, indeed, I consider it myself. So late as the eighteenth century, David Hume writes in an essay *Of the Standard of Taste*: "Besides, every kind of composition, even the most poetical, is nothing but a chain of propositions and reasonings; not always indeed the justest and most exact, but still plausible and specious, however disguised by the coloring of the imagination." And even today the writer on logic whom I quoted earlier asserts, in denial of the commonplace: "Every poem, except in rare extreme cases, contains judgements and implicit propositions, and thus becomes subject to logical analysis."[3]

4. But may the chain of propositions and reasonings be not merely plausible and specious but even sufficiently just and exact? May the poem be not merely subject to logical analysis but logical in form? May, to return to our point, the subject and structure of a poem be conceived and expressed syllogistically? Anyone at all acquainted with modern criticism and the poems that are currently in fashion will think in this connection of Marvell's "To His Coy Mistress." The apparent structure of that poem is an argumentative syllogism, explicitly stated. "Had we but world enough and time," the poet says,

> This coyness, Lady, were no crime . . .
>
> But at my back I always hear
> Time's winged chariot hurrying near . . .

[3] Scholiast cited in Otto Bird, "The Seven Liberal Arts," in Joseph T. Shipley, ed., *Dictionary of World Literature* (New York, 1943), p. 55; J. E. Spingarn, *A History of Literary Criticism in the Renaissance*, 2d ed. (New York, 1908), pp. 24-27; David Hume, *Philosophical Works* (Boston and Edinburgh, 1854), III, 264; von Mises, *loc cit.*

Now, therefore . . .
. . . let us sport us while we may.

If we had all the space and time in the world, we could delay consummation. But we do not. Therefore. The structure is formal. The poet offers to the lady a practical syllogism, and if she assents to it, the appropriate consequence, he hopes, will follow:

Had we but world enough, and time,
This coyness, Lady, were no crime;
We would sit down and think which way
To walk and pass our long love's day.

Thou by the Indian Ganges side
Shouldst rubies find; I by the tide
Of Humber would complain. I would
Love you ten years before the Flood,
And you should, if you please, refuse
Till the conversion of the Jews.

My vegetable love should grow
Vaster than empires, and more slow.
A hundred years should go to praise
Thine eyes and on thy forehead gaze;
Two hundred to adore each breast;
But thirty thousand to the rest;
An age at least to every part,
And the last age should show your heart;
For, Lady, you deserve this state,
Nor would I love at lower rate.

But at my back I always hear
Time's winged chariot hurrying near;
And yonder all before us lie
Deserts of vast eternity.
Thy beauty shall no more be found,
Nor in thy marble vault shall sound
My echoing song; then worms shall try
That long preserved virginity,
And your quaint honor turn to dust,
And into ashes all my lust:
The grave's a fine and private place,
But none, I think, do there embrace.

Now, therefore, while the youthful hue
Sits on thy skin like morning dew,
And while thy willing soul transpires
At every pore with instant fires,
Now let us sport us while we may,
And now, like amorous birds of prey,
Rather at once our time devour
Than languish in his slow-chapt power.
Let us roll all our strength and all
Our sweetness up into one ball,
And tear our pleasures with rough strife
Thorough the iron gates of life:
Thus, though we cannot make our sun
Stand still, yet we will make him run.[4]

5. The logical nature of the argument here has been generally recognized, though often with a certain timidity. Mr. Eliot hazards: "the three strophes of Marvell's poem have something like a syllogistic relation to each other." And in a recent scholarly work we read: "The dialectic of the poem lies not only or chiefly in the formal demonstration explicit in its three stanzas, but in all the contrasts evoked by its images and in the play between the immediately sensed and the intellectually apprehended."[5] That is, the logic is recognized, but minimized, and our attention is quickly distracted to something more reputable in a poem, the images or the characteristic tension of metaphysical poetry. For Mr. Eliot the more important element in this case is a principle of order common in modern poetry and often employed in his own poems. He points out that the theme of Marvell's poem is "one of the great traditional commonplaces of European literature . . . the theme of . . . *Gather ye rosebuds*, of *Go, lovely rose*." "Where the wit of Marvell," he continues, "renews the theme is in the variety and order of the images." The dominant principle of order in the poem, then, is an implicit one rather than the explicit principle of the syllogism, and implicit in the succession of images.

[4] Modernized from H. M. Margoulliouth, ed., *The Poems and Letters* (Oxford, 1927), Vol. II.

[5] T. S. Eliot, *Selected Essays*, new ed. (New York, 1950), p. 254; Helen C. White, Ruth C. Wallerstein, and Ricardo Quintana, eds., *Seventeenth Century Verse and Prose* (New York, 1951), I, 454.

6. Mr. Eliot explains the implicit principle of order in this fashion:

> In the first of the three paragraphs Marvell plays with a fancy that begins by pleasing and leads to astonishment. . . . We noticed the high speed, the succession of concentrated images, each magnifying the original fancy. When this process has been carried to the end and summed up, the poem turns suddenly with that surprise which has been one of the most important means of poetic effect since Homer:
>
> But at my back I always hear
> Time's winged chariot hurrying near,
> And yonder all before us lie
> Deserts of vast eternity.
>
> A whole civilization resides in these lines:
>
> Pallida Mors aequo pulsat pede pauperum
> tabernas
> Regumque turres . . .
>
> A modern poet, had he reached the height, would very likely have closed on this moral reflection.

What is meant by this last observation becomes clear a little later, where it is said that the wit of the poem "forms the crescendo and diminuendo of a scale of great imaginative power."[6] The structure of the poem, then, is this: It consists of a succession of images increasing in imaginative power to the sudden turn and surprise of the image of time, and then decreasing to the conclusion. But is there any sudden turn and surprise in the image of time? and does the poem consist of a succession of images?

7. This talk of images is a little odd, since there seem to be relatively few in the poem if one means by "image" what people usually do—a descriptive phrase that invites the reader to project a sensory construction. The looming imminence of Time's winged chariot is, no doubt, an image, though not a full-blown one, since there is nothing in the phrasing that properly invites any elaboration of sensory detail. But when Mr. Eliot refers to "successive images" and cites "my *vegetable* love," with *vegetable* italicized, and "Till the conversion of the Jews," one suspects that he is provoking images where they do not textually exist. There is about as much

[6] Eliot. pp. 253-55.

of an image in "Till the conversion of the Jews" as there would be in "till the cows come home," and it would be a psychiatrically sensitive reader who would immediately visualize the lowing herd winding slowly o'er the lea. But "my *vegetable* love" will make the point. I have no doubt that Mr. Eliot and subsequent readers do find an image here. They envisage some monstrous and expanding cabbage, but they do so in ignorance. *Vegetable* is no vegetable but an abstract and philosophical term, known as such to the educated man of Marvell's day. Its context is the doctrine of the three souls: the rational, which in man subsumes the other two; the sensitive, which men and animals have in common and which is the principle of motion and perception; and, finally, the lowest of the three, the vegetable soul, which is the only one that plants possess and which is the principle of generation and corruption, of augmentation and decay. Marvell says, then, my love, denied the exercise of sense but possessing the power of augmentation, will increase "Vaster than empires." It is an intellectual image, and hence no image at all but a conceit. For if one calls any sort of particularity or detail in a poem an "image," the use of the wrong word will invite the reader to misconstrue his experience in terms of images, to invent sensory constructions and to project them on the poem. . . .

8. But if the poem is not a succession of images, does it exhibit that other principle which Mr. Eliot ascribes to it—the turn and surprise which he finds in the abrupt introduction of Time's chariot and which forms a sort of fulcrum on which the poem turns? Subsequent critics have certainly felt that it has. In a current textbook we read:

> The poem begins as a conventional love poem in which the lover tries to persuade his mistress to give in to his entreaties. But with the introduction of the image of the chariot in l. 21, the poem becomes obsessed by the terrible onrush of time, and the love theme becomes scarcely more than an illustration of the effect which time has upon human life.

And the leading scholar in the field, a man who is generally quite unhappy with Mr. Eliot's criticism, nevertheless says:

> the poet sees the whole world of space and time as the setting for two lovers. But wit cannot sustain the pretence that youth and beauty and love are immortal, and with a quick change of tone—like Catullus' *nobis*

cum semel occidit brevis lux or Horace's *sed Timor et Minae*—the theme of time and death is developed with serious and soaring directness.[8]

9. These, I believe, are not so much accounts of the poem as accounts of Mr. Eliot's reading of the poem. Let us question the fact. Does the idea of time and death come as any surprise in this context? The poem began, "Had we but world enough and Time." That is, it bagan with an explicit condition contrary to fact, which, by all grammatical rules, amounts to the assertion that we do not have world enough and time. There is no surprise whatever when the proposition is explicitly made in line 21. It would rather have been surprising if it had not been made. Indeed, the only question we have in this respect, after we have read the first line, is: How many couplets will the poem expend on the ornamental reiteration of the initial proposition before he comes to the expected *but*? The only turn in the poem is the turn which the structure of the syllogism had led us to await. . . .

10. In brief, the general structure of Marvell's poem is syllogistic, and it is located in the Renaissance tradition of formal logic and of rhetoric. The structure exists in its own right and as a kind of expandable filing system. It is a way of disposing of, of making a place for, elements of a different order: in this case, Clevelandizing conceits and erotic propositions in the tradition of Jonson and Herrick. These reiterate the propositions of the syllogism. They do not develop the syllogism and they are not required by the syllogism; they are free and extra. There could be more or less of them, since there is nothing in the structure that determines the number of interpolated couplets. It is a matter of tact and a matter of the appetite of the writer and the reader.

11. The use of a structure as a kind of expandable filing system is common enough in the Renaissance. The narrative structure of a Shakespearean play can be regarded as a structure of this order. It exists in its own right, of course, but it is also a method for disposing various kinds of material of other orders—a set speech or passion here, an interpolated comic routine in another place. The structure offers a series of hooks upon which different things can be hung. Whether the totality will then form a whole, a unity,

[8] Wright Thomas and Stuart Gerry Brown, eds., *Reading Poems* (New York, 1941), p. 702; Douglas Bush, *English Literature in the Earlier Seventeenth Century* (Oxford, 1945), p. 163.

is a question of interpretation and a question of value. It is a question, for example, of what sort of unity is demanded and whether there are various sorts.

12. In Marvell's poem, only the general structure is syllogistic; the detail and development are of another order, and critics have been diligent in assigning the poetic quality of the whole to the non-syllogistic elements. Is it possible, then, to write a lyric that will be wholly or almost wholly syllogistic? It is. There is such a lyric in the *Oxford Book of English Verse*, a lyric of somewhat lesser repute than Marvell's but still universally conceded to possess the true lyrical power. It is Dunbar's "Lament for the Makaris."

13. The structure of Dunbar's poem is the structure of the traditional syllogism with which everyone is acquainted: *All men are mortal, I am a man*; together with a concluding practical syllogism, *What must be, must be accepted, but I must die.* The syllogism is developed in two ways, both characteristic methods in the logical tradition of the later Middle Ages. It begins with the immediate induction from experience of the leading principle, the major premise:

I that in heill wes and gladnes,
Am trublit now with gret seiknes,
An feblit with infermite;
Timor mortis conturbat me.

The experience, then, is the sudden alteration from health to illness, and this yields the generalization:

Our plesance heir is all vane glory,
This fals warld is bot transitory,
The flesche is brukle, the Fend is sle;
Timor mortis conturbat me.

The premise, then, is: This false world is but transitory; and it is presently expressed in more restricted terms:

The stait of man dois change and vary,
Now sound, now seik, now blith, now sary,
Now dansand mery, now like to dee;
Timor mortis conturbat me.

The syllogism is now developed by another form of induction, and this development accounts for the remainder of the poem, except for the last stanza. It is developed through induction by simple enumeration in support and explication of the major premise, but with this special feature, that the induction proceeds by a hierarchical method. Nothing could be more characteristic of medieval logic. The argument is: If everything sublunary changes and varies, is mortal, then every estate of man is mortal; and the poet enumerates the estates:

On to the ded gois all Estatis,
Princis, Prelotis, and Potestatis,
Baith riche and pur of al degre;
  Timor mortis conturbat me. . . .

He takis the campion in the stour,
The capitane closit in the tour,
The lady in bour full of bewte;
  Timor mortis conturbat me.

He sparis no lord for his piscence,
Na clerk for his intelligence;
His awful strak may no man fle;
  Timor mortis conturbat me.

Art, magicianis, and astrologgis,
Rhetoris, logicianis, and theologgis,
Thame helpis no conclusionis sle;
  Timor mortis conturbat me.

If all estates must die, then poets, too, must die. And now Dunbar proceeds by a simple enumeration, a roll call, of poets:

He has done petuously devour
The noble Chaucer, of makaris flour,
The Monk of Bery, and Gower, all thre;
  Timor mortis conturbat me.

The gud Syr Hew of Eglintoun,
And eik Heryot, and Wyntoun,
He has tane out of this cuntre;
  Timor mortis conturbat me.

He continues to enumerate poet after poet whom death has taken, until he comes finally to his friendly enemy, the poet, Kennedy, and to himself:

Gud Maister Walter Kennedy
In point of dede lyis veraly,
Gret reuth it were that so suld be;
Timor mortis conturbat me.

Sen he has all my brether tane,
He wil nocht lat me lif alane,
Of forse I man his nyxt pray be;
Timor mortis conturbat me.

Therefore, I must die, concludes the syllogism. And now follows the practical syllogism, the act of resignation:

Sen for the deid remeid is none,
Best is that we for dede dispone,
Eftir our deid that lif may we;
Timor mortis conturbat me.[10]

Almost every proposition in the poem is strictly controlled by the syllogistic structure. The exceptions are the refrain and a certain number of affective sentences: "He has done petuously devour / The noble Chaucer" and "Gret reuth it wer that so suld be." These direct the feeling of the poem. Yet, though the poem is so completely determined by logical method and logical structure, it has seemed, and justly, to generations of readers to be a moving poem and properly poetical.

14. I shall conclude with another poem of the same sort, a lyric of even greater renown in modern criticism. This is the song from *Summer's Last Will and Testament* by Thomas Nashe, "Adieu, farewell, earth's bliss." It, too, has a refrain, though in English, a response from the Litany of Saints which was customarily recited through the streets of London in time of plague. The poem, like Dunbar's, consists of a series of discrete, self-inclosed stanzas, in which each line is end-stopped. The structure of the poem is, like Dunbar's and Marvell's, a practical syllogism explicitly propounded, though not quite so formally as in the preceding poem. It opens with the rejection of earthly happiness. The argument is, to begin with the suppressed premise: True happiness is certain, but the world is uncertain; therefore worldly happiness is not true happiness. The world is uncertain since it is subject to the certainty of death and change. Nor can the goods of this world buy continued

[10] W. Mackay Mackenzie, ed., *The Poems* (Edinburgh, 1932), pp. 20-23.

life, or the art of medicine procure it: the plague increases. What is best in this life—and here we have the structure of the next three stanzas—beauty, prowess, and wit, all fade:

Haste therefore each degree
To welcome destiny.

For the world after death is certain, and its happiness true happiness:

Adieu, farewell, earth's bliss!
This world uncertain is:
Fond are life's lustful joys,
Death proves them all but toys.
None from his darts can fly;
I am sick, I must die–
  Lord, have mercy on us.

Rich men, trust not in wealth,
Gold cannot buy you health;
Physic himself must fade;
All things to end are made;
The plague full swift goes by;
I am sick, I must die–
  Lord, have mercy on us.

Strength stoops unto the grave,
Worms feed on Hector brave;
Swords may not fight with fate;
Earth still holds ope her gate;
Come, come! the bells do cry–
I am sick, I must die–
  Lord, have mercy on us.

Wit with his wantonness
Tasteth death's bitterness;
Hell's executioner
Hath no ears for to hear
What vain art can reply;
I am sick, I must die–
  Lord, have mercy on us.

Haste therefore each degree
To welcome destiny;
Heaven is our heritage;

Earth but a player's stage;
Mount we unto the sky;
I am sick, I must die—
Lord, have mercy on us.[11]

15. The poem is a series of fairly literal propositions, some exactly in logical form: *This world uncertain is, All things to end are made. Queens have died young and fair, Haste therefore each degree.* They are such propositions as might have been translated from the *Summa contra Gentiles* of Thomas Aquinas, and they are located in that general tradition. Thomas, for instance, discusses the following questions: That human happiness does not consist in carnal pleasures; that man's happiness does not consist in glory; that man's happiness does not consist in wealth; that happiness does not consist in worldly power; that happiness does not consist in the practice of art; that man's ultimate happiness is not in this life, "for if there is ultimate happiness in this life, it will certainly be lost, at least by death."[12] But these are the propositions of Nashe's lyric, some literally, some more figuratively put.

16. Of the propositions in the poem, perhaps the most figurative is *Strength stoops unto the grave,* which yet is fairly literal as we see the suggestion of an aged figure bent over more and more until he is almost prone. And there are, of course, affective elements in the poem, as in *death's bitterness* and *Hell's executioner.* But the special distinction of the poem and the source of an unusual quality of feeling perhaps lies in the meter as much as in anything else. The six-syllable line glides from a regular iambic pattern into a triple movement—accented, unaccented, accented—and back again as if both were its mode of being and neither had precedence over the other:

Beauty is but a flower
Which wrinkles will devour;
Brightness falls from the air;
Queens have died young and fair.

[11] Modernized from Ronald B. McKerrow, ed., *Works* (London, 1904-10), III, 283.

[12] *Contra Gentiles* iii. 27, 29-31, 36, 48, in *Opera omnia* (Rome, 1882-1948), Vol. XIV; Anton C. Pegis, ed., *Basic Writings of Saint Thomas Aquinas* (New York, 1945), Vol. II.

The poem in this respect belongs to a curious episode in the history of English meter; for this phenomenon appears only, to my knowledge, in the songs written within a fairly short period, of perhaps ten or twenty years, in the 1590's and early 1600's. Of a similar sort is Shakespeare's:

> Come away, come away, death
> And in sad cypress let me be laid;
> Fly away, fly away, breath;
> I am slain by a fair cruel maid.

17. But the special distinction of the poem has usually been found in the line, *Brightness falls from the air.* This is certainly a proposition of a different order from those we have discussed, and one that has excited the sensibilities of innumerable modern readers. It is a line in the symbolist tradition. One remembers how Stephen Dedalus in the *Portrait of the Artist as a Young Man* recalls the line, though at first in an altered form:

> She had passed through the dusk. And therefore the air was silent save for one soft hiss that fell. And therefore the tongues about him had ceased their babble. Darkness was falling.
>
> *Darkness falls from the air.*
>
> A trembling joy, lambent as a faint light, played like a fairy host around him. But why? Her passage through the darkening air or the verse with its black vowels and its opening sound, rich and lutelike?
>
> He walked away slowly towards the deeper shadows at the end of the colonnade, beating the stone softly with his stick to hide his revery from the students whom he had left: and allowed his mind to summon back to itself the age of Dowland and Byrd and Nash.
>
> Eyes, opening from the darkness of desire, eyes that dimmed the breaking east. What was their languid grace but the softness of chambering? And what was their shimmer but the shimmer of the scum that mantled the cesspool of the court of a slobbering Stuart. And he tasted in the language of memory ambered vines, dying fallings of sweet airs, the proud pavan. . . .
>
> The images he had summoned gave him no pleasure. They were secret and enflaming but her image was not entangled by them. . . .

Yes; and it was not darkness that fell from the air. It was brightness.

Brightness falls from the air.

He had not even remembered rightly Nash's line. All the images it had awakened were false.[13]

18. But all the images it had awakened were false for still another reason. The line as Joyce quotes it is certainly an evocative line, a line in the symbolist tradition, and hence apt and fitted to entangle itself in reverie. But it seems out of place in the poem. It is so much a line in the symbolist tradition that the historical scholar grows wary and suspicious. He turns to the text. He looks in the great modern edition of Nashe, the edition of McKerrow, and he finds that the editor records with a sigh: "It is to be hoped that Nashe meant 'ayre,' but I cannot help strongly suspecting that the true reading is 'hayre,' which gives a more obvious, but far inferior, sense."[14] So we have the alternatives: *Brightness falls from the air* or *Brightness falls from the hair*. But the latter is a literal account of the effect of age and death. The proposition so read is of the same order as all the other propositions in the poem, of the same order as *Queens have died young and fair.* There is no doubt, then, as to the correct reading. In fact, the symbolistic line, however good, is a bad line in context, since it is out of keeping. And so the poem loses its last claim to modernity. It becomes a Renaissance poem. It returns to the park of logic from the forest of reverie. The experience of the poem is the experience of syllogistic thinking with its consequences for feeling, attitude, and action. It is a mode of experience that the Renaissance practiced and cherished, and expressed with power, dignity, and precision. It is a poetical experience and a logical, and it is both at once.

[13] James Joyce, *A Portrait of the Artist as a Young Man* ("Modern Library" ed.; New York, 1928), pp. 273-75.

[14] McKerrow, IV, 440.

CHAPTER SIX

Form and Use of the Hypothetical Syllogism

J. V. CUNNINGHAM's essay "Logic and Lyric" explicitly takes a controversial position: that the notion of an opposition between logic and poetry is false. Cunningham's procedure in establishing this proposition is two-fold. First, he makes clear the precise nature of his dispute with those critics who hold an opposing view. Then he proceeds to a logical argument to establish his own position. In effect, he proposes that if poetry which is generally recognized as good is logically organized, then it is false to say that logic and poetry are incompatible. He uses analyses of three poems to establish the factual truth of the if-clause of his proposed hypothesis; and he concludes that since the truth of the if-clause is established, the then-clause must follow and all contradictory positions must be false. Although most of the essay consists of his attempt to establish the factual truth of the if-clause, this large portion of the essay, important as it is, is a means to an end, not the end itself.

Cunningham wishes to refute a misconception of the nature of poetry which leads, he believes, to a serious misreading of many poems. This misconception grows out of the romantic notions that there is an antipathy between reason and emotion and that poetry is spontaneous and emotive rather than logical and rational. This attitude, he says, has been carried over into modern criticism and modern linguistic theory, where it is common practice to analyze the uses of language and place them on a scale with logical and descriptive uses at one end and poetic and emotive uses at the other. This is the position, for example, of Richard Von Mises, a philosopher and linguist, whom Cunningham quotes in the second paragraph of his essay.

Cunningham finds support for his own position from Aristotle, the medieval and Renaissance rhetoricians, and David Hume, an eighteenth-century empiricist. These men believed that poetry and logic are not at opposite poles, not antipathetic; rather, they believed that logic itself may very well provide the form for a poem or the means to an understanding of the poet's main intention. For these men—as for Cunningham—poetry is almost a subdivision of logic. Citation of these men as authorities, however, does not sufficiently establish Cunningham's case, though it may make his position command more respect. Use of authorities is seldom sufficient to establish a controversial position. Hence, rather than rely on authority, Cunningham turns to logical argument to establish his position. He cites authority but he relies on reason.

Analysis of the method and form of Cunningham's argument is instructive both to our understanding of his essay and to our grasp of the function of logic in responsible rhetoric. His argument begins with the assumption that *if* it can be shown that much poetry generally recognized as good, even by those critics who disagree with him, is logically organized, then it will follow that the notion of an opposition between logic and poetry, maintained by many of these critics, is false. This is his major premise. Like the major premise of the categorical argument, it is assumed—nothing can be proved, regardless of the method employed, unless something is assumed without proof. Cunningham's major premise has the specific logical form of the if-then, or hypothetical, proposition. A hypothetical proposition is a complex proposition (that is, it consists of two simple propositions) in which the second half, or CONSEQUENT, is represented as following from the first half, or ANTECEDENT. Finally, Cunningham's major premise is implicit, not explicit, in his writing. In any essay the major premise may or may not be stated explicitly; the important thing is that it be apparent as a basic assumption. The syllogism's sentences are a convenient and abstract way to express the propositions of an argument explicitly; yet it is neither necessary nor always desirable that the bare bones of the syllogism appear in an essay.

The latter two-thirds of Cunningham's essay consists of his attempt to show that, as a matter of fact, a number of poems generally recognized as good are logically (syllogistically) organized. This is his minor premise. The minor premise, in this case, affirms the if-clause (or antecedent) of the major premise. This affirmation is not assumed; it is factually established.

If we consider carefully Cunningham's attempt to affirm that poetry is logical by analyzing three poems, we may discover not only something of his own method of logical argument but also a good deal about the forms and methods of logic itself. Since his argument is that poetry, like prose, may use logic as an organizational element, and our full understanding of a poem may depend upon our ability to perceive its logical structure, Cunningham's essay provides us with an analysis of the way in which logic operates in writing; it is also itself an example of logical organization.

The first poem which Cunningham discusses is Andrew Marvell's "To His Coy Mistress," a poem almost universally praised; its organization is specifically and consistently that of the syllogism. It begins with an if-then proposition explicitly stated: If we had "world enough and time" then "this coyness . . . were no crime." The second stanza, or strophe, consists of a denial of the antecedent, the simple if-proposition of the major premise. We do not have world enough and time: "at my back I always hear/Time's winged chariot hurrying near." The third stanza, beginning "Now, therefore. . . ," states the conclusion of the argument that coyness is a crime: "Now let us sport us while we may."

The various couplets of each stanza, Cunningham points out, are largely elaborations of the syllogistic proposition which the stanza is intended to convey. They "reiterate the propositions of the syllogism. They do not develop the syllogism and they are not required by the syllogism." Indeed, Cunningham contends that misreading of the poem has often resulted because readers refused to consider seriously the logical structure of the poem as a whole. Both T. S. Eliot and Douglas Bush, noted contemporary literary critics, see the second stanza as constituting an "abrupt turn and surprise" in the poem. If we recognize the syllogistic structure of the whole, however, the second stanza is not an "abrupt turn" or "surprise" at all. For, since the poem begins with an explicit statement of a hypothetical proposition, which is obviously contrary to fact, the explicit statement at the beginning of the second stanza is not only not a surprise but altogether expected. Our recognition of the major premise in the first line leads us to anticipate the necessary statement of the minor premise in line 21. "The only turn in the poem is the turn which the structure of the syllogism had led us to await."

Though there are nonlogical (which is not to say illogical) elements in the poem, such as rhythm, figures of speech, change of tone, and connotatively affective words, its general structure is syllogistic and we must be aware of this if we are to read the poem responsibly. And, though the detail and development of each stanza are in themselves nonlogical, the detail and development contribute to and exemplify the logical structure of the whole.

The other two poems which Cunningham discusses are also generally highly praised, and they are both "wholly or almost wholly syllogistic," without so many nonlogical elements as Marvell's poem. The first is Dunbar's "Lament for the Makaris." In this poem the structure of the syllogism is categorical rather than hypothetical. The syllogism is the traditional "All men are mortal / I am a man / Therefore I am mortal." The poem opens with the categorical proposition "This false world is but transitory." Dunbar continues by listing all the estates of men and finally of poets and of himself and shows them to be a part of the world and therefore transitory (mortal). This may be restated in the following syllogistic pattern:

Major premise:	All in this world is transitory.
Minor premise:	All the estates of men, of poets, and of myself are in this world.
Conclusion:	Therefore all the estates of men, of poets, and of myself are transitory.

"Yet," Cunningham concludes, "though the poem is so completely determined by logical method and logical structure, it has seemed, and justly, to generations of readers to be a moving poem and properly poetical."

The last poem which Cunningham discusses in support of his minor premise—that many poems universally recognized as good are logically conceived and organized—is Nashe's great lyric "Litany in Time of Plague." "The structure of the poem," Cunningham suggests, "is, like Dunbar's and Marvell's, a practical syllogism."

Nashe's major premise, unlike Marvell's and Dunbar's, but like Cunningham's in this essay, is unstated or "suppressed". It is "All the goods of this world are uncertain." His minor premise is "Worldly happiness is of this world," and he concludes that worldly happiness "is therefore uncertain."

Nashe's poem, also, introduces a second complication; it uses two syllogisms. The first was summarized above; the second goes somewhat as follows: "Since worldly happiness is uncertain (conclusion of the first syllogism), we should seek for that happiness which is certain; that happiness which is certain is heavenly happiness; therefore we should seek for heavenly happiness." The poem, Cunningham concludes, is misinterpreted as being a forerunner of the "symbolist tradition." "The experience of the poem is the experience of syllogistic thinking with its consequences for feeling, attitude, and action."

After his analysis of these three poems in support of his minor premise, Cunningham's conclusion—that the notion of an opposition between logic and poetry is false—though unstated, obviously follows. Thus, if one grants Cunningham his major premise and if one is convinced by his analysis of the three poems, his conclusion must necessarily be granted. Perhaps his refusal to *state* the conclusion is more effective than an explicit statement of it. We are led by the logic, which he has made uppermost in our attention, to the conclusion; *we* state it, and thus we are more convinced.

It is, however, not the concern of this chapter to agree or disagree with Cunningham's thesis, but to discover the formal structure of the argument by which the conclusion is established. Cunningham's hypothetical syllogism has only two terms, compared to three in the formal or categorical syllogism discussed in Chapter V. Further, the terms always bear precisely the same relation to each other, that is, if *A* . . . , then *B*. . . . In the categorical syllogism there were three possible relationships—all, some, none. Consequently the possibilities for variation in the hypothetical syllogism are much reduced; there are, as a matter of fact, only four. With the form if *A* then *B*, one may either affirm the antecedent (as Cunningham has done), deny the antecedent (as Marvell has done in "To His Coy Mistress"), affirm the consequent, or deny the consequent. Of these four forms, two are valid and two are invalid. If we assume that if *A* then *B*, then, clearly, if we can affirm *A*, *B* will follow necessarily;

thus to affirm the antecedent is a valid form. It does not, however, follow necessarily that to deny *A* is to deny *B;* thus to deny the antecedent is an invalid form. Still assuming if *A* then *B*, if we deny *B* then *A* will necessarily be denied; thus to deny the consequent is a valid form. On the other hand, if we affirm *B*, we do not necessarily affirm *A;* thus to affirm the consequent is invalid.

Consider a simple illustration. Assume that if it is raining then the streets are wet. Now, if it *is* raining (affirm the antecedent) then the streets will be wet. However, if it is *not* raining (deny the antecedent) this does not mean, necessarily, that the streets will not be wet. After all, there are other causes than rain for wet streets. However, if the streets are not wet (deny the consequent), it cannot be raining. On the other hand, if the streets are wet (affirm the consequent), it is not necessarily raining, for, as noted above, there are other causes than rain for wet streets.

Given the above rules, we can see that Cunningham's argument is valid; the conclusion may or may not, of course, be true. On the other hand, the argument of Marvell's poem is invalid, whatever one may think of the truth or falsity of the conclusion, because the antecedent is denied.

Note that in any hypothetical syllogism, the antecedent is a *sufficient* condition for the consequent and the consequent is a *necessary* condition of the antecedent. That is, if one affirms *A*, this is sufficient to establish *B*, but *A* is not necessary to *B*. On the other hand, *B* is necessary to *A;* you cannot at the same time have *A* and not *B*. The consequent, however, though necessary for the antecedent, is not sufficient to imply it; you can have *B* and not *A*.

The hypothetical syllogism may use words other than *if* and *then*, without changing the argument. For example, "If *A* then *B*" may be stated "*A* implies *B*," "*B* is necessary to *A*," "*A* is sufficient to establish *B*," "Only if *B* then *A*" (or "*A* only if *B*"), "Provided that *A* then *B*," or "In case of *A* then *B*." Though these sentences are all different and may suggest different emphases, the proposition in each remains the same. Care should be taken, however, to avoid the supposition that "If *A* then *B*" means "*A* if *B*." For "*A* if *B*" is merely a grammatical inversion of "If *B* then *A*," and, as the foregoing discussion should have made clear, this does not have at all the same meaning as "If *A* then *B*." Some caution should also be observed with "*A* if and only if *B*." Since "if" states a sufficient condition and "only if" a necessary condition, "*A* if and only if *B*" means that *A* is both a necessary *and* a sufficient condition for *B* and *B* is both a necessary *and* a sufficient condition for *A*. In short, the two terms are equivalent and to affirm or deny *A* is to affirm or deny *B* and vice versa. Some critics maintain that what Marvell really meant in his poem was "If and only if we have 'world enough and time' is coyness not a crime." If this is the case, the denial of "world enough and time" is also a denial of the second proposition and Marvell's logic is sound.

The way in which a given proposition will be expressed in a particular essay, and, for that matter, whether it will be expressed explicitly, is, once again, a pragmatic consideration. Cunningham might have chosen to make all of his propositions explicit; he might have argued to the same conclusion by means of a categorical, rather than a hypothetical, syllogism. That he did not means simply that for his purposes in this essay another method was more effective. Each writer must choose his own course; but in order to choose intelligently and responsibly, he must know the possibilities.

Whatever logical form a writer may use, he must choose legitimate assumptions. If his premises are not accepted by the reader, nothing follows. Even if his assumptions are accepted, he still must insure the validity of the conclusion drawn from them. Only thus can he write logically sound, accurate, and effective prose.

EXERCISES

1. Which of the following arguments are valid? Which invalid? Why?
   a. If the pressure on the gas increases, the gas contracts. The gas contracted. Therefore, the pressure was increased.
   b. If the pressure on the gas increases, the gas contracts. The pressure was not increased. Therefore gas did not contract.
   c. If the pressure on the gas increases, the gas contracts. The gas did not contract. Therefore the pressure was not increased.
   d. If the theory of evolution is true, we should be able to find fossil remains of extinct animal forms. As a matter of fact, Darwin and others have found such remains. The theory of evolution, therefore, must be true.
   e. If the earth is a sphere, then a pendulum of specified length will make two swings per second at every point of the earth's surface. But it can be shown experimentally that there is a variation in

the number of swings per second such a pendulum makes as it is moved along a meridian circle. It follows that the earth is not a sphere.

f. If China abandons her intention of invading Formosa, the U.S. will not become embroiled in a war with China. As a matter of fact, however, Chinese leaders realize that they could not invade Formosa with their weak navy and with the U.S. Seventh Fleet in the Formosa Straits. Therefore the U.S. will not become embroiled in a war with China.

g. If water could be held by gravity on the surface of a tetrahedron so as to cover seven-tenths of the area, it would correspond in plan to the oceans of the world. It is, however, impossible to hold water on the surface of a tetrahedron so as to cover seven-tenths of its surface. Consequently water on a tetrahedron cannot be made to correspond in plan to the oceans of the world.

h. If Einstein is correct when he argues that both science and ethics are logical, then it follows that ethical norms may be defended. Einstein has, in fact, provided us with such a defense. It follows that his argument is correct.

i. If the nonlogical elements in Marvell's poem, "To His Coy Mistress," are not necessary to the syllogistic organization of the poem and if the poem can be understood only syllogistically, it follows that the nonlogical devices of Marvell's poem are not essential to our understanding of the poem. Cunningham has shown that the nonlogical devices are not necessary to the syllogistic organization of the poem and he has shown that the poem can be understood only syllogistically. It follows that the nonlogical elements in the poem are not essential to our understanding of it.

j. If the account of the creation of the world in Genesis is accepted as literally true, the sun was not created until the fourth day. And if the sun was not created until the fourth day it could not have been the cause of the alternation of day and night for the first three days. If the sun was not the cause of the alternation of day and night during the first three days, then the word "day" must have been used in a different sense in the book of Genesis than that which is accepted now. Consequently, if the account of the creation of the world in Genesis is accepted as literally true, the word "day" must have been used in a different sense in the book of Genesis than that which is accepted now.

k. If minorities generally are to receive equal rights, long standing prejudices must be overcome. But as long as minority groups provide economic competition for majority groups, in the South and elsewhere, prejudice will not be overcome and minority groups do provide economic competition. Therefore minorities generally will not receive equal rights.

l. Only if we are able to solve the problems of the cold war can we be assured of a peaceful world. But we cannot solve the problems of the cold war unless we learn to co-operate with the Russians. But co-operation with Russia is impossible, for the Russians are unwilling to live up to their agreements. Thus a peaceful world is impossible.

2. Using *P* to stand for "the pressure on the gas increases" and *C* to stand for "the gas contracts," translate each of the following into if-then propositions:

a. If the pressure on the gas increases, the gas contracts.
b. The pressure on the gas increases if the gas contracts.
c. If the pressure on the gas does not increase the gas will not contract.
d. If the gas contracts, the pressure increases.
e. Only if the pressure on the gas increases will the gas contract.
f. Only if the gas contracts does the pressure increase.
g. It is necessary that the gas contract if the pressure on the gas increases.
h. Provided that the pressure on the gas increases, the gas will contract.
i. If and only if the pressure on the gas increases will the gas contract.
j. Only if the gas does not contract can we say that the pressure is not increased.

3. Which of the sentences in the preceding exercise express the same propositions?

NOTE: Suggestions for theme assignments appear in the general exercises following Chapter 7.

BERTRAND RUSSELL

*A Free Man's Worship**

TO Dr. Faustus in his study Mephistopheles told the history of the Creation, saying:

2. "The endless praises of the choirs of angels had begun to grow wearisome; for, after all, did he not deserve their praise? Had he not given them endless joy? Would it not be more amusing to obtain undeserved praise, to be worshipped by beings whom he tortured? He smiled inwardly, and resolved that the great drama should be performed.

3. "For countless ages the hot nebula whirled aimlessly through space. At length it began to take shape, the central mass threw off planets, the planets cooled, boiling seas and burning mountains heaved and tossed, from black masses of cloud hot sheets of rain deluged the barely solid crust. And now the first germ of life grew in the depths of the ocean, and developed rapidly in the fructifying warmth into vast forest trees, huge ferns springing from the damp mould, sea monsters breeding, fighting, devouring, and passing away. And from the monsters, as the play unfolded itself, Man was born, with the power of thought, the knowledge of good and evil, and the cruel thirst for worship. And Man saw that all is passing in this mad, monstrous world, that all is struggling to snatch, at any cost, a few brief moments of life before Death's inexorable decree. And Man said: 'There is a hidden purpose, could we but fathom it, and the purpose is good; for we must reverence something, and in the visible world there is nothing worthy of reverence.' And Man stood aside from the struggle, resolving that God intended harmony to come out of chaos by human efforts. And when he followed the instincts which God had transmitted to him from his

* Bertrand Russell "A Free Man's Worship". *Mysticism and Logic* (London, George Allen and Unwin Ltd., 1929).

ancestry of beasts of prey, he called it Sin, and asked God to forgive him. But he doubted whether he could be justly forgiven, until he invented a divine Plan by which God's wrath was to have been appeased. And seeing the present was bad, he made it yet worse, that thereby the future might be better. And he gave God thanks for the strength that enabled him to forgo even the joys that were possible. And God smiled; and when he saw that Man had become perfect in renunciation and worship, he sent another sun through the sky, which crashed into Man's sun; and all returned again to nebula.

4. " 'Yes,' he murmured, 'it was a good play; I will have it performed again.' "

5. Such, in outline, but even more purposeless, more void of meaning, is the world which Science presents for our belief. Amid such a world, if anywhere, our ideals henceforward must find a home. That Man is the product of causes which had no prevision of the end they were achieving; that his origin, his growth, his hopes and fears, his loves and his beliefs, are but the outcome of accidental collocations of atoms; that no fire, no heroism, no intensity of thought and feeling, can preserve an individual life beyond the grave; that all the labours of the ages, all the devotion, all the inspiration, all the noonday brightness of human genius, are destined to extinction in the vast death of the solar system, and that the whole temple of Man's achievement must inevitably be buried beneath the debris of a universe in ruins—all these things, if not quite beyond dispute, are yet so nearly certain, that no philosophy which rejects them can hope to stand. Only within the scaffolding of these truths, only on the firm foundation of unyielding despair, can the soul's habitation henceforth be safely built.

6. How, in such an alien and inhuman world, can so powerless a creature as Man preserve his aspirations untarnished? A strange mystery it is that Nature, omnipotent but blind, in the revolutions of her secular hurryings through the abysses of space, has brought forth at last a child, subject still to her power, but gifted with sight, with knowledge of good and evil, with the capacity of judging all the works of his unthinking Mother. In spite of Death, the mark and seal of the parental control, Man is yet free, during his brief years, to examine, to criticise, to know, and in imagination to create. To him alone, in the world with which he is acquainted, this

freedom belongs; and in this lies his superiority to the resistless forces that control his outward life.

7. The savage, like ourselves, feels the oppression of his impotence before the powers of Nature; but having in himself nothing that he respects more than Power, he is willing to prostrate himself before his gods, without inquiring whether they are worthy of his worship. Pathetic and very terrible is the long history of cruelty and torture, of degradation and human sacrifice endured in the hope of placating the jealous gods: surely, the trembling believer thinks, when what is most precious has been freely given, their lust for blood must be appeased, and more will not be required. The religion of Moloch—as such creeds may be generically called—is in essence the cringing submission of the slave, who dare not, even in his heart, allow the thought that his master deserves no adulation. Since the independence of ideals is not yet acknowledged, Power may be freely worshipped, and receive an unlimited respect, despite its wanton infliction of pain.

8. But gradually, as morality grows bolder, the claim of the ideal world begins to be felt; and worship, if it is not to cease, must be given to gods of another kind than those created by the savage. Some, though they feel the demands of the ideal, will still consciously reject them, still urging that naked Power is worthy of worship. Such is the attitude inculcated in God's answer to Job out of the whirlwind; the divine power and knowledge are paraded, but of the divine goodness there is no hint. Such also is the attitude of those who, in our own day, base their morality upon the struggle for survival, maintaining that the survivors are necessarily the fittest. But others, not content with an answer so repugnant to the moral sense, will adopt the position which we have become accustomed to regard as specially religious, maintaining that, in some hidden manner, the world of fact is really harmonious with the world of ideals. Thus Man creates God, all-powerful and all-good, the mystic unity of what is and what should be.

9. But the world of fact, after all, is not good; and, in submitting our judgment to it, there is an element of slavishness from which our thoughts must be purged. For in all things it is well to exalt the dignity of Man, by freeing him as far as possible from the tyranny of non-human Power. When we have realised that Power is largely bad, that Man, with his knowledge of good and evil, is

but a helpless atom in a world which has no such knowledge, the choice is again presented to us: Shall we worship Force, or shall we worship Goodness? Shall our God exist and be evil, or shall he be recognised as the creation of our own conscience?

10. The answer to this question is very momentous, and affects profoundly our whole morality. The worship of Force, to which Carlyle and Nietzsche and the creed of Militarism have accustomed us, is the result of failure to maintain our own ideals against a hostile universe: it is itself a prostrate submission to evil, a sacrifice of our best to Moloch. If strength indeed is to be respected, let us respect rather the strength of those who refuse that false "recognition of facts" which fails to recognise that facts are often bad. Let us admit that, in the world we know, there are many things that would be better otherwise, and that the ideals to which we do and must adhere are not realised in the realm of matter. Let us preserve our respect for truth, for beauty, for the ideal of perfection which life does not permit us to attain, though none of these things meet with the approval of the unconscious universe. If Power is bad, as it seems to be, let us reject it from our hearts. In this lies Man's true freedom: in determination to worship only the God created by our own love of the good, to respect only the heaven which inspires the insight of our best moments. In action, in desire, we must submit perpetually to the tyranny of outside forces; but in thought, in aspiration, we are free, free from our fellow-men, free from the petty planet on which our bodies impotently crawl, free even, while we live, from the tyranny of death. Let us learn, then, that energy of faith which enables us to live constantly in the vision of the good; and let us descend in action, into the world of fact, with that vision always before us.

11. When first the opposition of fact and ideal grows fully visible, a spirit of fiery revolt, of fierce hatred of the gods, seems necessary to the assertion of freedom. To defy with Promethean constancy a hostile universe, to keep its evil always in view, always actively hated, to refuse no pain that the malice of Power can invent, appears to be the duty of all who will not bow before the inevitable. But indignation is still a bondage, for it compels our thoughts to be occupied with an evil world; and in the fierceness of desire from which rebellion springs there is a kind of self-assertion which it is necessary for the wise to overcome. Indignation is a submission of

our thoughts, but not of our desires; the Stoic freedom in which wisdom consists is found in the submission of our desires, but not of our thoughts. From the submission of our desires springs the virtue of resignation; from the freedom of our thoughts springs the whole world of art and philosophy, and the vision of beauty by which, at last, we half reconquer the reluctant world. But the vision of beauty is possible only to unfettered contemplation, to thoughts not weighted by the load of eager wishes; and thus Freedom comes only to those who no longer ask of life that it shall yield them any of those personal goods that are subject to the mutations of Time.

12. Although the necessity of renunciation is evidence of the existence of evil, yet Christianity, in preaching it, has shown a wisdom exceeding that of the Promethean philosophy of rebellion. It must be admitted that, of the things we desire, some, though they prove impossible, are yet real goods; others, however, as ardently longed for, do not form part of a fully purified ideal. The belief that what must be renounced is bad, though sometimes false, is far less often false than untamed passion supposes; and the creed of religion, by providing a reason for proving that it is never false, has been the means of purifying our hopes by the discovery of many austere truths.

13. But there is in resignation a further good element: even real goods, when they are unattainable, ought not to be fretfully desired. To every man comes, sooner or later, the great renunciation. For the young, there is nothing unattainable; a good thing desired with the whole force of a passionate will and yet impossible, is to them not credible. Yet, by death, by illness, by poverty, or by the voice of duty, we must learn, each one of us, that the world was not made for us, and that, however beautiful may be the things we crave, Fate may nevertheless forbid them. It is the part of courage, when misfortune comes, to bear without repining the ruin of our hopes, to turn away our thoughts from vain regrets. This degree of submission to Power is not only just and right; it is the very gate of wisdom.

14. But passive renunciation is not the whole of wisdom; for not by renunciation alone can we build a temple for the worship of our own ideals. Haunting foreshadowings of the temple appear in the realm of imagination, in music, in architecture, in the untroubled kingdom of reason, and in the golden sunset magic of lyrics, where

beauty shines and glows, remote from the touch of sorrow, remote from the fear of change, remote from the failures and disenchantments of the world of fact. In the contemplation of these things the vision of heaven will shape itself in our hearts, giving at once a touchstone to judge the world about us, and an inspiration by which to fashion to our needs whatever is not incapable of serving as a stone in the sacred temple.

15. Except for those rare spirits that are born without sin, there is a cavern of darkness to be traversed before that temple can be entered. The gate of the cavern is despair, and its floor is paved with the gravestones of abandoned hopes. There Self must die; there the eagerness, the greed of untamed desire must be slain, for only so can the soul be freed from the empire of Fate. But out of the cavern the Gate of Renunciation leads again to the daylight of wisdom, by whose radiance a new insight, a new joy, a new tenderness, shine forth to gladden the pilgrim's heart.

16. When, without the bitterness of impotent rebellion, we have learnt both to resign ourselves to the outward rule of Fate and to recognise that the non-human world is unworthy of our worship, it becomes possible at last so to transform and refashion the unconscious universe, so to transmute it in the crucible of the imagination, that a new image of shining gold replaces the old idol of clay. In all the multiform facts of the world—in the visual shapes of trees and mountains and clouds, in the events of the life of Man, even in the very omnipotence of Death—the insight of creative idealism can find the reflection of a beauty which its own thoughts first made. In this way mind asserts its subtle mastery over the thoughtless forces of Nature. The more evil the material with which it deals, the more thwarting to untrained desire, the greater is its achievement in inducing the reluctant rock to yield up its hidden treasures, the prouder its victory in compelling the opposing forces to swell the pageant of its triumph. Of all the arts, Tragedy is the proudest, the most triumphant; for it builds its shining citadel in the very centre of the enemy's country, on the very summit of his highest mountain; from its impregnable watch-towers, his camps and arsenals, his columns and forts, are all revealed; within its walls the free life continues, while the legions of Death and Pain and Despair, and all the servile captains of tyrant Fate, afford the burghers of that dauntless city new spectacles of beauty. Happy those sacred ram-

parts, thrice happy the dwellers on that all-seeing eminence. Honour to those brave warriors who, through countless ages of warfare, have preserved for us the priceless heritage of liberty, and have kept undefiled by sacrilegious invaders the home of the unsubdued.

17. But the beauty of Tragedy does but make visible a quality which, in more or less obvious shapes, is present always and everywhere in life. In the spectacle of Death, in the endurance of intolerable pain, and in the irrevocableness of a vanished past, there is a sacredness, an overpowering awe, a feeling of the vastness, the depth, the inexhaustible mystery of existence, in which, as by some strange marriage of pain, the sufferer is bound to the world by bonds of sorrow. In these moments of insight, we lose all eagerness of temporary desire, all struggling and striving for petty ends, all care for the little trivial things, that, to a superficial view, make up the common life of day by day; we see, surrounding the narrow raft illumined by the flickering light of human comradeship, the dark ocean on whose rolling waves we toss for a brief hour; from the great night without, a chill blast breaks in upon our refuge; all the loneliness of humanity amid hostile forces is concentrated upon the individual soul, which must struggle alone, with what of courage it can command, against the whole weight of a universe that cares nothing for its hopes and fears. Victory, in this struggle with the powers of darkness, is the true baptism into the glorious company of heroes, the true initiation into the overmastering beauty of human existence. From that awful encounter of the soul with the outer world, renunciation, wisdom, and charity are born; and with their birth a new life begins. To take into the inmost shrine of the soul the irresistible forces whose puppets we seem to be—Death and change, the irrevocableness of the past, and the powerlessness of Man before the blind hurry of the universe from vanity to vanity—to feel these things and know them is to conquer them.

18. This is the reason why the Past has such magical power. The beauty of its motionless and silent pictures is like the enchanted purity of late autumn, when the leaves, though one breath would make them fall, still glow against the sky in golden glory. The Past does not change or strive; like Duncan, after life's fitful fever it sleeps well; what was eager and grasping, what was petty and transitory, has faded away, the things that were beautiful and eternal shine out of it like stars in the night. Its beauty, to a soul not worthy

of it, is unendurable; but to a soul which has conquered Fate it is the key of religion.

19. The life of Man, viewed outwardly, is but a small thing in comparison with the forces of Nature. The slave is doomed to worship Time and Fate and Death, because they are greater than anything he finds in himself, and because all his thoughts are of things which they devour. But, great as they are, to think of them greatly, to feel their passionless splendour, is greater still. And such thought makes us free men; we no longer bow before the inevitable in Oriental subjection, but we absorb it, and make it a part of ourselves. To abandon the struggle for private happiness, to expel all eagerness of temporary desire, to burn with passion for eternal things—this is emancipation, and this is the free man's worship. And this liberation is effected by a contemplation of Fate; for Fate itself is subdued by the mind which leaves nothing to be purged by the purifying fire of Time.

20. United with his fellow-men by the strongest of all ties, the tie of a common doom, the free man finds that a new vision is with him always, shedding over every daily task the light of love. The life of Man is a long march through the night, surrounded by invisible foes, tortured by weariness and pain, towards a goal that few can hope to reach, and where none may tarry long. One by one, as they march, our comrades vanish from our sight, seized by the silent orders of omnipotent Death. Very brief is the time in which we can help them, in which their happiness or misery is decided. Be it ours to shed sunshine on their path, to lighten their sorrows by the balm of sympathy, to give them the pure joy of a never-tiring affection, to strengthen failing courage, to instil faith in hours of despair. Let us not weigh in grudging scales their merits and demerits, but let us think only of their need—of the sorrows, the difficulties, perhaps the blindnesses, that make the misery of their lives; let us remember that they are fellow-sufferers in the same darkness, actors in the same tragedy with ourselves. And so, when their day is over, when their good and their evil have become eternal by the immortality of the past, be it ours to feel that, where they suffered, where they failed, no deed of ours was the cause; but wherever a spark of the divine fire kindled in their hearts, we were ready with encouragement, with sympathy, with brave words in which high courage glowed.

21. Brief and powerless is Man's life; on him and all his race the slow, sure doom falls pitiless and dark. Blind to good and evil, reckless of destruction, omnipotent matter rolls on its relentless way; for Man, condemned to-day to lose his dearest, to-morrow himself to pass through the gate of darkness, it remains only to cherish, ere yet the blow falls, the lofty thoughts that ennoble his little day; disdaining the coward terrors of the slave of Fate, to worship at the shrine that his own hands have built; undismayed by the empire of chance, to preserve a mind free from the wanton tyranny that rules his outward life; proudly defiant of the irresistible forces that tolerate, for a moment, his knowledge and his condemnation, to sustain alone, a weary but unyielding Atlas, the world that his own ideals have fashioned despite the trampling march of unconscious Power.

CHAPTER SEVEN

Form and Use of the Alternative Syllogism

BERTRAND RUSSELL'S essay "A Free Man's Worship" is an eloquent plea, by the British philosopher and atheist, for freedom not only from the tyranny of the outside forces of nature but from doctrines, religious and otherwise, which direct our worship to any nonhuman power. Much of the effectiveness of Russell's essay derives from his use of nonlogical techniques. However he has also taken pains to insure the logical accuracy of what he says. Thus he provides us with an exceptionally fine example of the use of logic as an organizing and formulative principle even in persuasive writing.

To begin with, Russell presents to us the background of a purposeless universe. Modern science shows us "that man is the product of causes which had no prevision of the end they were achieving; that his origin, his growth, his hopes and fears, his loves and beliefs, are but the outcome of accidental collocations of atoms." There is no God who had a divine Plan for the universe and there is no end for which the world generally or men individually were created. There is merely matter and motion. Man is an accident and his achievements are doomed to extinction. Given this background of "unyielding despair," how, Russell asks, can man live most effectively?

He may, Russell answers, seeing his impotence before the mechanistic forces that control his outward life, prostrate himself before their irresistible power. Or he may, through the freedom which is given to man alone, refuse to be subject to power and choose to worship the ideal. Only these two alternatives are open to man in a universe of chance.

Throughout the essay Russell stresses these alternatives, and they establish a thematic unity in the essay as a whole. The savage, he says, "having in himself nothing that he respects more than Power, . . . is willing to prostrate himself before his gods, without inquiring whether they are worthy of his worship." This is the religion of Moloch[1]—the religion of the slave. Naked power as worthy of worship is also found, Russell suggests, in the Old Testament story of Job and in the modern evolutionary doctrine of the survival of the fittest.

Some, accepting the claim of the ideal world, try to escape the dilemma by arguing that the world of fact and the world of ideals are the same. But this is an illusion. "The world of fact," Russell states, "after all, is not good; and in submitting our judgment to it, there is an element of slavishness . . . ." In short, he maintains that the conventional religious view—that God is "all powerful and all-good, the mystic unity of what is and what should be"—is just another variety of the worship of Power. "Shall we worship Force, or shall we worship Goodness? Shall our God exist and be evil, or shall he be recognized as the creation of our own conscience?" These are the two alternatives and, Russell insists, we must choose between them. This is his major premise.

As a matter of fact, Russell continues, Power is largely bad, and "the worship of Force, to which Carlyle and Nietzsche and the creed of Militarism have accustomed us, is the result of failure to maintain our own ideals against a hostile universe; it is itself a prostrate submission to evil, a sacrifice of our best to Moloch." Although we live in a world where our ideals cannot be completely realized, they must be maintained. Since the worship of power is bad, reject it; worship human ideals. Thus, in effect, he argues *Either A or B, not A, therefore B*. "In action, in desire, we must submit perpetually to the tyranny of outside forces; but in thought, in aspiration we are free, free from our fellow men, free from the petty planet on which our bodies impotently crawl, free even, while we live, from the tyranny of death." Though we must submit our desires to the world of fact, we do not need to submit our thoughts. And if we keep our thoughts free we "half reconquer the reluctant world." Yet we must, in order to keep our thoughts free, recognize a degree of submission to power—the submission of our desires.

[1] An ancient Phoenician god, to whom children were sacrificed by burning.

When we resign our desires and refuse to worship Nature or God or anything nonhuman, we can build through our own ideals a world of beauty. "In this way mind asserts its subtle mastery over the thoughtless forces of nature." Though the slave is doomed to worship Power, the free man by refusing such worship absorbs Power and makes it a part of himself. Courage and beauty are the result of his refusal.

Russell concludes his essay by formulating once again the alternative of the major premise and its resolution. The free man must, he says, "disdain the coward terrors of the slave"—the worship of power. He must "worship at the shrine his own hands have built"—the shrine of his own thoughts and ideals. He must not be dismayed by the natural universe, "the wanton tyranny that rules his outward life." He must defy power and its worship to "sustain alone . . . the world that his own ideals have fashioned despite the trampling march of unconscious power."

If an alternative, *either . . . or . . .*, proposition as a major premise is combined with a categorical proposition as a minor premise, as in this essay, the argument forms an ALTERNATIVE SYLLOGISM. We have seen that the number of possible valid and invalid forms in the categorical syllogism is considerable because there are three terms and three possible relationships among them and that the number is reduced to four in the hypothetical syllogism, since there are only two terms and only one relationship. The alternative syllogism, however, has only two possibilities, although it has two terms and one relationship. In the minor premise we may affirm one of the two alternatives or we may deny one. Since an alternative proposition implies that at least one of its alternates is true, the denial of one must, of necessity, entail the truth of the other. But the affirmation of one does not necessarily entail the denial of the other. Thus, an alternative syllogism is valid if and only if the minor premise denies one of the alternates. This is precisely what Russell has done. He sets up the alternative: *Either* we must worship power *or* we must worship the ideals which our own minds have wrought. He proceeds to show that the worship of power is evil: we must not worship power and be slaves. Thus he concludes that we must worship at the shrine our own ideals have wrought and be free men.

If the minor premise of an alternative syllogism affirms one of the alternates, no conclusion may be drawn, for "or" means "at least one" but not necessarily "not both." For example, if I say "you may buy a loaf of bread either at the bakery or at the grocery store" and you agree that this is a true premise, then if you discover that the bakery has sold all its bread, it follows that you must be able to buy one at the grocery, or the major premise would be untrue. However, if you can buy a loaf of bread at the grocery, this does not necessarily mean that you cannot buy one at the bakery, for there is nothing in the major premise to suggest that bread is not available at both.

Sometimes we encounter an argument which goes something like this:

Not both *A* and *B*
A
∴ not *B*

This is known as a DISJUNCTIVE SYLLOGISM. Here the major premise states specifically that at least one of the disjuncts is false. Hence, if one disjunct is categorically asserted by the minor premise to be true, the other must be false; and this is the conclusion of the argument. The following argument is disjunctive.

It cannot both be that labor unions can protect the rights of their members and improve the status of the laboring man *and* be politically inactive. But since it is the primary function of labor unions to protect the rights of the laboring man and improve his status, it follows that they must be politically active.

Alternative and disjunctive propositions may, upon occasion, be combined. When this occurs the major premise of the argument takes the form:

Either *A* or *B* and not both *A* and *B*.

In this case an affirmation or denial of either *A* or *B* in the minor premise results in a denial or affirmation in the conclusion. Of these three forms, alternative, disjunctive, and combined, the alternative syllogism, which Russell has used, is the most common.

An alternative argument is effective only if the two alternatives exhaust the possibilities. This is why Russell is particularly concerned to show, in paragraph 8, that the apparent third alternative, maintaining that "in some hidden manner the world of fact is really harmonious with the world of ideas," is really not a third alternative at all but merely another form of one of his proposed alternatives—slavishness to non-human power. If there were really a third possibility to be added to Russell's alternatives, his whole argument would fail. He must insist that *any* worship of a nonhuman entity is a worship of Power and hence included under the two alternatives he has set up. If, for example, we were to argue that a man is either a socialist or a fascist and prove that he is not a socialist, we could not assume that he is a fascist unless we could also show that there is no third alternative—that the major premise exhausts all the possibilities. It is, of course, altogether possible that a man may be neither a socialist nor a fascist; if this were the case, the major premise would not exhaust the possibilities. If, however, the reader agrees that Russell's alternatives are complete and if he is convinced by Russell's attempt to show that worship of Power is evil and destructive, then the conclusion follows inevitably.

An analysis of Russell's essay in purely logical terms, however, is inadequate. After analyzing the logical structure of the Einstein and Cunningham essays, one has the feeling that the analysis catches the substance and spirit of the essay itself. There are, of course, in both of these essays certain nonlogical elements; but the basic intent of each is logical demonstration, and thus a logical analysis is very nearly equivalent to the essay itself. The intent of "A Free Man's Worship," however, is not logical demonstration, and a logical analysis of the essay leaves us with the feeling that far too little has been noticed. This is because Russell is not primarily concerned with proof or demonstration but with persuasion. Logical forms of discourse appeal to the reason; their function is to demonstrate, to convince by reason. Persuasion, on the other hand, appeals to the emotions. The two are not, of course, necessarily separate; a brilliant syllogistic demonstration, like that of Einstein's essay, will persuade through its sheer reasoning. Nonetheless, there are many nonlogical techniques which are used almost exclusively for emotive appeal and they are often significant for responsible rhetoric. There is a tendency for many people to look down their noses at emotional appeals, to feel that somehow they are less respectable than a precise rational demonstration. This is not necessarily the case, and Russell's essay, whether one agrees with his point of view or not, is an example of an altogether legitimate and very effective use of various nonlogical, rhetorical devices of persuasion.

Consider, for example, the following sentence:

A strange mystery it is that Nature, omnipotent but blind, in the revolutions of her secular hurryings through the abysses of space, has brought forth at last a child, subject still to her power, but gifted with sight, with knowledge of good and evil, with the capacity of judging all the works of his unthinking Mother.

Emotional heightening here is achieved, in part, through inverted word order. Normal English word order consists of a subject, followed by a verb, followed by a complement, if any. By inverting the expected order at the beginning of the sentence—"A strange mystery it is" rather than "It is a strange mystery"—Russell gives special emphasis to "a strange mystery." He wishes to create a sense of awe—not primarily to convey information—and this is precisely the effect of the inversion. Further, the position of the adjectives in normal sentence order is relatively fixed; they commonly come before the nouns they modify. By placing the adjectives "omnipotent" and "blind" after the noun "Nature," Russell again gives special emphasis to these key terms. For the two characteristics of Nature—blindness and omnipotence—are the very characteristics which make the production of man "a strange mystery." The mystery, indeed, is a paradox—that a "blind" force, even though "omnipotent," should produce a man gifted with "sight." Finally, the whole sentence achieves emotive unity and life through Russell's use of personification. Nature is a "Mother" who has brought forth a "child" capable of "judging" her "unthinking" power. The emotive force of Russell's sentence may be gauged by comparing it with the following paraphrase, which contains the logical content of the original, but lacks its inversion, paradox, and personification: "It is a strange mystery that omnipotent and blind nature has produced man, who is capable of judging nature itself."

Consider, also, the following sentence:

That man is the product of causes which had no prevision of the end they were achieving; that his origin, his growth, his hopes and fears, his loves and his beliefs, are but the outcome of accidental collocations of atoms; that no fire, no heroism, no intensity of thought and feeling, can preserve an individual life beyond the grave; that all the labours of the ages, all the devotion, all the inspiration, all the noonday brightness of human genius, are destined to extinction in the vast death of the solar system, and that the whole temple of man's achievement must inevitably be buried beneath the debris of a universe in ruins—all these things, if not quite beyond dispute, are yet so nearly certain, that no philosophy which rejects them can hope to stand.

This is a very long sentence, but it is extremely effective. First, because by holding up the sense of the sentence through five long *that*-clauses, Russell creates suspense and builds a climax; second, because the heavy rhythmic stresses come where they should, on key words like *man*, *origin*, *end*, *hopes*, *fears*, *loves*, *beliefs*, and so on; third, there is variety and change of pace in the rhythm. Each that-clause builds and then drops back to the next that-clause, but each receives a little greater emphasis than the one preceding, giving a kind of cumulative, battering effect like the waves of the sea. Although all sentences have rhythm, some have more than others; and very pronounced rhythmical effect is a means of heightening emotional overtones by stressing key, and usually emotively significant, words. Further, phrase balances phrase. The series which opens each that-clause is balanced by a corresponding series in the next; thus "his origin, his growth, his hopes and fears, his loves and beliefs" parallels and balances "no fire, no heroism, no intensity of thought and feeling," which in turn parallels "all labours of the ages, all devotion, all the inspiration, all the noonday brightness of human genius." Throughout his essay, Russell uses these nonlogical, persuasive devices to compel acceptance of his rational intent, which is embodied in the propositions of the alternative syllogism.

The most effective and thoroughgoing of the nonlogical devices which Russell uses in this essay, however, is imagery. Throughout he has provided illustration for and emotive expansion of his syllogistic structure by developing a pattern of images with strong emotional associations. For example, the world of fact, of natural forces, and of Power, the worship of which, Russell says, man should reject, is identified with the "Forces of Darkness," cold, danger, armies of evil, and the transitory things destroyed by time. On the other hand, the world of the mind, of human ideals, which Russell says man should worship, is identified with light, joy, comradeship, the armies of the blest; it is a temple, a bulwark, a fortress of righteousness; it is unchanging, out of time, a part of eternity. Man is a pilgrim torn between these two alternatives—the alternatives of Russell's major premise. The pilgrim's way is a road fraught with dangers; his progress is a struggle against the forces of evil, darkness, and cold. He is able to win through to the temple of light and joy and to worship there only if he renounces Power, the forces of Time and desire—in short, only through renunciation, which is seen as a gate that leads to the temple, to light, and to joy.

Paragraphs 14 through 22 of Russell's essay develop this consistent pattern of emotive images. In paragraph 14 he suggests that we must build a temple for the worship of our own ideals "in the untroubled kingdom of reason, . . . remote from the fear of change, remote from the failures and disenchantments of the world of fact." This is Russell's image of heaven, a kind of Eternal City of the mind. A part of the power of this vision lies in its correspondence to the traditional Christian view of heaven. There, too, all is light and joy and the pilgrim is freed from his bondage to time. Russell here uses the emotive power of a great religious tradition in Western culture for his own very different ends.

In paragraph 15, Russell notes that "there is a cavern of darkness to be traversed before the temple can be entered." The cavern is entered through the "gate of despair"; the floor is paved with "abandoned hopes"; but there is another gate that leads out of the cavern into the light and radiance of the temple: this is the "gate of renunciation." We must, he urges, renounce all desire for the things of this world before we can be fit for eternal things—all "personal goods subject to the mutations of time." In this cavern the "self must die." In paragraph 16, Russell continues this line of imagery, suggesting that the idols of this time-bound world are idols of clay, which do not endure; in the Eternal Kingdom, however, "a new image of shining gold replaces the old idol of clay." Those who worship Power, the things of this world, worship, in effect, false gods. Those who worship in the temple of the human mind worship eternal things. The alternative of Russell's original major premise, then, is carried out in the imagery. And the resolution of the alternative, the rejection of the worship of Power, is not only stated, but powerfully and emotively reinforced in the imagery. Who wants to worship an idol of clay? Who doesn't desire to worship in the temple of wisdom and share the joy of the Eternal City?

In paragraph 16, Russell expands this pattern of imagery still further. The temple becomes a citadel as well. The eternal kingdom is not the remote heaven of traditional theology; it is built in this life, "in the very midst of the enemy's country." The enemy, of course, is Force and Power, the world of fact, which must be renounced. From the citadel's "watchtowers" may be viewed the enemy's "camps and arsenals, his columns and forts." The "legions of Death and Pain and Despair" are camped 'round about. But to those who dwell in the citadel these legions not only hold no fear but provide "new spectacles of beauty." In the citadel live the "brave warriors," who "through countless ages of warfare have preserved the priceless heritage of liberty." This is "the home of the unsubdued."

In the last five paragraphs of the essay, Russell continues to develop and to amplify his basic propositions through imagery. He compares our life to a narrow raft tossed on rolling waves in a dark ocean—this is the world as science presents it to our view. He compares life to a battle in which the individual must fight alone, although he may have the "flickering light" of human comradeship to guide him. But he insists that, through faith, we can reach our goal. And victory over the powers of darkness provides "a true baptism" into the glorious company of heroes. Note here the continuing religious overtones of the images, not only in the emphasis on faith and in the use of the word *baptism* but in the whole concept of wayfaring and warfare. Russell's pilgrim walks the same road, meets the same enemies, and has a goal remarkably parallel to that of the pilgrim Christian in Bunyan's famous allegory *Pilgrim's Progress.* But it is not only to Bunyan's work that Russell's essay may be compared; his fabric of imagery is woven from the whole Protestant Christian tradition as revealed in innumerable sermons and religious tracts. Russell draws on the emotive force of a whole tradition which is deeply embedded in our society. He has at hand a full and deep reservoir of emotive power on which to draw, and he uses it with consummate skill.

The slave worships the darkness and the night—Power—because they are greater than himself and he has not renounced desire and self; all his thoughts are of things which Time and Fate and Death devour. The victor in the struggle, on the other hand, has abandoned the slave's struggle for private happiness; he has given up self and desire; he burns with a "passion for eternal things." The free man conquers because he worships timeless things at the shrine of his own self-created ideals. Though man's life is "brief and powerless" he can, in the time given him, cherish the ideals that his mind has created. He can sustain the world of the mind, a "world that his own ideals have fashioned, despite the trampling march of unconscious Power."

What Russell has done here by means of imagery is to create a movement of conception and feeling which parallels and reinforces the movement of the propositions of his underlying syllogism. His method is analogous to the method of Marvell in his poem, "To His Coy Mistress," which Cunningham has discussed. The images in Russell's essay and in Marvell's poem "reiterate the propositions of the syllogism. They do not develop the syllogism and they are not required by the syllogism." But they *do* develop and they *are* required by Russell's intention in the essay. For Russell, as mentioned earlier, is not primarily concerned to demonstrate or to *prove* a contention; he wishes to persuade the reader. And the strong emotional overtones of the images Russell uses are a part of his strategy of persuasion. So, too, is his syllogism. Einstein's purpose in his essay is primarily explication; he uses the syllogism as a device for organizing and clarifying his ideas. Cunningham, on the other hand, is concerned to prove; he uses the syllogism as a basis for establishing a controversial position. But, as we have said, Russell's central concern is persuasion. If he has succeeded in moving the reader, if he has, by means of the syllogism, imagery, sentence rhythm, word order, and word choice, persuaded the reader to a new belief, he has had his way.

The various uses of the syllogism in these three essays suggest, once again, the necessity of individual responsibility and pragmatic choice. The uses of the syllogism are as various as the author's intentions. Though there are rules for accurate and valid use of any logical form and though these forms may be seen used well in a variety of essays, the particular way in which a form is valuable to the individual writer is a matter not reducible to rules.

In Russell's essay the syllogism provides a logical and responsible basis for his emotive appeal. The essay demonstrates his firm grasp of the rational basis on which his persuasion rests. An appeal to the emotions may well be irresponsible unless the writer has done the work required for a rational understanding of the legitimate basis of his appeal. An attempt to stir the emotions is responsible when it has the sort of rational basis which Russell's essay has. A rationally based emotive appeal is not only legitimate; it lies at the heart of most great literature; it provides us with more than the mechanically contrived demonstration of the bare syllogism; it gives us the very stuff of human experience. This is not to say that syllogistic organization of an essay, poem, or of any writing whatever is the only means of providing a legitimate basis for emotive appeal. But it is one means, and Russell's essay shows that it can be an effective one.

EXERCISES

1. Which of the following arguments are valid? Which invalid? Why?
   a. Either there is a fault in the gas line or the stove is defective.
   There is a fault in the gas line.
   Therefore the stove is not defective.
   b. Either there is a fault in the gas line or the stove is defective.
   The stove is not defective.
   Therefore there is a fault in the gas line.
   c. It is not the case both that it is noon and my watch is right. It is noon. My watch must be wrong.
   d. Conscience is either the voice of God within us or it is a reflection of group custom. Examination of primitive societies reveals that, as a matter of fact, what one culture considers wrong another considers right, and that the conscience by which men act reflects the customs of the culture within which they live. Therefore, conscience is a reflection of group custom and not the voice of God within us.
   e. Either Russia must abandon its policy of repudiating debts incurred by the Czar or France will lose the money she loaned Russia. Russia, however, will not abandon its policy of repudiating debts incurred by the Czar, for the present government of Russia feels that the Czar's regime was illegitimate. Consequently, France will not be paid.
   f. It is not possible for the country as a whole to be prosperous while a major segment of the country is in economic trouble. At the present time our farmers are in severe economic difficulty. Therefore the illusion that the country as a whole is prosperous is false.
   g. Either China must abandon her intention of invading Formosa or the U.S. will become embroiled in a war with China. As a matter of fact, however, the Chinese leaders realize that they

could not possibly invade Formosa with their weak navy and with the U.S. Seventh Fleet in the Formosa Straits; the present Chinese policy is merely a bluff. Therefore, the U.S. will not become embroiled in a war with China.

h. Either present government security measures must be abandoned or they will, by closing the channels of information available to scientists, undermine the possibility of scientific advance. The present mood of the Congress and the people, however, insures the continuance of present government security measures. Thus the possibility of scientific advance will be undermined.

i. Governments arise either out of the people or over the people. The English government is one of those which arose out of conquest and not out of the people; consequently it arose over the people. (From Thomas Paine, *The Rights of Man*)

2. Using the discussion in this chapter as a guide, write an analysis of the nonlogical elements in the last paragraph of Russell's essay.

GENERAL REVIEW EXERCISES

Analyze the logical (syllogistic) structure of the following arguments.

NOTE: These arguments usually involve more than one kind of syllogism.

a. Either we must work to establish individual freedom everywhere in the world or imperialism and militarism will continue to flourish. If we continue to expand our foreign aid program we will be working to establish individual freedom everywhere in the world. Thus, if we continue to expand our foreign aid program, imperialism and militarism will be destroyed.

b. Either Emily Dickinson is a great poet or there are no great American poets. Yet if there are no great American poets, surely America is spiritually diseased. But America is not spiritually diseased. Therefore Emily Dickinson is a great poet.

c. If God is the creator of all that exists and if God is good, it follows that what He creates must be good. But evil is not good. Therefore, if God is the creator of all that exists and if God is good, evil does not exist. We know, however, that evil does exist. Therefore either God is not the creator of all that exists or God is not good.

d. In order to train the mind we must study exact disciplines like mathematics and languages. Yet, even though we must either train the mind or perish, we do not study exact disciplines such as mathematics and languages. Consequently, we will perish.

e. The Federal Government cannot both build and own public power projects and stay out of active economic competition with private industry. Nonetheless the government continues to build and own public power projects. But if the government is in active economic competition with private industry our free enterprise system is endangered. Anything which endangers our free enterprise system should be discontinued.

f. It is not the case both that it is midnight and the sun is shining; and it is either noon or midnight. The sun is shining. Therefore it must be noon.

g. If the child is repressed the adult will suffer psychologically. But either the child is repressed or he is allowed free expression. Thus if the adult does not suffer psychologically he must have been allowed free expression as a child.

h. If Algernon is in jail, then he is not a nuisance to his family. If he is not in jail, then he is not a disgrace. If he is not a disgrace then he is in the army. If he is drunk he is a nuisance to his family. Therefore if he is drunk then he is in the army.

SUGGESTIONS FOR THEME ASSIGNMENTS

1. Write an essay which logically affirms or denies either the antecedent or the consequent of the following proposition:

If Einstein is correct in arguing that both science and ethics are logical, then it follows that all ethical norms may be logically defended.

2. Write an essay in which you argue logically from the major premise to an affirmation or denial of one of the alternatives in the following proposition:

Either Cunningham's argument demonstrates that there is not antipathy between logic and poetry or Cunningham has failed in his major purpose.

3. In paragraphs 11 and 12 of "A Free Man's Worship" Russell refers to the Prometheus myth. Look up this myth in any general encyclopedia or mythology text. Write an essay in which you discuss the following:

How is the myth relevant to Russell's thesis in these paragraphs?

What is the effect of his allusion?

What proposition in the syllogistic pattern of his essay does it reinforce?

4. Write an essay in which you logically affirm or deny one of the following alternatives:

Either ethical norms can be traced to axioms or Einstein's thesis is false.

5. Write an essay in which you logically affirm or deny one of the propositions of the following hypothesis:

If the nonlogical elements in Marvell's poem are not necessary to the syllogistic organization of the poem and if the poem can be understood only syllogistically, then the nonlogical devices of Marvell's poem are not necessary to our understanding of the poem.

6. Cunningham states, in effect, at one point in his essay that poetry is a subdivision of logic. Using this proposition as a conclusion to your argument, write an essay in which you logically demonstrate its truth or falsity.

7. Write an essay in which you logically either affirm or deny the consequent of the following proposition:

If Russell's thesis is correct then traditional Christian worship, because it is a worship of power, is evil.

8. Einstein concludes his essay by stating "Truth is what stands the test of experience." Using this proposition as a conclusion to your argument, write an essay in which you logically demonstrate its truth or falsity.

9. One of the subsidiary lines of thought in Russell's essay yields the following categorical syllogism:

All worship of power is evil.
The Old Testament book of Job urges the worship of power.
∴ The book of Job urges a kind of worship which is evil.

Read the book of Job (especially chapter 38) and, on the basis of your reading, logically defend or attack Russell's minor premise in the above syllogism. (Some of the more ambitious students may wish to attack or defend the major premise; this is fair game, but much more difficult.)

FRED L. WHIPPLE

The Dust Cloud Hypothesis[*]

IF the earth should disappear some day in a chain-reacting cloud of dust, a possibility which is mentioned half-seriously in these deranged times, philosophers on another planet might find a certain poetic symmetry in its birth and death. Recent astronomical studies have given us reason to surmise that the earth was born in a cloud of dust. This dust cloud hypothesis, as it is called, suggests that planets and stars were originally formed from immense collections of submicroscopic particles floating in space. Although it is still being developed, the dust cloud hypothesis possesses a plausibility that other theories about the origin of planets and stars have lacked.

2. The beginnings of our physical universe are necessarily beclouded in the swirling mists of countless ages past. What cosmic process created the stars and planets? Are new ones still being formed? Or were all that now exist made in one fell swoop? Scientists are making progress in their study of these fascinating questions, although they still cannot answer them with certainty.

3. The dust cloud theory begins with the fact that there are gigantic clouds of dust and gas in the abyss of space that lies between the stars. Observations by the world's astronomers during the past twenty years have proved the existence of these clouds. Interstellar space, formerly supposed to be empty, is now known to contain an astonishing amount of microscopic material. Jan Oort of the Netherlands has calculated that the total mass of this interstellar dust and gas is as great as all the material in the stars themselves, including all possible planet systems. In other words, for every star there is an equal amount of dust and gas dispersed in space. The immensity of this quantity of material is beyond the grasp of human imagina-

* Fred L. Whipple, "The Dust Cloud Hypothesis," *Scientific American* (May, 1948). Used with permission.

tion. In the Milky Way alone, it comes to 300 million million earth masses. Yet interstellar space itself is so vast that this dust and gas is scattered more thinly than in the highest vacuum that can be created on earth.

4. We have a good deal of information about the composition of this nebulous star dust. The gases that we can detect are the ordinary elements with which we are familiar—hydrogen, helium, oxygen, nitrogen, carbon, and so on. Dutch astronomers have recently shown that these gas atoms slowly coalesce into chemical combinations and dust particles. While the structure of the dust particles is uncertain, it appears that most of them are very small—of the order of a fifty-thousandth of an inch in diameter. Evidence of their size and of the fact that they actually are dust particles is afforded by the way in which they scatter the light from distant stars. This scattering produces dark clouds on a photographic plate. The small amount of starlight that filters through these dust clouds is reddened—for the same reason that the sun appears reddened during a dust storm: the long waves of red light are less scattered by small dust particles than are the shorter waves of other colors.

5. What collects these dust particles into clouds? Lyman Spitzer, formerly of Yale and now at Princeton, suggested that it might be the pressure of light. The pressure of light, which is so exceedingly small that it cannot ordinarily be observed, is strikingly demonstrated in comets' tails, which are formed by the pressure of sunlight forcing fine material away from the head of the comet.

6. The writer, following the approach suggested by Spitzer, found that under rather unusual, but possible, circumstances the light from stars would tend to force interstellar dust into larger and larger clouds. In the starlight of space, each dust particle casts a shadow. The shadow is minute. Nonetheless, it results in less light shining from the direction of one particle on another near by, and vice versa. Hence the two particles tend to attract each other, by a force varying inversely as the square of the distance between them. The mathematics of this principle is similar to that of Newton's law of gravitation.

7. After a few particles are collected into a small cloud, the cloud casts a larger shadow in the starlight on the particles in its neighborhood. These particles are drawn into the cloud, making it larger and larger. If such a cloud is not too much stirred by its motion through

other banks of dust and gas, and if too bright a star does not pass through it and scatter the particles by its light pressure, the cloud will continue to draw in dust. Finally it will attain a mass and density sufficient for gravity to become stronger than light pressure. The cloud will then begin to contract. Calculations show that for a dust cloud with the same mass of material as the sun, the two forces would be about equal when the diameter of the cloud was some 6,000 billion miles. This distance is 60,000 times the distance of the earth from the sun. It has been further calculated that such a cloud might develop and collapse into a star in less than a billion years.

8. These calculations were made before any dust clouds of this nature had actually been observed. During the war, Bart J. Bok of Harvard, while musing one day over some familiar photographs of the Milky Way, noticed some very small, round, dark patches that had not seemed important before. He studied a number of photographs of each region in the Milky Way and found the same dark patches in all the photographs. These were not photographic blemishes but truly dense, dark clouds in space! When Bok estimated their distances and calculated their diameters, he found that the smaller clouds in this group were about the same size as the hypothetical dust cloud for which gravity equals the light pressure on dust. Many were larger but few much smaller.

9. Bok's discovery suggested the fascinating possibility that the small dark clouds might be stars in the making. That new stars are constantly being formed from cosmic dust seems more than likely. There is no other reasonable explanation for the brightness of certain stars. A star's intensity of radiation, which shows how fast it is burning up its energy in nuclear reactions, indicates its maximum age. Some stars are so brilliant that they could not have radiated for two billion years, the minimum time we can allow since the "beginning." Hence they must have been born later than the solar system. The discovery of these clouds encouraged the writer to study the possibility that not only a star but also a system of planets might condense out of such clouds.

10. Let us consider our solar system, therefore, as a case study of the formation of a star and its satellites. We have a huge dust cloud, as described above, which has begun to condense under gravity. There will be minor turbulent motions of the material within it—sub-clouds, or streams of dust—that slide by each other

or collide. In order to explain the present slow rotation of our sun, we must assume that the motions of the streams in the original dust cloud canceled each other and that the cloud as a whole did not rotate. This point can be illustrated by a well-known parlor game. The victim is persuaded to sit on a piano stool with his arms outstretched and holding some books. The stool is started turning slowly. Its occupant is then instructed to draw in his arms and the books. He now spins so rapidly that he may fall off the stool. This phenomenon demonstrates the law of "conservation of angular momentum," or what might be called "rotational obstinacy." Angular momentum, or rotation around the center, may be variously distributed among the parts of the system, but the total momentum for the system as a whole remains constant. Thus if the great dust cloud from which the sun was formed had had any appreciable rotation to begin with, after its collapse the condensed sun would have rotated with great speed. But actually our sun turns very slowly; it takes nearly a month to make a complete rotation. Consequently the original dust cloud must have been almost stationary.

11. This, by the way, would not necessarily be true of other dust clouds in our galactic system. The Milky Way itself rotates; hence we might expect many coalescing dust clouds within it to possess a great amount of rotation. In that case, according to our theory, they could not condense into single stars but would form double stars or even clusters. As a matter of fact, most stars *are* double or multiple, so that in this respect the dust cloud hypothesis is consistent with observations. The sun can be considered a somewhat unusual case.

12. Having accounted for the sun's slow rotation, let us go back to the original dust cloud. Under the force of its own gravity, it has begun to condense. At first it collapses very slowly, because the motions of its internal currents and streams resist its contraction. A group of moving particles is of course harder to collect and compress than one which is standing still. But in the course of millions of years the random motions of the stream within the cloud are damped out by collisions and friction. Meanwhile the cloud contracts more and more powerfully as it becomes smaller, because as its density increases, the force of gravity among the particles increases. The net result, with resistance diminishing and gravity increasing, is that the cloud collapses faster and faster. Its final col-

lapse from a size equal to that of the solar system (i.e., the diameter of the orbit of Pluto, the farthest known planet) would require just a few hundred years. Due to the increased pressure in the contracting cloud, its temperature rises enormously. In the last white-hot phase of its collapse, the sun would begin to radiate as a star. Its central temperature would become great enough to start the cycle of nuclear reactions among carbon, hydrogen and helium which keeps the sun radiating.

13. Now we must account for the evolution of the planets from the same great dust cloud. We return to the cloud before it has begun to shrink appreciably, and follow the largest stream in the cloud. If the dust in this stream is sufficiently dense, the stream condenses into minor clouds. As these clouds drift along together, roughly in the same direction, they will pick up material less compact than themselves; hence they will grow slowly, feeding on portions of the great cloud. As they grow, the minor clouds, now "proto-planets," begin to spiral slowly in toward the center of the main cloud. They have gained in mass but not in angular momentum, so they move towards the center of gravity, somewhat as a whirling ball on a rubber string, if no force is exerted to keep it whirling, spirals in an ever-narrowing circle as its motion is slowed by friction. Some of the proto-planets move in more rapidly than others, their rate depending on their size and on chance encounters with other streams.

14. If the great cloud remained spread out forever, all the proto-planets would eventually wind up at its center. But long before some of them have completed their spiral, the main cloud collapses and forms the sun. Its rapid final collapse leaves a number of proto-planets stranded in their orbits, outside the collapsing cloud. Some are trapped too near the center and are pulled in or destroyed in the sun's heat. Others are far enough away to remain intact. They condense and become planets. Some of them may be at enormous distances from the sun. For all we know, there may be planets in our system beyond Pluto, the farthest one that we can see.

15. When first formed, the planets are hot, perhaps hot enough to be in a molten condition. But since they are relatively small, their heat of contraction is not sufficient to start the nuclear reactions that would make them radiate permanently like a star. Gradually they cool off.

16. We have described, then, how the dust cloud hypothesis accounts for the origin of the solar system. Now let us see how well our theory accounts for the system's peculiarities.

17. Any theory about the evolution of our planetary system must explain certain striking characteristics: (1) The planets all move in the same direction and, with one exception, very nearly in the same plane as the earth's orbit, called the plane of the ecliptic. (2) Their orbital paths around the sun are nearly circular. (3) Almost all the planets rotate, or spin, on their axes, in the same direction in which they revolve about the sun. (4) Most of them have moons or satellites—Jupiter has eleven—which usually revolve about the planet in the plane of its rotation and in the same direction.

18. Thus the theory must account for a great deal of regularity in the system. But it must also explain some irregularities. For example the orbit of Uranus and its system of five satellites, including probably the one recently discovered by G. P. Kuiper at the McDonald Observatory in Texas, is tipped up roughly at right angles to the plane of the ecliptic. Neptune's single satellite revolves backwards, as compared with the rest of the solar system, although Neptune itself turns in the forward direction and is thus properly oriented. Some of the satellites of Jupiter and Saturn also are contrary.

19. To begin with, the theory explains why the planets generally revolve in the same direction and in nearly the same plane. Their plane and direction are determined by the motion of the original stream from which they were created. The planets' circular paths around the sun are accounted for by the spiraling phase of their evolution. Spiraling reduces the orbit of a revolving body more and more to the circular form.

20. The spacing of the planets at their present distances from the sun is not explained by the dust cloud hypothesis. This spacing, as every astronomy student knows, follows a regular mathematical relationship known as Bode's Law. It is possible that the planets' distances from the sun were determined by gravitational effects over a long period of time rather than at the very beginning. The great mathematical astronomer Ernest W. Brown, of Yale, doubted that the planet distances could have remained constant for more than 100 million years or so.

21. The planets' rotation or spinning is adequately explained by the dust cloud theory. As the great cloud condenses, it is denser

towards the center than in its outer regions. Thus a proto-planet, when it spirals in, tends to pick up more material on the side that faces towards the center than on the side away from it. This process produces a result something like the rolling of a snowball. The side that picks up more material becomes heavier and is slowed up. The outer side of the planet, being lighter, travels faster and moves forward. Thus the process imparts a forward spin to the whole planet.

22. On the assumption that the planets actually gained all of their rotation in this fashion, we can estimate how large they must have been when they condensed. The size of the planet when it started to rotate can be calculated from its present speed of rotation and its mass. The results of these calculations are very encouraging to the dust cloud hypothesis, for the calculated diameter of each proto-planet figures out to about the same as or a little more than the diamater of the orbit of that planet's farthest present satellite. This indicates that the satellites were formed while the planets were still distended as clouds. When a planet-cloud collapsed, the outer material collected into satellites or fell to the surface of the planet. Thus the satellites developed in just about the same way as the planets did when the sun-cloud collapsed.

23. We have no difficulty in accounting for the rapid revolutions of the satellites around their planets. The planets themselves rotate rapidly. We would also expect the satellites to revolve in the same direction as their planets' rotation and in the plane of the equator. In most cases, as we have seen, they do. But what about the exceptions? Neptune's only satellite, the three outer ones of Jupiter, and one of Saturn's revolve in a direction opposite from all the others and generally in planes different from those of their planets' equators. The answer is probably very simple: the maverick satellites were not a part of these planets' initial systems but were captured later, when they could no longer be completely controlled. Very likely there were originally many dense minor clouds, or potential planets, which did not develop into full-fledged planets. Some of these were small and outside the main stream. If a small cloud of this sort ran into a planet-cloud before the planet had collapsed, it would be captured and become a satellite. Normally the planet-cloud's rotation would carry the captured cloud along in the same direction, and would reduce the size of the satellite's orbit. But a satellite that was captured by a planet's gravity after the planet had collapsed would be less

strongly influenced. If it was revolving backwards when it was captured, it would continue in a retrograde orbit, even though held a prisoner by the planet's force of gravity.

24. Our hypothesis has another major irregularity to explain. Why are some of the planets so much larger than others, and why are the large planets so much less dense than the earth? The average density of Jupiter, for example, is only a little greater than that of water, while the earth is five and one-half times as dense as water. Saturn, if it could be put into a huge sea, would actually float. The explanation of these differences probably lies, as Henry Norris Russell of Princeton has suggested, in the fact that the giant planets were bigger to begin with. Their size gave them a huge gravitational attraction so that they could hold the light gases, such as hydrogen and helium, which would float away from a less massive planet. Their ability to attract and hold light elements would have a double result: they would grow rapidly, and they would be relatively light in proportion to their volume. On the other hand, a smaller proto-planet such as the earth, which has less ability to hold hydrogen or helium, would soon reach the limit of its growth. Lyman Spitzer has recently shown that hydrogen and helium are escaping from the earth's atmosphere even today.

25. There is still another odd peculiarity of the solar system that the dust cloud hypothesis seems to explain quite well. This is the fact that the planets which are closest to the sun have relatively few satellites and comparatively thin atmospheres. The explanation is this: When the sun was collapsing to its final form, the energy released by its contraction made it hot. The inner planets—Mercury, Venus, the Earth and Mars—were then in a fairly dense region of the condensing sun. As a result, their atmospheres and surfaces were heated to very high temperatures. Most of their satellites would boil away. Fortunately for the theory, this boiling period was very short—perhaps a few months or years—else the planets would have boiled away also. As it was, the earth and moon probably were not entirely spared by this "bath of fire"; both may have been appreciably reduced in size by the evaporation of their outer rocks. The outer planets, being outside this bath of fire, would not have been much affected, which accounts for the fact that they still have thick gaseous envelopes and a comparative abundance of satellites.

26. One other puzzling phenomenon, perhaps the most fascinating

of all, remains to be explained. This is the great collection of asteroids, or minor planets, found in the region between Mars and Jupiter. There are at least 1,600 of these "flying mountains," ranging from a mile or two or three or four hundred miles in diameter. All revolve in the same forward direction and near the plane of the ecliptic, although not as close to it as the planets. Their grouping suggests that the asteroids had a common origin. Are they the building stones of a planet that was stillborn, or the debris of one that was smashed? Present opinion favors the latter possibility. The proof, though not yet complete, is fairly convincing. Harrison Brown and his associates have shown that meteorites—pieces of interplanetary material that fall on the earth as shooting stars—must be fragments of a broken planet. Other studies by C. C. Wylie in Iowa indicate that these shooting stars or fireballs swing about the sun in orbits resembling those of some asteroids. Though the chain of evidence at this point is weak, we may reasonably accept the tentative conclusion that meteorites are baby asteroids, and that the asteroids, in turn, are broken pieces of a once completely formed planet. Harrison Brown calculates that the planet was about the size of Mars.

27. How was the planet smashed? Probably by collision with another planet; there may even have been more than two planets involved. On the dust cloud theory, we can easily assume the formation of an eccentric planet which would cross the path of one in the main stream. If it did, sooner or later we would expect the two planets to collide. The resultant cosmic explosion would produce the scattered asteroids.

28. We have seen, then, that the dust cloud hypothesis accounts for a great many of the facts about our solar system. The chief difficulty in the theory has to do with the question of how the protoplanets maintained themselves during the early stages. At that period the dust clouds had to be very rare, their average density being more nearly a vacuum than the vacuum in a Thermos bottle. Yet they had to hold together sufficiently to pick up material from the rarer spaces between them, and had to be massive enough to grow and to spiral in towards the sun. Such a situation is difficult to imagine, but there is some theoretical evidence that it is possible.

29. We must now consider whether the dust cloud theory is more convincing, or has fewer weaknesses, than other theories that have been proposed. The famous Nebular Hypothesis of the French

mathematical astronomer, the Marquis Pierre Simon de Laplace, suggested that the sun and planets derived from a great revolving nebula, or cloud. In this respect Laplace's theory sounds somewhat like the present one. But he assumed that the planets were formed from rings of matter left behind when the dish-shaped nebula collapsed. The nebular hypothesis meets with the overwhelming difficulty that it requires that most of the solar system's rotation be carried by the sun. As we have seen, the slowly rotating sun actually contains only a small percentage of the system's total rotation or angular momentum, while Jupiter contains more than half. It is not possible to account for the observed motions by Laplace's theory.

30. Another famous and extremely important theory, known as the Planetary Hypothesis, was proposed by the geologist T. C. Chamberlain and the astronomer F. R. Moulton, of the University of Chicago, early in this century. They postulated that the planets were formed as the result of a near-collision between the sun and another star. The star came very close to the sun, perhaps even grazing its surface. Huge tides were raised on the sun and great quantities of material were torn from it. This material is then supposed to have condensed into droplets which eventually coalesced into planets. The planetary hypothesis has many attractive features, and has dominated thinking in this field for many years.

31. One of its principal difficulties, which is also common to other theories that require a stellar collision or near-collision, was pointed out by Henry Norris Russell and proved by Lyman Spitzer. Let us consider the physical state of the hot, gaseous material which, according to this theory, is to be removed from beneath the surface of the sun very rapidly, say within an hour or two. While this gas remains in the sun, it is held by the sun's enormous gravity, some 28 times that of the earth. If it were not extremely hot, the gas would collapse into a very dense mass. It is kept distended by solar temperatures which range from 10,000 degrees F. at the surface to some 40 million degrees at the center. Suppose, then, that we scoop enough material out of the sun to make the planets, allowing for a considerable loss into space. We are drawing out gas at a temperature of perhaps 10 million degrees. At the instant when it is released from the sun's great gravity, the explosive pressure of this superheated gas is fantastically great. Released suddenly, the gas expands

in an explosion of almost inconceivable force. Most of the gas is lost forever from the solar system. Furthermore, it is very difficult to conceive of a process whereby the remaining gas would cool and condense into droplets, or collect in masses as large as the planets.

32. Recently the German physicist C. F. von Weizsäcker has developed a new mathematical theory for the evolution of planets from a gas-and-dust cloud rotating about the sun. His theory can be made to predict the Bode's Law relationship of planet distances from the sun. There is still some question, however, whether the Weizsäcker theory really works. Moreover, it leaves wide open the question as to how the gas cloud came into existence and into motion about the sun.

33. All of the current theories about the birth of the stars and planets leave much to be desired. The truth is that we are still groping in the haze of a poorly illuminated and ancient past. Perhaps an entirely new advance in science will be required to light our way. On the other hand, it is possible that we have already stumbled on the correct path but cannot see clearly enough to recognize its worth.

CHAPTER EIGHT

Form and Method of Explanation, Hypothesis, Induction

TO explain facts in the world of experience is one of the primary objectives of human reasoning. Both individually and collectively man attempts to push beyond mere descriptions to provide explanations for the things which he observes and the feelings which he has—explanation is a way of giving meaning to these bare facts of experience. To know, for instance, that the price of orange juice varies from season to season and year to year may be useful information. It may be of interest to know that the shape of a pygmy's nose differs from the shape of an Eskimo's nose, and that both differ from the nose shapes of chimpanzees, tarsiers, and polar bears. However, we also wish to know why: What economic factors influence the pricing of orange juice? What physiological and anatomical factors, such as teeth and forces of mastication, enter into an explanation of the differences in nose shapes. Similarly, to know that there are nine planets, to know their order and distance from the sun, to be able to name them and perhaps to point out the visible ones in the sky—all this is interesting and perhaps useful. But if we know only the "what" and not the "why" or "how," then we neither understand the processes or causes behind the occurrence of a fact nor are we able to predict future events.

In "The Dust Cloud Hypothesis" Fred L. Whipple, Director of the Astrophysical Observatory of the Smithsonian Institute, presents an explanation to account for the facts of the present observable form and operation of the solar system. He attempts to show the "how" and "why" of the "what" which makes up our factual knowledge of the solar system. If we analyze this essay not only to discover *what* the elementary principles of explanation are, but also to learn *how* and *why* an explanation functions as it does, we shall be in a position both to understand explanations (as well as to recognize them) and to control them better as we use them in our own writing.

One of Whipple's more detailed explanations deals with the slow rotation of the sun (paragraph 10). The fact to be explained may be stated in the sentence—called the EXPLANANDUM[1]—*The sun rotates very slowly*. How is it explained? The dust cloud, from which the sun was formed by contraction, probably did not rotate as a whole, and had very little motion among its parts in the form of general rotation. Angular momentum, we know as a general law, is constant within a rotating system. According to this law, the more distant mass is from its center of rotation the more slowly it rotates, and conversely, the closer it is to its center the faster it rotates, so long as the angular momentum remains constant. Thus, the very slight angular momentum within the widely scattered dust cloud, a large portion of which remains in the powerfully contracted sun, appears in the slow rotation of the sun. These sentences, called the EXPLANANS, which account for the occurrence of the fact, can be sorted out into two types: first, those which state *certain conditions* which occur prior to, or at the same time as, the event we are explaining—in this case the dispersed and contracted forms of the mass (in the dust cloud and in the sun), and the speed with which the dust cloud moves; second, those which state *general laws*—in this case the law of conservation of angular momentum.

By restating the explanation we can discover the *form* which binds the explanandum and explanans into an explanation:

1. If angular momentum remains constant within a rotating system, then if the rotation of the mass of a system when widely scattered from its center is very slight, the rotation of the mass when concentrated at its center will be slow.
2. Angular momentum remains constant within a rotating system.

[1] The terms *explanandum* and *explanans* have been taken from the essay "The Logic of Explanation," by Carl G. Hemple and Paul Oppenheim, *Philosophy of Science*, Vol. XV (1948).

3. Thus, if the rotation of the mass of a system when widely scattered from its center is very slight, the rotation of that mass when concentrated at its center will be slow.
4. Moreover, the rotation of the mass of the solar system when widely scattered from its center (in the dust cloud) was (Whipple assumes) very slight.
5. Thus, the rotation of that mass when concentrated at its center (in the sun) is slow.

Arranged in this way it becomes obvious that the form of explanation is a form of deductive argument we have already studied. The hypothetical premise (1) employs the law of conservation of angular momentum, and states that it implies a certain relation between rates of rotation as the mass in a rotating system varies in its distribution from the center. The consequent in this premise is implied by the antecedent according to an established physical law; it is therefore a legitimate major premise. The minor premise (2) affirms the antecedent of the major premise, making the conclusion (3) a valid inference from (1) and (2). Then the conclusion from the first two premises becomes, in turn, the major premise for a second argument. The minor premise (4) of this second argument Whipple has assumed to be true. The conclusion (5) then follows from the second pair of premises and the form of the argument is valid. In other words, the form of explanation utilizes the form of deductive argument in this manner: the explanandum is the conclusion deducible from the explanans which constitutes the premises.

Stated explicitly as a syllogism, an explanation, such as the one above, is somewhat stilted. Whipple's version is much smoother. With even less formality we might answer the question "Why does the sun rotate slowly?" like this: According to the law of conservation of angular momentum, the sun rotates slowly because the dust cloud from which it is contracted had almost no rotational movement. Or, even more briefly, we might say: The sun rotates slowly because it is a contraction of a dust cloud that hardly moved at all. In all these versions the underlying form of explanation is the same. They differ in the extent to which the parts of the explanation are made complete and explicit, and in the directness and completeness with which the form of explanation is expressed. In the last brief version, part of the explanans—the general law—is suppressed, and the form of explanation is not directly shown; in the next-to-last version all the parts are given implicitly, and the form of explanation appears indirectly.

The form of explanation is a simple form of logical deduction. And it is its simplicity which imparts clarity and efficiency to the organization of Whipple's explanation of the sun's rate of rotation. Though his knowledge is greater than that of most men, his technique of explanation is a common logical form available to anyone. Moreover, because deliberate analysis of an explanation involves reducing it to its logical components, use of the form of explanation requires explicit statement of assumptions: it demands that we know what our assumptions are. The form of explanation, therefore, also serves responsible writing by bringing assumptions to light.

To have a sense that an event is explained is to have a sense of familiarity with the pattern of events leading up to and including that event. In writing an explanation, this sense of familiarity is produced by identifying the event to be explained and the pattern of events leading up to it, and then showing that the antecedent events actually could have occurred to fill out the familiar deductive pattern. Put into the terminology of explanation, we can say that a successful written explanation makes clear the explanandum and both parts of the explanans, and then shows logically that these elements in fact constitute an explanation. Whipple's paragraph explaining the slow rotation of the sun embodies all these requirements of explanation.

Similarly, the technique of explanation informs all other parts of Whipple's essay where his purpose is to explain. For instance, in paragraph 17 he states: "Any theory about the evolution of our planetary system must explain certain striking characteristics." In paragraphs 17 and 18 he enumerates these characteristics; that is, he identifies or describes the facts of the solar system which any theory needs to explain, facts which he undertakes to explain with the dust cloud hypothesis. Paragraph 19 names first the two-part explanandum "why planets generally revolve in the same direction and in nearly the same plane," and then provides the explanans, showing the logical relation between them. Paragraph 21 again begins with another explanandum, the statement that planets rotate. The antecedent conditions of the condensing dust cloud, the spiraling of a partially condensed planet, the continuing attraction of dust particles on one side more than on the other, together with general laws regarding mass and momentum, are combined in the form of explanation. In this way Whipple accounts, paragraph by paragraph, for the observed characteristics of the solar system, including its regularities and irregularities. Each time he not only tells us the "what" about the facts of the solar system, but the "why" and "how" as well.

Taken together, the series of paragraph-length explanations in paragraphs 17-28 constitute a larger explanation—an explanation of the salient characteristics of the solar system. In this larger explanation Whipple shows how the presently observable characteristics of the solar system are deducible from the antecedent conditions described by the dust cloud hypothesis and the universally accepted laws of physics. Earlier, in paragraphs 10-16, he had explained the origin of the solar system, again using the antecedent conditions described by his hypothesis, along with the laws of physics.

Then, in paragraphs 29-32 Whipple considers the adequacy of other theories which attempt to account for the formation and present characteristics of the solar system. Three other prominent hypotheses he discovers to be inadequate. That is, some aspects of the solar system as we now know it are not deducible from the antecedent conditions which these theories assume, in accordance with accepted physical laws. None of the other theories adequately *explains* the origin and characteristics of the solar system.

Whipple concludes from his comparison of the dust cloud theory with other theories, not that the dust cloud hypothesis is true, but that it seems to be the best explanation yet proposed for the origin and characteristics of the solar system. As he had said at the end of his first paragraph, his hypothesis "possesses a plausibility that other theories about the origin of the planets and stars have lacked." The claim of superiority for his theory, though certainty is remote and facts are obscure, lies in the adequacy with which the dust cloud hypothesis enables us to deduce the observable facts of the solar system.

We are now in a position to understand the "why" as well as the "what" of the organization of Whipple's entire essay. In outline form we can review what he has done:

Paragraphs 1-2 constitute a brief *introduction*, acquainting us with the subject of the essay, and informing us that the author will explain a theory of the origin and characteristics of the solar system.

Paragraphs 3-9 provide the *background* of this theory, which both informs us of the factual basis on which the theory rests and recounts the development of the theory.

Paragraphs 10-16 *explain the origin of the solar system*, by means of a series of subsidiary explanations.

Paragraphs 17-28 *explain the characteristics of the solar system*, again by means of a series of subsidiary explanations.

Paragraphs 29-32 *examine other theories*, in terms of their adequacy in explaining the origin and characteristics of the solar system.

Paragraph 33 *assesses* the possibilities for the author's theory being correct.

The reason for the success of this organization is apparent. The introduction identifies the theory which the essay will explain, announcing the subject and purpose of the essay. The background provides, among other things, factual information about the solar system which the reader will need if he is to realize what facts need to be explained and if he is to understand the explanations which follow. Only then can Whipple proceed with his explanations of the origin and characteristics of the solar system without having to interrupt his explanation to supply necessary factual information. And only when his own explanations are complete and his theory tested is it plausible for him to compare his theory with others by testing their adequacy in explaining the solar system. The simplicity and reasonableness of Whipple's organization and procedure are not deceptive; the procedure, once understood, is as easily available to our own writing as the logical form of explanation is.

Having analyzed the form of explanation and observed how Whipple's essay explains the facts of the solar system, we can now view the essay in another way. Just as he tests other theories of the origin of the solar system by showing their adequacy or inadequacy in accounting for observable facts, so his deductions of observable facts from the hypothesis that the solar system began as a dust cloud constitute a test of his own hypothesis. The facts are described in paragraphs 17-18. When a valid deduction (or explanation) yields one of these facts as a conclusion the hypothesis is said to be CONFIRMED. If any one of these facts cannot be explained by the given hypothesis, or if the deduction yields a conclusion which is not factually true, the hypothesis is said to be DISCONFIRMED. Viewed in this way the essay presents a series of tests which, except for one or two unsolved problems, confirm the dust cloud hypothesis. Furthermore, the deductive form of explanation may function for prediction. The same deductions which explain aspects of our solar system also predict the formation of new stars and perhaps even new solar systems from dust clouds we can now observe.

The same logical form, thus, enables us to explain, to test a hypothesis, or to predict future events. The difference is one of emphasis. In explaining the origin and characteristics of the solar system, Whipple is concerned to find initial conditions and general laws on the basis of which he may deduce the given phenomena. In testing a hypothesis either the antecedent conditions or the general laws are considered problematic: when the conclusion which they are able to predict is compared with the results of experience, the hypothesis is confirmed (or disconfirmed). In prediction the initial conditions and the general laws are given but the conclusion is problematic: it is a statement about an event that has not yet occurred. Sometime in the future the occurrence or nonoccurrence of a predicted event may serve to test the accuracy of the prediction. The decision as to which use to make of the form of explanation in writing is pragmatic; it depends on what information we take to be given and on the intention with which we approach a subject.

So far we have been concerned with the form of explanation and its use in *organizing* writing, whether our intention is to explain, predict, or test a hypothesis. In light of what we have just learned we can discover how hypotheses provide a useful method for *selecting* information when we write. In writing research papers we need to select facts, since more facts turn up during research than can appear conveniently in the paper. Not only do we turn up more facts than can be used, we also turn up many that should not be used, simply because they have no direct bearing on our purpose in writing. Overabundant and random facts are cumbersome and meaningless. If, for instance, Whipple had included, in addition to the facts he employs, these additional facts—that there are dark spots on the sun, that Mars has three main types of clouds, that Venus is continually shrouded in a vapor of carbon dioxide, that the nucleus of a comet is a conglomerate of ices and solids—his essay would stray from the point and, probably, exasperate the reader if not confuse him hopelessly. These additional facts are not necessary parts of the logical deductions from the dust cloud theory and the laws of physics. Thus, they are irrelevant. It is Whipple's hypothesis, the subject of his essay, that decides whether they are relevant or not. By forming a hypothesis, constructing a tentative pattern for arranging facts, it is possible to distinguish relevant from irrelevant facts.

Three observations about facts and hypotheses may be useful here. To be relevant, a fact must be relevant *to* something. The additional facts about the solar system introduced in the preceding paragraph are not relevant to Whipple's purpose in his essay, since they do not participate in his explanations. They may, of course, be relevant to other hypotheses or purposes. Second, facts are not relevant merely to other facts. The additional facts we have introduced are not relevant to each other as they stand, and taken together they do not *mean* anything. Even if we combine more facts from Whipple's essay with them—that there are gigantic clouds of dust and gas in space, that the mass of this dust and gas equals the mass of the stars, that the dust particles are about a fifty-thousandth of an inch in diameter, that light exerts pressure, that stars radiate in nuclear reactions, and so on—still the facts do not *mean.* Meaning does not lie in the facts by themselves; meaning lies in the form imposed on the facts by the individual. And it is by connecting facts with other facts that we can create a form to give them meaning. Because a hypothesis connects facts of one kind with facts of another kind, it enables us to impose meaning on the discrete facts of experience. Whipple's training put thousands of facts at his disposal; his hypothesis functions at one and the same time as a method of selecting facts and of giving them meaning.

Third, although a hypothesis enables us to select some facts and discard others, since it functions as something for facts to be relevant *to,* it does not necessarily select only those facts which enter into deductions that confirm the hypothesis. Relevant facts may contribute to either confirmation or disconfirmation of hypotheses. Thus, hypotheses render explanation possible; they function as a basis for selecting facts; but they may select facts which help to discredit them. This is the reason new hypotheses, like Whipple's dust cloud theory, often need to be sought.

Factual conditions, as distinguished from logical conditions, necessary to confirm or disconfirm a hypothesis may be illustrated by a simple example. The hypothesis *(All) Water freezes at tempera-*

tures lower than 32° F. may be said to be confirmed when we have observed repeated instances of water actually freezing at temperatures below 32°. We ourselves have observed perhaps a dozen instances of this. If we let *T* and *F* stand respectively for *Water at 32° or lower* and *Water freezing*, we may schematize our reasoning as follows:

T_1 was followed by F_1
T_2 was followed by F_2
. . . .
T_{12} was followed by F_{12}

On the basis of these twelve confirming circumstances, supposing no negative (or disconfirming) circumstances, we say that the hypothesis has been established. Although any hypothesis is tentative to some extent, since twelve (or any finite number) instances of one kind of fact (water at 32° F.) accompanied in each instance by another kind of fact (water freezing) cannot with absolute certainty establish the generalization "All," we do, nonetheless, regularly assume the reliability of this "leap" from "some" to "all" in explanation.

This kind of reasoning is called INDUCTIVE. Inductive reasoning, then, is a method of confirming a general statement (hypothesis) connecting facts of one kind with facts of another kind. In explanation, induction is an essential part of the over-all deduction. In the over-all deductive pattern, the conclusion is deduced, validly or invalidly, from the premises; deduction moves from a general rule to a specific instance (from premise to conclusion). Induction moves from specific instances to a general rule within the deductive frame. Both types of reasoning are essential to and complement one another.

To explain an event, as we have seen, means to derive deductively a statement which describes that event, using as premises universal laws together with sentences describing antecedent conditions. The hypothesis from which the deduction proceeds is confirmed when, by observing particular cases (induction), we discover that the facts which make up the event to be explained are regularly preceded, in all observed instances, by the facts which make up the initial conditions. The situation described by the initial conditions is usually referred to as the CAUSE of the event to be explained.

The form and tests of causal explanation serve not only the physical sciences, with which Whipple is concerned, but they serve as well for explanation in other fields. In history, for example, we find explanations like the following:

> . . . Here again [in 18th century England] there was no inspection of domestic conditions of service. The evil-minded and avaricious master could abuse his apprentice with little fear of anything beyond a bad reputation among his neighbours. Pauper children, apprenticed to the lower type of master or mistress, perished as miserably as the same class of child in the worst factories of a later generation. So far from originating cruelty to children, the factory system called attention to the evil by concentrating it where all could see, and so stimulated indignation that brought it to an end.[2]

One of the explanations here has the explanandum *The master could abuse his apprentice* or, more specifically, *Pauper children, apprenticed to the lower type of master or mistress, perished miserably.* Only the general rule, that there was no inspection of domestic conditions of service, is stated explicitly for the explanans, but the antecedent conditions, that the master often wished to abuse his apprentice and could get away with it, is plainly enough implied. There is also explanation of abolition of cruelty to children under adverse working conditions. In syllogistic form, it states that

If cruelty is seen, it stimulates public indignation.
The factory system concentrated cruelty so that all could see it.
Thus, public indignation was stimulated under the factory system.
Moreover, stimulated public indignation produces action which abolishes its cause.
Hence manifest cruelty (the cause of public indignation) was abolished.

Although the emphasis of history, and of the humanities generally, is on particular events, whereas the emphasis of physics, and of the sciences generally, is toward discovering universal laws, the difference is not in the logical method of their explanations, but in the intention. The intention of the historian, for example, unlike that of the astrophysicist, is generally not to explicate or corroborate (confirm) a general law but to report the occurrence of particular events. Nonetheless, general laws, often not explicitly stated,

[2] G. M. Trevelyan, *History of England*, 2d ed., rev. (New York, Longmans, Green and Co., 1942), p. 523. Used with permission of the publishers.

are as essential to explanation in the social sciences and humanities as particular statements are to scientific explanation.

Further, in the social sciences and humanities hypotheses usually cannot be tested in so conclusive a way as in the physical sciences; historical situations cannot be set up in the laboratory and quantitatively measured. Hence, we often speak of historical trends or configurations rather than laws. The general statements (trends) in Trevelyan's explanation—if cruelty is seen, it stimulates public indignation, and public indignation produces action which abolishes its cause—cannot be given the same sort of precise corroboration which is available to test the law that water freezes at 32° F. Nonetheless, Trevelyan's laws can be inductively tested by referring to other historical occurrences of seen cruelty resulting in public indignation which produced action to eliminate the cruelty. Thus Trevelyan's hypothesis may be tested and confirmed (or disconfirmed) by the same method as any hypothesis in the physical sciences. We find in other fields, then, the same form of explanation, the same use of hypothesis, the same kinds of tests which we found in the physical sciences. Each may supply a pattern for responsible writing.

Though some account of the process of formulating a hypothesis may be appropriate in an essay of explanation, such an account is not a part of the logical explanation itself and does not provide a form for writing. Whipple uses an account of the formulation of the dust cloud hypothesis to introduce factual information which his readers will need to understand his theory. Because this account does not show us *why* the solar system has the characteristics we observe, the rest of the essay, if it is to explain these characteristics, must be cast in the form of logical explanation.

Sometimes hypotheses seem to come as momentary intuitive insight. We may suddenly get an idea, see a pattern in our material, realize an arrangement of facts which enables us to understand them and proceed to explanation. One of the famous examples of this occurred when Galileo, while in a cathedral at Pisa, suddenly wondered whether, perhaps, the oscillations of the lamps hanging by long chains from the high ceiling of the church occupied the same time regardless of the range (or length) of their swing. His hypothesis of the isochronous oscillations of the pendulum—a revolutionary hypothesis in his day—came as sudden insight. His only means of testing it at the time was with the only clock he had with him—his pulse. His test confirmed the theory. He later tested and re-tested his theory with more and more accurate measurements, and always with the same results. In this way he established the hypothesis which had come to him apparently by intuition.

Chance often seems to bring about formulation of new hypotheses. Fortuitous circumstances contributed to the discovery of radium. By accident, Pierre and Marie Curie left a piece of pitchblende in a drawer with some photographic plates. They later discovered that the plates had been exposed, and, since there was no other explanation for the exposure, they theorized that some hitherto unknown element, capable of radiation that can affect photographic plates, was contained in the pitchblende.

Hypotheses may be the result of observing similarities between different sets of facts. For instance, the similarities between the whirling masses which surround the nucleus of observed dust clouds and the rotation of the planets around the sun may very well have been the observation which, along with other observed similarities, led Whipple to formulate the dust cloud theory. Analogy, the transferrence of a pattern which organizes one set of facts to another set of facts, is another way of arriving at hypotheses.

Very often, hypotheses appear to be formulated as generalizations of, or extensions from, a series of factual observations. In reciting the facts upon which his dust cloud theory was formed (paragraphs 3-9), Whipple indicates that his hypothesis was an extension of certain astronomical facts. A familiar illustration of this process is that from the distaste (or pleasure) we feel toward a few members of a race, nationality, economic class, or religious group, we may generalize that all members of that group are distasteful (or pleasing). Ordinarily we call a generalization of this type a *prejudice* when it is untested, and perhaps untestable, and call it a *fact* (technically, a corroborated hypothesis) when it has been tested and shown to be useful for prediction. Hypotheses formed in this way are often called inductive hypotheses, since they develop general statements from particular facts.

Whether we obtain a hypothesis by intuitive insight, by stumbling over it through sheer chance, by analogy, by generalizing an observed pattern, or by some combination of these means is irrelevant to the value of a hypothesis. It is the hypothesis itself, however arrived at, which has value as a basis for selecting and arranging facts in our writing, and it is the testing of the hypothesis which provides the fertile ground for making new observations.

In summing up our analysis, we can see the value of understanding the form and uses of explanation, hypothesis, and induction. Our responsibility as writers demands that understanding and requires careful use of it. The form of explanation demands that we articulate our assumptions, bringing them to light for examination; it demands that we ensure the rationality of our explanations; and it provides the model by which we can test the completeness and organization of written explanations. Use of this logical form provides a touchstone for prediction and hypothesis. To understand the function of hypotheses enables us to judge the relevance of facts. And the role of induction in corroborating hypotheses assists both our responsible choice among hypotheses and our organization of evidence to support or refute them. For hypotheses are not true; they become true. "Truth is what stands the test of experience."

EXERCISES

State in separate assertions (propositions) the explanandum and the two parts of the explanans for each explanation in the following paragraphs.

1. [According to one theory, new species of plants and animals develop as a result of mutation.] It was found that hereditary characters, with minor exceptions, are transmitted from parent to offspring by well-defined, complex microscopic chemical units, called chromosomes, in the germ cells. Particular hereditary effects are localized at points, designated as genes, within each separate chromosome. Variations occur, among other ways, by the inheritance of different sorts of genes or chromosomes from the two parents, in sexual reproduction. New sorts of hereditary characters appear suddenly when some change, called a mutation, occurs in a set of chromosomes, in an individual chromosome, or in a gene within a chromosome. Such changes can be induced artificially in the laboratory, but their exact nature and effect cannot yet be predicted in individual cases. In nature, so far as has been determined, they occur spontaneously and at random.[1]

[1] From "Evolution, Organic," *Collier's Encyclopedia*. Used with permission of the publishers, P. F. Collier & Son Corp.

2. This age [late eighth century] was one of the blackest in history, as are all those when an old order disappears, leaving men at the mercy of their own passions. The Gallo-Romans were no longer governed by an administration of the Roman variety. The Barbarians had wrecked the idea of law, and everyone pleaded the customs of his tribe; they had wrecked the idea of State finances and the Merovingian kings had squandered the kingdom through gifts bestowed on their boon companions; they had wrecked the idea of a State justice, and the nobles, like the Church, thenceforth claimed the administration of their own justice.[2]

3. To the end of his life this love of an obsolete England persisted in William Joyce, to be rebuffed by contemporary England. . . . It was this love, slanting across time, which made him a Fascist. He had been brought up to believe in an England who held Ireland by force, and felt betrayed when Home Rule was given. This meant an actual, material betrayal. The family had to leave Ireland, like many other loyalist Irishmen. Thus William Joyce found himself exiled from his real motherland, Ireland, which his blood must have loved, and confined in England, for love of which he had betrayed Ireland, and which showed no gratitude for that sacrifice.[3]

4. The President's power, if any, to issue the order [seizing the steel mills] must stem either from an act of Congress or from the Constitution itself. There is no statute that expressly authorizes the President to take possession of property as he did here. Nor is there any act of Congress . . . from which such a power can fairly be implied. . . .

[Thus] it is clear that if the President had authority to issue the order he did, it must be found in some provisions of the Constitution. . . . The contention [of the government] is that presidential power should be implied from the aggregate of his powers under the Constitution. . . .

[But] the Constitution does not subject the law-making power of Congress to presidential or military supervision or control. . . .

The founders of this Nation entrusted the lawmaking power to Congress alone in both good and bad times. . . . [Thus] this seizure order cannot stand.[4]

5. In passing upon the question of Presidential powers in this case [President Truman's seizure of the steel mills], we must first consider the context in which those powers were exercised. . . .

[2] From Andre Maurois, *A History of France* (New York, Farrar, Straus, and Cudahy, Inc., 1957). Used with permission of the publishers.

[3] From *The Meaning of Treason* by Rebecca West. Copyright 1947 by Rebecca West. Reprinted by permission of the Viking Press, Inc.

[4] From Mr. Justice Black's majority opinion: Youngstown Sheet and Tube Co. *vs.* Charles Sawyer, June 2, 1952.

For almost two full years, our armed forces have been fighting in Korea, suffering casualties of over 108,000 men. Hostilities have not abated. . . . Congressional support of the action in Korea has been manifested by provisions for increased military manpower and equipment. . . .

. . . The central fact in this case [is] that the Nation's entire basic steel production would have shut down completely if there had been no Government seizure. . . . The uncontroverted affidavits . . . amply support the finding that "a work stoppage would immediately jeopardize and imperil our national defense."

. . . Accordingly, if the President has any power under the Constitution to meet a critical situation in the absence of express statutory authorization, there is no basis for criticizing the exercise of such power in this case.

A review of executive action demonstrates that . . . with or without explicit statutory authorization . . . Presidents have . . . dealt with national emergencies by acting promptly and resolutely. . . . Congress and the courts have responded to such executive initiative with consistent approval. [There follows a summary of numerous cases in which Presidents have acted to deal with national emergencies without explicit Congressional or Constitutional authorization and have been upheld by the courts.]

No basis for claims of arbitrary action, unlimited powers or dictatorial usurpation of Congressional power appears from the facts of this case. On the contrary, judicial, legislative, and executive precedents throughout our history demonstrate that in this case the President acted in full conformity with his duties under the Constitution. Accordingly, we would reverse the order of the District Court [holding the seizure unconstitutional].[5]

6. A general demand for restatement or explanation seems to have arisen from time to time. . . . Such a demand presumably indicates a disharmony between traditional explanations and current needs. It does not necessarily imply the "falsehood" of the older statement; it may merely mean that men wish to live and act according to a different formula. This is especially evident . . . whenever a "scientific" explanation replaces a theological one. For example, the spots on the moon's surface might be due, theologically, to the fact that it was God's will they should be there; "scientifically" they might be "explained" as craters of extinct volcanoes. The newer explanation may be said, not so much to contain "more" truth than the older, as to supply the *kind* of truth

[5] From Mr. Chief Justice Vinson's dissenting opinion: Youngstown Sheet and Tube Co. *vs.* Charles Sawyer, June 2, 1952.

which was now demanded. An event was "explained" . . . when its history had been traced and described. . . . No one . . . wishes to deny that this [kind of] explanation had and still has a more "satisfying" quality than the one it superseded. But why was it more satisfying? It was more satisfying . . . because, . . . instead of the kind of "truth" which is consistent with authoritative teaching, men began [from the 17th century on] to desire the kind which would enable them to measure, to weigh, and to control the things around them. . . . For a scientific type of explanation to be satisfying, for it to convince us with a sense of its necessary truth, we must be in the condition of needing and desiring that type of explanation and no other.[6]

[6] From Basil Willey, *The Seventeenth Century Background*, published in London by Chatto and Windus and in America by Columbia University Press, 1942. Used with permission of the publishers.

PETER F. DRUCKER

*Henry Ford: Success and Failure**

HENRY FORD'S hold on America's imagination—indeed on the imagination of the world's masses—was not due to his fabulous financial success. And it can only partly be explained by the overwhelming impact of the automobile on our way of life. For Henry Ford was less the symbol and embodiment of new wealth and of the automobile age than the symbol and embodiment of our new industrial mass-production civilization.

2. He perfectly represented its success in technology and economics; he also perfectly represented its political failure so far, its failure to build an industrial order, an industrial society. The central problem of our age is defined in the contrast between the functional grandeur of the River Rouge plant, with its spotless mechanical perfection, and the formlessness and tension of the social jungle that is Detroit. And the two together comprise Henry Ford's legacy.

3. Both his success and his failure can be traced to his being thoroughly representative of that most native and most dominant of all American traditions, the one which in Populism found its major political expression. Indeed, Henry Ford was both the last Populist and perhaps the greatest one. He owed all his basic convictions to Bryan: pacifism, isolationism, hatred of monopoly and of "Wall Street" and of "international bankers," firm belief in a sinister international conspiracy, and so forth. He also made true the great dream of the political crusaders of 1896: that industrial production

* From *Harper's Magazine*, July, 1947. By permission of the author. Copyright 1947 by Harper & Brothers.

might be made to serve the common man. This dream had obsessed the American people since Brook Farm and Robert Owen's New Lanark, half a century before Bryan.

4. The Populists had believed that a Jeffersonian millennium would result automatically from eliminating "monopoly" and the "money power" and the "satanic mills" of crude industrialism—as these terms were understood in the nineteenth century. Ford fulfilled the dream. He succeeded without benefit of monopoly, he defied the big bankers, he gave his factories a clean and airy efficiency which would have delighted nineteenth-century reformers. But in fulfilling the dream he dispelled it. And in the place of the old enemies which he vanquished we have today, in the industrial system which Ford did so much to develop, new problems to face: the long-term depression, and the political and social problems of industrial citizenship in the big plant. Henry Ford's solution of the industrial problems with which the nineteenth century had wrestled unsuccessfully constituted his success, his achievement. His inability to solve the problems of the new industrial system, his inability to see even that there were such problems, was the measure of his final and tragic failure.

5. It may seem paradoxical to interpret Henry Ford's importance in terms of a concept—especially a political concept such as Populism. He himself had nothing but contempt for concepts and ideas, and prided himself on being neither a theoretician nor a politician but a "practical man." And the main criticism which has been leveled against him and against everything he stood for—the criticism embodied in, for instance, Charlie Chaplin's "Modern Times"—has been that he made mechanical perfection an end in itself. But even his contribution to technology was not really a technical but a conceptual one—superb production man and engineer though he was. For he invented nothing, no new technique, no new machine, not even a new gadget. What he supplied was *the idea of mass production itself*—organization of man, machines, and materials into one productive whole.

6. In economics too Ford discovered no new facts; the data showing the effect of volume production on costs had all been collected and analyzed. But Ford was the first manufacturer to understand that these data disproved the traditional theory that restricted production and a high profit margin—that is, monopoly—provided the

most profitable form of industrial production. He demonstrated that one could raise wages, cut prices, produce in tremendous volume, and still make millions.

7. Above all Ford himself regarded his technical and economic achievements primarily as means to a social end. He had a definite political and social philosophy to which he adhered to the point of doctrinaire absurdity. Concern with the social effects of his actions determined every one of his steps and decisions throughout his entire life. It underlay the break with his early partners who wanted to produce a luxury car for the rich rather than follow Ford's harebrained idea of a cheap utility car for the masses. It motivated the radical wage policy of the early Ford who in 1914 fixed his minimum wage at the then utopian figure of $5.00 a day for unskilled labor. It showed in Ford's lifelong militant pacifism, of which the tragicomic Peace Ship episode of 1915-16 was only one manifestation. It showed in his isolationism, in his hostility to Wall Street, and in the raucous pamphleteering of the Dearborn *Independent* in the twenties. This social philosophy explains the millions he poured into "chemurgy" or into utopian village communities of self-sufficient, sturdy, yeoman farmers. It was responsible for his belief in decentralization, and for his nostalgic attempt to recreate the atmosphere of an earlier and simpler America in a museum community—right next door to the River Rouge plant.

8. It might almost be said that Henry Ford's life work, despite these moves of his, brought about the opposite kind of world from the one he hoped for and believed in. Thus Ford, the pacifist, built up one of the world's greatest armament plants and helped to make possible the mechanized warfare of our age. Ford, the isolationist, more than any other man has made it impossible for this country to stay out of international politics and international wars: for he made this country the most powerful industrial nation on earth. Ford, the agrarian decentralist, left as his life's work the River Rouge plant, the most highly centralized and most completely mechanized concentration of industrial power in the world. The enemy of finance-capital and bank credit, he made installment buying a national habit. An orthodox Jeffersonian, he has come to stand for the extreme application of the assembly-line principle, with its subordination of the individual to the machine. And the very workers at the Ford Motor Company whose mass production was to give

economic security and full industrial citizenship to all, are today organized in the most class-conscious union in America—and in a Communist-dominated local at that.

9. Yet it would be wrong to argue from the failure of Ford's social ideas that they never were anything but "eccentric hobbies," as the obituaries rather condescendingly called them. The tragic irony with which his every move turned against him in the end does not alter the fact that his was the first, and so far the only, systematic attempt to solve the social and political problems of an industrial civilization. There is also little doubt that Ford himself believed—certainly until 1941 when the Ford workers voted for the CIO, and perhaps even afterward—that he had actually found the answer for which the American people had been searching for almost a century: the realization of the Jeffersonian society of independent equals through industrial technology and economic abundance.

10. Nor was he alone in his appraisal of the meaning of his work. It was shared by the American people as a whole in the years immediately following the first World War—witness Wilson's urging in 1918 that Ford run for the Senate, and the powerful "Ford for President" boom of 1923. The view was also held abroad, especially in the Europe of the early twenties and in Lenin's Russia—perhaps even more generally there than here. Indeed, it was the performance of Henry Ford's America which in 1918 and 1919 gave substance to Wilson's promise of the millennium of peace, democracy, and abundance, and which established America's moral and political authority in those years. And the Ford spell remained potent long after Wilson's promise had faded under the cold light of the international realities of the nineteen-twenties.

11. The postwar world of today is at least as much under the spell of Franklin D. Roosevelt's name as an earlier generation was under that of Wilson. But Henry Ford today no longer symbolizes an America that has successfully solved the basic social problems of an industrial world. He stands instead for the lack of a solution. And that surely accounts in large measure for the difference between 1919 and 1947 in the acceptance and the effectiveness of America's moral and economic leadership.

II

12. Henry Ford took the conveyor belt and the assembly line from the meat-packing industry where they had been in general use as early as 1880. The interchangeability of precision-made parts was an even older principle; it went back to the rifle plant which Eli Whitney built in Bridgeport for the War of 1812. The idea of breaking down a skilled job into the constituent elementary motions, so that it could be performed by unskilled men working in series, had been thoroughly explored—by Taylor among others—and had been widely used in American industry twenty years before Ford came on the scene, as for example by Singer Sewing Machine and National Cash Register. Yet we associate all these principles with Henry Ford, and rightly so. For each of them had been employed only as an auxiliary to the traditional manufacturing process. It was Ford who first combined them and evolved out of them consciously and deliberately a new concept of industrial production, a new technology. It is this new concept of mass production which in scarcely more than one generation has given us a new industrial civilization.

13. To Ford the importance of this new principle lay in its impact upon society—as the means for producing an abundance of cheap goods with the minimum of human effort and toil. Mass production itself, however, he considered as something purely technical, as simply a new method of organizing *mechanical* forces. Ford disciples, heirs, and imitators, the engineers and production men who today run our big industries, are certainly as convinced as their master that mass production is a mechanical technique; many use it as if it were a mere gadget. And Charlie Chaplin took the same view when, in "Modern Times," he caricatured our modern industrial civilization.

14. But if mass production were indeed only a technique, and primarily mechanical—if it were different in degree but not in kind from pulley, lever, or wheel—it could be applied only to mechanical tasks similar to the ones for which it was first developed. But long before the recent war, mass-production principles were used for such jobs as the sorting and filling of orders in a mail-order house or the diagnosis of patients in the Mayo Clinic. Henry Luce even used

it successfully to organize writers—traditionally regarded as extreme individualists—for the mass production of interchangeable "formula-writing." And during the war we applied mass-production principles to thousands of new products and processes and to such problems as the selection and training of men in the armed services. In all these uses the mechanisms of the assembly line are purely subordinate if indeed applied at all. In other words, mass production is not, fundamentally, a mechanical principle but *a principle of social organization.* It does not co-ordinate machines or the flow of parts; it organizes men and their work.

15. Ford's importance lies precisely in the fact that his principle of mass production substitutes the co-ordination of human beings for the co-ordination of inanimate parts and of mechanical forces on which industry was originally based. When we talk of the Industrial Revolution, we think at once of Watt's steam engine. It is true that there was a lot more to the Industrial Revolution than new machines; but the steam engine is a good symbol for it because the essence of early industry was the new organization of mechanical forces. Mass production is based, however, on the organization of human beings and of human work—something radically different from anything that was developed in the early days of industry. Indeed it has brought about a new Industrial Revolution. The assembly line is a symbol for a new principle of social organization, a new relationship between men who work together in a common task, if not for a common purpose.

16. On what basis does this mass-production principle organize men? What kind of society does it either assume or create? It assumes or creates a society in which things are produced by the co-operation of individuals, not by a single individual. By himself the individual in modern mass-production industry is completely unproductive and ineffectual. But the organized group produces more, better, and more effectively than any individual or any number of individuals working by themselves ever could. In this society the whole—the organized group—is clearly not only more than, but different from, the sum of its parts.

17. Proof of this is what happens when a man loses his place in the organized group, or his access to the productive organism; when, in other words, he becomes unemployed. Under modern mass-production conditions, the man who has lost his job is not just out of

luck economically; in fact, in a rich country such as ours, the direct economic consequences of unemployment can be minimized almost to the vanishing point. But he is incapable of producing anything, of being effective in society; in short, he is incapable of being a citizen, he is cast out. For he derives his productiveness, his function in the community, his citizenship—at least his effective rather than purely formal citizenship—from his position in the group effort, in the team, in the productive organism.

18. It is this social effect of unemployment, incidentally, rather than the economic effect, that makes it the major catastrophe it is. That unemployment endangers people's standards of living is, of course, bad enough; but that it endangers their citizenship and self-respect is its real threat and explains our panicky fear of the "next depression."

19. In the society of the modern mass-production plant everyone derives his effectiveness from his position in an organized group effort. From this follow some important consequences. One is that such a society needs a government, a direction, a management responsible to no one special-interest group, to no one individual but to the over-all purpose, the over-all maintenance and strengthening of the whole without which no individual, no special-interest group could be effective. It also follows that in such a society there must be rank: a difference of authority and prestige based on the differentiation of functions. But at the same time, in such a society no one individual is less important or more important than another. For while no one individual is irreplaceable—only the organized relationship between individuals is irreplaceable and essential—every single operation, every single function is equally necessary; the whole order would collapse, the entire productive machine would come to a stop, were one to take out one function, one job—just as the whole chain becomes useless if one takes out one link. That is why, in such a society, there should be simultaneously an inequality of subordination and command based on the differentiation of functions, and a basic equality based on membership and citizenship. . . .

20. [That mass-production society is a hierarchical one] shows clearly when we analyze what popularly passes for a clear explanation of the essence of mass production: the saying that it replaces skilled by unskilled labor. That is pure nonsense, if taken literally. Of course, in mass production manual skill is eliminated by breaking up

each operation into the component simple operations, with each worker performing only one unskilled operation or a series of such. But this presupposes a fantastic skill in analyzing and breaking up the operation. The skill that is taken out of the manual operation has to be put back again further up the line, in the form of much greater knowledge, much more careful planning for the job; for there is such a thing as a law of the preservation of skill. And in addition mass production needs a new skill: that of organizing and leading the human team. Actually "unskilled" mass production needs proportionately more and more highly skilled men than "skilled" production. The skills themselves have changed from those of the craftsman to those of engineer, draftsman, and foreman; but the number of trained and skilled men in American industry has been growing twice as fast since 1910 as that of unskilled and semi-skilled men.

21. Above all, the co-operation and co-ordination which are needed to make possible the elimination of manual skill presuppose an extraordinarily high level of social skill and social understanding, of experience in working together. . . .

22. What we mean when we say that mass production is based on unskilled labor is simply that the individual becomes effective and productive only through his contribution to the whole, and not if viewed separately. While no individual does the job, each one is necessary to get the job done. And the job, the end-product of co-operative effort, is more skilled than anything the most skilled person could have produced by himself. As in every hierarchical society, there is no answer in the mass-production plant to the question who does the job; but there is also no answer to the question who does not do the job. For everybody has a part in it.

23. There are a good many industries today which do not use the mass-production principle. Among them are some of the most efficient ones, for instance, the modern cotton mills (in which one worker may manage a great many looms) and a good many of our chemical industries (in which one worker may perform a number of different functions). Nevertheless, the mass-production industries are representative of our American industry as a whole because they express in the purest form the essence of industrial production, i.e., a principle of social organization. The real Industrial Revolution of our day—the one which Henry Ford led and symbolized—was not

a technological one, was not based on this or that machine, this or that technique, but on the hierarchical co-ordination of human efforts which mass production realizes in its purest form.

III

24. It is understandable that Henry Ford's disciples and imitators failed to see the political and social implications of mass production until they were confronted by them in the form of an aggressive union movement—and very often not even then. For most of these men were really only concerned with technical problems, and really believed in mechanical efficiency as an end in itself. But Henry Ford's own blindness cannot be so simply explained as due to a lack of social or political concern—not even as due to a lack of social or political imagination. The real explanation is that Ford was concerned exclusively with the solution of the *social and political problems of the pre-Ford, the pre-mass-production industrial civilization.* And because his answers really did solve these problems, or at least the more important of them, it never entered his mind to subject this answer of his in turn to a social and political analysis. His gaze was firmly fixed on the industrial reality of his own youth, the industrial reality against which Populism had revolted in vain. He never even saw what he himself had called into being. As a high official of his own company once said: "What Mr. Ford really sees when he looks at River Rouge is the machine shop in which he started in 1879."

25. Though Henry Ford may never have heard of Brook Farm, of Robert Owen's New Lanark, or of any of the many other utopian communities that had dotted the Midwest not so many years before his birth in 1863, they were his intellectual ancestors. He took up where they had left off; and he succeeded where they had failed. . . .

26. The utopias of the 1830's and 1840's were in themselves the reaction to a failure: the abortive attempt during Jackson's administration to bring back to America the lost innocence of the Jeffersonian society of self-sufficient independent farmers. The utopians no longer hoped to be able to do away with the modern division of labor or even with industry. On the contrary, they promised to obtain for mankind the full benefits of industrial productivity, but without its having to pay the price of subjecting itself to the "money

power" or to "monopoly," or of having to work in the "satanic mills" of Blake's great and bitter poem. These were to be eliminated by a blend of pious sentiment, community regulations, and social science.

27. Of all the utopians only the Mormons survived—and they only by flight from the land of the Gentiles. But though they failed, Brook Farm, New Zion, New Lanark, and all the other attempts at the American industrial Jerusalem left a very deep imprint on the consciousness of the American people. Neither Fourier, whose ideas fathered Brook Farm, nor Robert Owen was an American. Yet it is possible, indeed probable, that the mixture of earnest, semi-religious sentiment and trust in a "scientific" principle which is so typical of the American "reformer" or "radical" has its roots in much older and deeper layers in our history than the utopias. But it is certain that the utopias determined the specific form which American radicalism was to take for a whole century. They provided the targets, the battle cries, and the weapons for Populism, for Wilson's New Freedom, and even for much of the early New Deal (such as the "scientific" gold magic of 1933). They fathered Henry George, Bellamy, and the anti-trust laws. They molded the beliefs and the hopes of America's inland empire in the Midwest. But they remained a futile gesture of revolt until Henry Ford came along.

28. Today we know that in depression and unemployment we have as serious an economic problem as "monopoly" and the "money power" ever were. We see very clearly that mass production creates as many new social and political questions as it answers. Today we realize that as a *final* solution to the problems of an industrial civilization Henry Ford's solution is a failure.

29. But Ford's mass production was not aimed at these new dangers but at the traditional devils of American radicalism. And these it actually did exorcise. Ford succeeded in showing that industrial production can be production *for* the masses—instead of production for the benefit of monopolist or banker. Indeed, he showed that the most profitable production is production for the masses. He proved that industrial production could give the workers increasing purchasing power to buy industrial products and to live on a middle-class standard; that was the meaning of his revolutionary $5.00-a-day minimum wage.

30. Finally—and to him most importantly—he proved that, properly analyzed and handled, industrial production would free the workers from arduous toil. Under modern mass-production conditions, the worker is confined to one routine operation requiring neither skill nor brawn nor mental effort. This fact would not have appeared to Henry Ford as a fatal defect but as a supreme achievement; for it meant that—in contrast to the tradition of the "satanic mills"—the worker's skill, intelligence, and strength would be fully available for his community life as an independent Jeffersonian citizen outside of the plant and after working hours.

31. At Brook Farm, too, the "real life" was supposed to come in the "communion of spirits" in the evening after the day's work had been done; but the day's work took so much time and effort that the "real life" could be lived only by neglecting the work. Mass production cuts both time and energy required for the day's work so as to give the worker plenty of scope for this "real life." No wonder that Ford—the Ford of 1919—thought he had built the "new Jerusalem" on a permanent foundation of steel, concrete, and four-lane highways.

IV

32. It was Ford's personal tragedy to live long enough to see his utopia crumble. He was forced to abandon his basic economic principle—the principle of the cheapest possible production of the most utilitarian commodity. First he scrapped the Model T. That was in 1927. Then, five years later, he abandoned the Model A and adopted the annual model change which substitutes the appeal of prestige and fashion for the appeal of cheapness and utility. When he did this he became just another automobile manufacturer. Even so his share in the market dropped from nearly half in 1925 to less than twenty per cent in 1940. Even more decisively proven was his failure to give the worker industrial citizenship; in 1941 the Ford workers voted to join the CIO almost three to one.

33. Up to the hour when the results were announced, the old man is said to have firmly believed that "his" workers would never vote for a union. All along he had fought off realization of his defeat by pretending to himself that his downfall was being caused by sinister conspiracies rather than by faults in the structure of the

community which he had built. This tendency to look for personal devils—itself a legacy from the utopians—had shown itself quite early in the tirades of the Dearborn *Independent* against international bankers, Wall Street, and the Jews during the nineteen-twenties. It became the basis on which he fought the unions all through the thirties. It also probably explains why Harry Bennett, starting as the plant's chief cop, rose to be the most powerful single individual in the Ford organization of the thirties, and the only one who really seemed to enjoy the old man's confidence. But the union victory—followed shortly by the unionization of the foremen—must have hit Henry Ford as a repudiation of all he had thought he had achieved, and had achieved primarily for the workers. The last years of the old man must have been very bitter ones indeed.

34. The lesson of Ford's ultimate failure is that we cannot hope to solve the problems of the mass-production society by technological devices or by changing the economics of distribution. These were the two approaches on which all nineteenth-century thought had relied, whether orthodox or rebel. Henry Ford went as far along these lines as it is possible to go.

35. For the time being, the political results of Ford's achievement were extraordinary. It took the wind out of the sails of the socialist critique of capitalist society. In this country it brought about the change from the fiery political action of Eugene Debs to the politically impotent moralism of Norman Thomas; in continental Europe it converted social democracy from a millenial fighting creed into a respectable but timid bureaucracy. Even more telling was the reaction of Communist Russia to Ford. In the twenties the Russians had to add to the messianic hopes of Karl Marx the promise of achieving eventually in a socialist society what Ford had already achieved in a capitalist one: a chance for the worker to drive to the plant in his own car and to work in collar and tie, and without getting calluses on his hands. And until 1929—as every meeting of the Third International affirmed—the Communists were completely convinced that Ford's America had actually solved the basic problems of capitalism and had restored it to ascendancy all the world over. Not until the great depression were the Communist leaders able to revitalize their creed, by making it appear to do what it cannot do: to solve, by the sheer force of the police state, the

new, the post-Ford problems of industrial society as they appeared after 1929.

36. As we in America confront these problems, the economic ones will not be the most difficult. Indeed the chief economic problem of our time—the prevention of depressions—should be solvable by basically mechanical means: by adapting our employment, fiscal, and budgeting practices to the time-span of industrial production —that is, to the business cycle. Much more baffling, and more basic, is the political and social problem with which twentieth-century industrialism confronts us: the problem of developing order and citizenship within the plant, of building a free, self-governing industrial society.

37. The fact that Henry Ford, after his superb success, failed so signally—that there is today such a grim contrast between his social utopia and our social reality—emphasizes the magnitude of the political task before us. But however treacherous the social jungle of our present mass-production society, however great the danger that it will fester into civil war and tyranny, the twentieth-century evils which Henry Ford left to us may well be less formidable than the nineteenth-century evils which he vanquished.

CHAPTER NINE

Paradox as Form

FROM the clarity and impact of Drucker's analysis of Henry Ford's success and failure, we see immediately the fine skill of his writing. He has dealt with a difficult and important subject and left us with a sense of its importance, not its difficulty. Drucker's accomplishment results largely from his technique of structuring his writing—from the individual phrase to the total essay—on a single formal concept. The essay is based on a nonlogical form—the *paradox*. The title itself is a paradox: "Henry Ford: Success and Failure." To discover how a formal concept may give shape to every aspect of an essay is the purpose of our analysis.

The brief opening paragraph dismisses Ford's financial success from the discussion and establishes Ford's real importance as a "symbol and embodiment of our new industrial mass-production civilization." It is as this symbol that Ford was "success and failure." Immediately in the second paragraph the formal concept of the essay appears in its characteristic shape:

> He perfectly represented its *success* in technology and economics; he also perfectly represented its political *failure* so far, its failure to build an industrial order, an industrial society.

The two terms *success* and *failure* not only occur here, but they occur in the order they did in the title (and will throughout the essay); each appears in its own clause of a balanced sentence; each has the same grammatical function and position in the structurally parallel clauses. In both clauses Ford ("he") is the subject which is at the same time both a success and a failure. This, by itself, would be contradictory nonsense, of course; the complements of each clause must explain how one person can be both success *and* failure in a single endeavor: he was a success from the standpoint of technology and economics, a failure from the standpoint of practical social politics.

The second sentence of this paragraph embodies the *idea* in the same shape, even though the *terms* are not repeated:

> The central problem of our age is defined as the contrast between the functional grandeur of the River Rouge plant, with its spotless mechanical perfection, and the formlessness and tension of the social jungle that is Detroit.

Clearly, both "the functional grandeur" and "the social jungle" are Ford's creations; one represents his success, the other his failure; the one is his product in the realm of technology and economics, the other his product in the realm of practical social politics. The obvious relation between these two sets of consequences is that of contrast, and in the sentence the word *contrast* reinforces the dichotomous nature of Ford's importance.

The second paragraph concludes: "And the two together comprise Henry Ford's legacy." Thus each sentence in the second paragraph puts before us the same idea, and the idea-pattern determines even the grammatical patterns of the two long sentences. Moreover, the order of these two important sentences repeats an order already established at the end of the opening paragraph of the essay—Henry Ford the man (sentence 1) was a symbol of a new industrial mass-production civilization (sentence 2). By the end of the second paragraph the man and his creations are interchangeable as symbol and thing symbolized, and they represent success and failure both literally and symbolically; the creations of Ford function as both source and effect of his success and his failure. The idea of the essay, as we have already seen, is presented in the shape of a complex paradox.

The third paragraph begins: "Both his *success* and *failure* can be traced to. . . ." The last four sentences of the fourth paragraph extend this pattern:

> (1) But in fulfilling the dream [Ford's success] he dispelled it [Ford's failure]. (2) And in place of the old enemies which he had vanquished [his success] we have today, in the industrial system which Ford did so much to develop, new problems to face . . . [his failure]. (3) Henry Ford's solution of the industrial problems with which the nineteenth century had wrestled unsuccessfully constituted his *success*, his achieve-

ment. (4) His inability to solve the problems of the new industrial system . . . was the measure of his *failure.*

This pattern reaches a climax in paragraph 8, where six of the seven sentences specify the paradoxical outcome of Ford's efforts. The final paragraph of the essay begins: "The fact that Henry Ford, after his superb *success, failed* so signally. . . ." Throughout this essay we find the "success and failure" *shape* of the idea informing the sentences, giving them structure and order.

If we turn our attention to the whole essay, we find that the structure of the idea informs the larger units of discourse as well. The four main sections are determined by this same shape. Besides defining the paradox of Ford's success and failure (as we have already seen) the first section demonstrates "Ford's importance in terms of a concept." Both his technical and economic achievements and their effects on practical social politics are included in this concept, the one as the source of the concept, the other as his hope of its success. Both the achievements and the effects are the concrete results of the concept; they are, in turn, those things in which Ford's importance has been recognized. In the first section of the essay, then, we have the idea of the essay defined and demonstrated, we see its "shape," and we become acquainted with its general nature.

Once we are familiar with the general nature of the idea, we are in a position to understand closer, detailed analysis from a more limited viewpoint. This is what Drucker provided in the second and third sections of his essay. In Section II we work from the technological effects of Ford's concept of mass production to its effect on social and political organization. We see again that the basis of his success is the basis of his failure. In Section III we work from the social effects of mass production to an understanding of Ford's goals and achievements: his success was a part of his failure.

Section II begins by explaining Ford's "new concept of industrial production," his "new technology." That it was a *concept* is clear since the principles of mass production—the conveyor belt and assembly line, and the interchangeability of precision-made parts—were not Ford's invention: rather, his invention was a concept of organization utilizing these two principles. Because Ford's concept used a principle of organizing *mechanical* forces he thought of mass production as a *mechanical* technique. So did everyone else. And insofar as mass production *is* a mechanical technique—a technology—it is Ford's success; by means of this technology it has been possible to produce "an abundance of cheap goods with a minimum of human effort and toil." It was by means of this technology that Ford *succeeded* in vanquishing the evils of nineteenth-century industrial society.

Paradoxically, mass production is not only a mechanical technique—a principle of organizing mechanical forces—it is also, and more fundamentally, a principle of organizing social forces. On the production line this principle "substitutes the co-ordination of human beings for the co-ordination of inanimate parts and of mechanical forces on which industry was originally based." But it assumes a social organization "in which things are produced by the co-operation of individuals, not by the single individual." The individual, by himself, "is completely unproductive and ineffectual." The principle of organizing *men* for the purpose of co-operative production has created a new social organization.

Subsequent paragraphs of Section II are devoted to demonstrating that the principles of mass production, which are clearly understood from the point of view of technology, are the principles of a new social organization. By this means Drucker uses familiar ideas to explain an unfamiliar concept and, at the same time, defines the new social organization. At the end of Section II, Drucker has established clearly the fact of a new social organization resulting from Henry Ford's concept of mass production.

Then, in Section III, having established the nature of the social organization that was a concomitant of Ford's technological success, Drucker shows us how, paradoxically, the new social organization constitutes Ford's failure. Ford failed, not in his attempt to solve the social and political problems which he saw clearly and which really existed, but in his creation of new social and political problems which he did not even attempt to solve. His failure was a failure of sight—of insight. Drucker makes this abundantly clear by repeatedly using words that suggest sight in the opening paragraph of this section: "Ford's disciples and imitators failed to *see*"; "Ford's own *blindness*"; "His *gaze*"; "He never *saw*"; "What Mr. Ford really *sees* when he *looks* at River Rouge is. . . ." Thus, Ford's failure was caused by his exclusive concern "with the solution of the *social and political problems of the pre-Ford, the pre-mass-produc-*

tion industrial civilization." As Drucker says later in this section, we can now see that Ford's solution of nineteenth-century problems in industrial society was his success; but "as a *final* solution to the problems of an industrial civilization Henry Ford's solution is a failure."

The last three paragraphs of Section III reinforce the paradox of Ford's success and failure *within* his attempt to solve social and political problems:

> . . . He proved that, properly analyzed and handled, industrial production would free the workers from arduous toil [his success]. Under modern mass-production conditions, the worker is confined to one routine operation requiring neither skill nor brawn nor mental effort [the new technology giving rise to the new social organization]. This fact would not have appeared to Henry Ford as a fatal defect [Ford's blindness] but as a supreme achievement [the failure of insight, hence his failure].

Finally, in Section IV we are in a position to understand fully the career of Henry Ford and his significance as a symbol of the new mass-production civilization. The first two paragraphs (like the opening sentence of the second paragraph of the essay) are devoted to Henry Ford the man—the bitter disappointment he must have felt when he at last "saw" the failure of his career. The remaining paragraphs of this section (like the remaining sentences in the second paragraph of the essay) concern the mass-production civilization of which Ford is the symbol. And just as Ford "saw" his failure, so we can see the significance of his failure: "The lesson of Ford's ultimate failure is that we cannot hope to solve the problems of the mass-production society by technological devices or by changing the economics of distribution." If success and failure comprise Henry Ford's legacy, it is for us to learn from his failure the means of success.

Our analysis of "Henry Ford: Success and Failure" shows that the form of the essay is based on the form of its central concept. If we pause to consider, we will realize that using the structure of an idea for the structure of discourse is not an unfamiliar practice. We have seen it in the earlier readings in this book and have used it ourselves, probably without being conscious of the technique. Whenever we tell a story or report on events we have observed, we organize our writing chronologically—that is, the concept of sequence in time provides the structure (or *form*) of our writing. Often, when we describe a physical object, we organize our writing "spatially"; ordinarily we try to proceed from top to bottom, from outside to inside, from bird's eye view to close-up, or in some "from-to" pattern of movement or position in space—that is, the concept of movement or position in space provides the *form* of our writing. These techniques are natural and easy because we use them frequently.

At the college level, though, we encounter new kinds of knowledge as well as additional facts. Accordingly, we need to learn new shapes for discourse and to learn to use them competently and with assurance. Among these are definition, classification, and logical relationships (deduction, explanation, induction), which we have already studied. Once we have learned to use these general forms in our writing, however, we have one more problem: we must find a way to give a sense of progression—in short, to make an essay interesting.

Drucker has successfully created interest by carefully managing his materials in terms of the reader's developing understanding. Section I acquaints us with Ford's success and failure and defines Ford's importance, all in general terms. Section II traces the causes of success and failure, beginning with analysis of mass-production technology much of which we probably understood, and leads us to an understanding of mass-production society. Section III deals with industrial society, analyzing Ford's achievements and creations in terms of his vision. Section IV, by drawing on our understanding of Ford's importance, of the nature of his success and failure, of the technology and social organization of mass-production civilization, and of Ford's own hopes, explores their significance to us. Each stage of the essay advances our knowledge of the facts of Henry Ford's career and advances our comprehension of the significance of those facts. To test this we have only to rearrange parts of the essay and find that the process of comprehension is interrupted.

It is progression of the mind in understanding the materials that sustains interest.

EXERCISES

1. Write a brief analysis of the principle(s) of organization in each of the following passages.

a. The late afternoon sun that still came over the brown shoulder of the mountain showed the bridge dark against the steep emptiness of the gorge. It was a steel bridge of a single span and there was a sentry box at each end. It was wide enough for two motor cars to pass and it spanned, in solid-flung metal grace, a deep gorge at the bottom of which, far below, a brook leaped in white water through rocks and boulders down to the main stream of the pass.[1]

b. We take it for granted that we can recognize our friends and acquaintances. This is possible only because no two of them are alike; there are sufficient differences of shape, movement, and voice to distinguish them. It is less obvious, but equally true, that such individual differences exist between animals. They are more difficult for us to recognize because we are less accustomed to looking closely at other animals than at human beings. Similar difficulties of recognition may arise between different human races. To Europeans, Chinese may all look alike at first appearance; a recent delegation of Englishmen to China found that the Chinese could not easily distinguish the members of the party. Such difficulties soon disappear on closer acquaintance with other racial groups.[2]

c. Fundamentally Grant was superior to Lee because in a modern total war he had a modern mind, and Lee did not. Lee looked to the past in war as the Confederacy did in spirit. The staffs of the two men illustrate their outlook. It would not be accurate to say that Lee's general staff were glorified clerks, but the statement would not be too wide of the mark. Certainly his staff was not, in the modern sense, a planning staff, which was why Lee was often a tired general. He performed labors that no general can do in a big modern army—work that should have fallen to his staff, but that Lee did because it was traditional for the commanding general to do it in older armies. Most of Lee's staff officers were lieutenant colonels. Some of the men of Grant's general staff, as well as the staffs of other Northern generals, were major and brigadier generals, officers who were capable of leading corps. Grant's staff was an organization of experts in the various phases of strategic planning.

[1] From Ernest Hemingway, *For Whom the Bell Tolls* (New York, Charles Scribner's Sons, 1940).

[2] From J. Maynard Smith, *The Theory of Evolution*, published as a Pelican Book by Penguin Books Inc., Baltimore, Md., 1958. Used with permission of the publishers.

The modernity of Grant's mind was most apparent in his grasp of the concept that war was becoming total and that the destruction of the enemy's economic resources was as effective and legitimate a form of warfare as the destruction of his armies. What was realism to Grant was barbarism to Lee. Lee thought of war in the old way as a conflict between armies and refused to view it for what it had become—a struggle between societies. To him, economic war was needless cruelty to civilians. Lee was the last of the great old-fashioned generals, Grant the first of the great moderns.[3]

d. But the tendency of the time is much better illustrated by a group of professors of education who have just recently proposed that the list of "required reading" in schools should be based upon a study which they have just sponsored of the tastes of school children. . . . Would any pediatrician base the diet which he prescribed for the young submitted to his care simply on an effort to determine what eatables they remembered with greatest pleasure? If he knew that the vote would run heavily in favor of chocolate sodas, orange pop, hot dogs and bubble gum, would he conclude that these should obviously constitute the fundamental elements in a "modern" child's menu?[4]

e. The history of the American people may be divided roughly into three periods. The first is the colonial period, in which different European groups, with differing cultural patterns, were adjusting themselves to one another and to the American environment and, thereby, evolving a new people and a new nation. The second is the national period, in which the young United States of America turned its back on Europe, marched steadily westward across the American continent, and transformed it, region by region, from a simple wilderness into a land of farms and towns and complex social-industrial institutions. Connections with the outside world were reduced to a minimum, and Americans, engaged in American tasks, sharpened and modified their own national characteristics, both personal and institutional, and emerged before the world as a powerful nation with positive interests and values uniquely its own. The third period is the one in which we find ourselves, at the present time, an integral part of the larger world. We are back where we started. The days of isolation are over. Just before the dawn of the twentieth century the United States found itself, half reluctantly, again facing outward. American goods and American capital had already invaded other lands; interests and values had forced a war with

[3] From T. Harry Williams, *Lincoln and His Generals* (New York, Alfred A. Knopf, Inc., 1952).

[4] From Joseph Wood Krutch, "Should We Bring Literature to Children, or Children to Literature," *New York Herald Tribune Book Review* (July 22, 1951). Used with permission of the publisher.

Spain and bequeathed us a colonial empire; and then the blunt fact of world interdependence pushed us into two great European wars. The cycle was thus completed, but the attitudes and assumptions inherited from the two earlier periods of American life, and their need of readjustment, have left much of mental confusion and much of uncertainty. We often appear to be a people whose bodies are in one age and whose minds are in an earlier one. The great task of adjustment still plagues the American people.[5]

f. There are two aspects, the formative and the conservative, to this process of self-development of man, and these correspond broadly to the roles of the individual and of the community. The first step in the development of new forms occurs in the individual, for though the inner tendency of the individual man is conservative, novelty arises from his response to fresh circumstances, new forms of thought and behavior being developed to their final expression in single brains. The individual is formative, but his life is short. On the other hand the community tradition is conservative and retains for long periods the records of all that it has absorbed from individuals. Social development thus depends on the interplay of the two. The individual forms the new and enriches the tradition; the tradition molds and matures the individual and enables him to carry the process further. The failure of the individual to maintain and further the tradition, or of the tradition of any community to organize the life of its members, represents an aberration from the proper relation which ultimately spells the collapse of the community.[6]

2. Examine textbooks for other college courses to see how the structure of the idea determines the structure of the writing. Then write a paper in which you analyze this method of organization as it functions in a single passage or brief chapter. For example, (*a*) how does a textbook for political science present the theoretical relations of the executive, judicial, and legislative powers in American government? the actual relations of these powers in a government agency like the Federal Communications Commission or the Civil Aeronautics Board? (*b*) How does a textbook for biology present the relation between adaptation and survival? between members of the order Primates? (*c*) How does a textbook for sociology present the relation between economic and cultural classes? between vocation and cultural classes?

[5] From Avery O. Craven and Walter Johnson, *The United States: Experiment in Democracy* (Boston, Ginn & Co., 1947). Used with permission of the publishers.

[6] From Lancelot Law Whyte, *The Next Development in Man* (New York, Henry Holt & Co., 1948).

STEPHEN SPENDER

From *World Within World**

OFTEN, during an air raid on London in 1940, I would hear a bomber diving downwards with a roar, as though its trajectory described a valley in the mountain-high air inhabited by aircraft. Then I would reassure myself by imagining that, in the whole area of the county of London, there were no more houses, but that the bomber was gyring and diving over an empty plain covered in darkness. This picture was both reassuring and exact: for it fixed my attention on my own smallness as a target compared with the immensity of London. And this was the reality. Only my fears were exposed.

2. If I thought of London as the London of my mind, and not as a geographical expanse, I only imagined places I knew and whose names occurred to me: Oxford Street, Piccadilly, St. Paul's, Liverpool Street, Kensington, Paddington, Maida Vale, Hampstead, and so forth. And even these places were represented in my mind only by the names of a few familiar features, churches, streets and squares, and not by all the other streets and the innumerable buildings which I did not know.

3. Although the raids stopped, or happened only at rare intervals, this picture of the aeroplane over the huge plain with the people concealed in crevices, can be enlarged to a vision of the new phase of domination and threat by machine-power politics, which the world had now entered and which did not end with the peace. The aeroplane filled ever-widening circles in the minds of people beneath it; but the pilot and even the officers who commanded him at bases, their masters in governments and the vanquished and victors of the war, were diminished, until it seemed that they no longer had wills

* From *World Within World*, copyright, 1948, 1949, 1951, by Stephen Spender. Reprinted by permission of Harcourt, Brace & World, Inc.

of their own, but were automata controlled by the mechanism of war.

4. It was a sign of this submission of human beings to the mechanical forces they had called into being and put into motion against one another that I was no longer interested in the personality of Hitler, since, having begun the war, he had not power to make it stop.

5. Everyone had shrunk in his own mind as well as in the minds of his fellow-beings, because his attention was diverted to events dwarfing individuals. These events could only lead to more battles and a victory catastrophic for the winning, as for the losing side. Personal misfortunes seemed of minor importance compared with the universal nature of the disaster overtaking civilization. So that in the summer of 1940, when invasion seemed imminent, a friend could say to me: "Within six weeks from now, if I blow out my brains and they spatter all over the carpet, in my own home and with my family in the room, no one will think it worth noticing."

6. We lived in a trance-like condition in which, from our fixed positions in our island-fortress-prison, we witnessed, as in a dream, not only armies, but whole populations controlled by the magnetic force of power. Even in the minds of those who knew them well, France and other continental countries had become mental concepts only, areas in our minds where incredible things happened; there, puppet dictators transmitted orders received from Germany, and Germany, a vast arsenal of mechanical power, added to its resources the industries of other nations and the slave labor of their peoples. Even today, *France under the Occupation* remains to me an idea only, to which I can attach little reality, a hallucinated vision of folly, betrayal, and despairing courage. So that, if some French friend begins to speak of his life during those years, I stare at him as though expecting to see him change into a different person.

7. During these months, a most poignant event, the suicide of Virginia Woolf, was observed by me as through a thick pane of glass, seen very clearly, but all sound shut out: the personal tragedy seen through the vast transparent impersonal one.

8. For the time being, the only hope was that the current of power should be reversed and turned back on those who had first employed it: that the pendulum of the bombers, swinging over us, should swing back again over Germany. Yet to admit this was an

admission of spiritual defeat: for it was to say that hope lay in power, in opposing despair with despair. We said this, with the result that we are still saying it. All this has implied the surrender of the only true hope for civilization—the conviction of the individual that his inner life can affect outward events and that, whether or not he does so, he is responsible for them.

9. From now on, the fate of individuals was more and more controlled by a public fate which itself seemed beyond control. For control implies not merely putting machinery into motion, but also being able to make it stop: modern war is a machine easy to make start, but it can only be stopped at the moment when it has destroyed or been destroyed by another war machine. Control means being able to relate a program of action to the results of that action. Now we had arrived at a stage when a large part of the resources of great nations were poured into programs of which no one could foresee the results. All this was only leading to subsequent plans for making atomic and hydrogen bombs to defend East against West or West against East in a meaningless struggle between potential ashes to gain a world of ashes. For, in the course of the struggle, the vast "machinery of production," together with its capitalist or proletarian owners, and all the sacred theories of whichever class, would be as outmoded as its own ruins, like the civilization and theories of Babylonian astrologers.

10. That part of living which was devoted to spiritual and personal values, became a marginal activity in society, and for individuals a side line, unless they happened to be old, sick, or socially unreliable. The most serious result was the effect on the minds of individuals, particularly the young, who found themselves in a world where no action of theirs, and nothing they created or thought, could alter the course of events. Here, though, on the level of thought and spiritual life, was the real challenge. For it is intolerable that men who, with their minds, have invented machines of destruction, and in their policies made themselves the half-slaves of these machines, should not be able to unthink what is a product of their intellects.

11. Within this situation of a world hypnotized by power, there were, none the less, two movements which expressed a faith in human values.

12. Firstly, there was a revival of interest in the arts. This arose

spontaneously and simply, because people felt that music, the ballet, poetry and painting were concerned with a seriousness of living and dying with which they themselves had suddenly been confronted. The audiences at the midday concerts of the National Gallery, or at the recitals of music and ballet in provincial towns and at factories, sat with rapt attention as though they were listening for some message from the artist, who, though perhaps he had lived in other times, was close to the same realities as themselves—and to the pressing need to affirm faith and joy within them. There was something deeply touching about this interest in the arts; it was one of the few things which can still make me regret the war.

13. The affirmation of these timeless qualities was the only answer of human personality to war. In a word, it was—survival. It answered that side of humanity which has produced the war with the indestructability of this other side—human love.

14. Lest it be objected that war is infinitely destructive and human love infinitely destructible, I repeat what I have said before: the inner life of man must create his outward circumstances. Perverted love, in the form of nationalism, or class solidarity (what is called "Communist love"), produce the forces of destruction in our time. Although we should support every outward movement for attaining peace and social improvement, it is only within the inner life that man can will himself to be a coherent whole and not a part set against another part.

15. One day, at a midday concert in the National Gallery, I listened to the playing of an early Beethoven Quartet (Opus 18, No. 1, I think). In the middle of the minuet there was a tremendous explosion. A delayed-action bomb had gone off in Trafalgar Square. In the trio of the minuet which they were playing, the musicians did not lift the bows from their strings. A few of the audience, who had been listening with heads bowed, straightened themselves for an instant and then resumed their posture.[1]

* * *

16. The second movement, expressing a faith in human values which developed during the war, was of those who believed that

[1] In the following section, which is here omitted, Spender describes the "writers who surmounted this situation of the world victimized by its own power"; they were "those who best resisted the imprisoning preoccupation of this age with its own time."

a better world could grow out of the war. They dreamed of planned cities which would rise above the bomb-damaged ruins. Thus dreaming, sometimes they seemed almost grateful to the Germans for destroying the slums. There would be better schools, and communal centers, and free medical care for the whole people. They did not seem aware that there might also be unparalleled poverty. An assumption of the planners was that an unplanned community was so wasteful that planning would soon make up for the losses of the war.

17. I supported the planners, though I reproached myself for not caring more about their plans. For one thing, these plans were hardly linked up with the war. War-time Britain tended to be divided between the military realists occupied in destroying the cities of Europe and the planners, who would come into action when the realists had destroyed enough for the war to be won. Just as planning was not fused with the spirit of the war, so I could not imagine it affecting greatly the spirit of the peace.

* * *

18. Reading over what I have written, I ask myself whether I would not have done better to write my autobiography as a novel. Many of the experiences would be easier to express in the kind of fiction which people recognize as autobiography, without their being confronted with the immediacy of the writer who says: "the hero is I."

19. Again, experiences are described here which some readers may think should have been confined to the anonymity of the psychological textbook.

20. Yet I think that I am justified in writing in the first person singular. Fiction and clinically analytic writing extend our knowledge of human personality, but they also offer avenues of escape from the glaring light of consciousness of him who says: "I am I." The writer of fictitious autobiography offers the truth about himself within the decent and conspiratorial convention of contemporary fiction, which invites the reader to identify himself with the writer-hero. Reader-writer walk together in a real-seeming dream-alliance leading into gardens inhabited by Stephen Daedalus and Marcel, out of which side-lanes wind obscurely to Dr. Kinsey's *The*

Sexual Behavior of the Human Male, or Sheldon's analysis of psychosomatic types.

21. I am I: hero of a potential autobiographic novel in which I give the hero and the other characters their real names and their attributes: curve on a psychiatrist's chart which I paste on my wall: and in spite of this, in fact because of it, I insist that I am a citizen, that I have views and take sides and accept responsibilities, and even hold opinions about public affairs. I am a citizen who revolts against the concept of himself as "social man," with a respectable, official outside life, and two secret selves—a fictitious hero and a clinical case history. It is in the individual who accepts the responsibility of his own complexity, that the diversity of society attains a unity of consciousness where opposites are reconciled.

22. The main narrative of this book is from my eighteenth year, in which I had attained the climax of a struggle beginning with my adolescence, until my fortieth year. When I was a child I was a naturalist with a long white beard and a clear blue gaze, like a portrait of such a child, which I have seen, by Dürer. That is to say, my early childhood was marked by a quite exceptional harmony, and it is perhaps this which has enabled me to retain throughout life a central calm and happiness, amid violent divisions of my own nature. But at the age of eighteen I could not reconcile my ideals either with myself or with the world. I was tormented by the feeling that nothing was as it should be, single and clear and pure.

23. My narrative describes how, in Germany and elsewhere, I sought to discover my real self by behavior which outraged my ideal self. The result of this was a series of relationships undertaken in a spirit of opportunism: yet I was too much an idealist to maintain a cynical attitude.

24. Then society, appearing in the conscious form of Communism, seemed to offer a way out of my dilemma. It suggested to me that after all I was not myself. I was simply a product of my bourgeois circumstances. By "going over to the proletariat" and entering a different set of circumstances I could become another kind of social projection. I would be "on the side of history" and not "rejected" by it, like one of the disused mines in Auden's early poems.

25. The Marxist criticism of my own position—sometimes publicly expressed as in Caudwell's *Illusion and Reality*, sometimes the voice

of social conscience in myself—told me I was wrong to think of myself as "separated from society." The solution of all my problems was to put myself in an "historically correct position."

26. But to believe that my individual freedom could gain strength from my seeking to identify myself with the "progressive" forces was different from believing that my life must become an instrument of means decided on by political leaders. I came to see that within the struggle for a juster world, there is a further struggle between the individual who cares for long-term values and those who are willing to use any and every means to gain immediate political ends—even good ends. Within even a good social cause, there is a duty to fight for the pre-eminence of individual conscience. The public is necessary, but the private must not be abolished by it; and the individual must not be swallowed up by the concept of social man.

27. Today, we are constantly told that we must choose between the West and the East. Confronted by such a choice, I can only say that, first and foremost, I am for neither West nor East, but for myself considered as a self—one of the millions who inhabit the earth. The conflict between East and West does not in itself involve a moral choice, if it is only a struggle between external forces: it becomes moral only if it is a choice within myself: that is to say, if having chosen my own self, my humanity, my conscience, I can then judge the rival claims of both sides. I do not *choose* America or Russia: I *judge* between them. If it seems absurd that an individual should set up as a judge between these vast powers, armed with their superhuman instruments of destruction, I can reply that the very immensity of the means to destroy proves that judging and being judged does not lie in these forces. For supposing that they achieved their utmost and destroyed our civilization, whoever survived would judge them by a few statements, a few poems, a few *témoignages*, surviving from all the ruins, a few words of those men who saw outside and beyond the means which were used and all the arguments which were marshaled in the service of those means.

28. Thus I could not escape from myself into some social situation of which my existence was a mere product, and my witnessing a willfully distorting instrument. I had to be myself, choose and not be chosen.

CHAPTER TEN

Responsibility and Form

HAVING analyzed some forms for discourse, we need, finally, to consider responsible choice among forms. If we examine the selections from *World Within World* in terms of formal aspects, we can begin to understand choice of method and form in writing. The three selections reprinted are from the book-length autobiography of Stephen Spender, a British poet and critic. They may be read as a single short essay, but what they demonstrate about choice of form is revealed fully only when they are viewed as part of an entire book.

Two characteristics of these selections immediately stand out: Spender relates events in generally chronological order, and he recounts the events as belonging specifically to his own life. He is writing personal narrative. A certain order and shape are given to his materials by the sequence of chronology and by the fact that all the events are parts of one person's experience. One formal aspect, then, emerges from the fact that this is personal narrative.

But the personal narrative is in a form neither of separate diary entries nor of a bare chronicle of events in Spender's life. Not only does the account record what happened in his life, it also includes examination of the significance of the happenings. Each event is interpreted. The first paragraph, for instance, relates Spender's experience of the 1940 air raids on London and his recurring feelings during them, together with his interpretation of the cumulative experience—that in reality he was a very small target, only his fears were exposed. The next paragraph reports his image of London at this time: rather than a distant, public, conventional London, he imagined the immediate, private London of his own experience. The third paragraph then pushes beyond personal interpretation of these experiences to their public, historical meaning: air raids were "a vision of the new phase of domination and threat by machine-power politics." Subsequent passages have a similar pattern—the friend talking of suicide, another friend describing France during the German occupation, the audience interrupted during the performance of a Beethoven quartet, and so on. The regular pairing of report of what happened with assessment of its significance—on either personal or public level, or both—constitutes a second element of the form of this essay.

Of particular interest is the effectiveness of the pairs of reports and interpretations. Each abstract statement, each interpretation and comment, appears with a strikingly memorable experience. In nearly every case the event reported is vivid because we see what Spender saw or we hear the words and sounds he heard. The events are concrete images, direct and lifelike, which not only form a record of Spender's life, but also serve effectively to demonstrate the accuracy and importance of his interpretation of his personal growth and the problems of his society.

Let us look at some of Spender's interpretations of events. The "picture of the aeroplane over the huge plain with the people concealed in crevices" is "enlarged to a vision of the new phase of domination and threat by machine-power politics." Caught within the machine of their own creating, all men—whether pilots, commanders, or "their masters in government"—became machine-like automata: "it seemed that they no longer had wills of their own" (paragraph 3). They had submitted to mechanical forces (paragraph 4). Moreover, "everyone had shrunk in his own mind as well as in the minds of his fellow-men" (paragraph 5). Even the suicide of another literary personality, a genuinely "personal tragedy [was] seen through the vast transparent impersonal one" (paragraph 7). In each event Spender saw the diminishing of the individual beneath the increasing pressure of machine-power, machine-war, machine-tragedy. Personal actions shrank in significance before the impersonal events of the war. These experiences exemplify the impending defeat of personal responsibility; he says explicitly: "All this has implied the surrender of the only true hope for civilization—the conviction of the individual that his inner life can affect outward events and that, whether or not he does so, he is responsible for them" (paragraph 8).

But surrender of individuality was more than the defeat of the self's importance and its responsibility for what happened. Spender felt that surrender of individuality was surrender of control. No one, no people, if their individuality was defeated, could have control of war; they could neither stop it nor forsee the ends to which action should be directed. With the highly destructive modern weapons, if control was not maintained, there could only be "a meaningless struggle between potential ashes to gain a world of ashes." In such a struggle there is no right side; political ideology becomes meaningless. The war, as Spender saw it, made personal actions only "a marginal activity, and for individuals a side line" (paragraph 10).

Later Spender describes two wartime movements which he interpreted to be reactions against the stifling of individual responsibility—reactions by a saving remnant of individuals with faith in human values (paragraphs 11-15). The renewed interest in the arts answered the destruction of war with indestructibility of human love. The musicians and audience at the midday concert seemed, in their responses to the quartet and the exploding bomb, to bear witness to the endurance of their individual inner lives. Again Spender finds that "it is only within the inner life that man can will himself to be a coherent whole." Although their movement expressed a faith in human values, the community planners who hoped for a better world growing out of the war's destruction were less important to Spender, because their plans were not realistic and immediate.

Finally, through analyzing his problem in writing personal narrative, and with a backward glance over the entire book, Spender restates his position (paragraphs 18-28). "It is in the individual who accepts the responsibility of his own complexity, that the diversity of society attains a unity of consciousness where opposites are reconciled." He shows how he learned that "progressive" social forces, such as Communism, inhibit individual freedom; that "within the struggle for a juster world, there is a further struggle between the individual who cares for long-term values and those who are willing to use any and every means to gain immediate political ends—even good ends. Within even a good social cause, there is a duty to fight for the pre-eminence of individual conscience. The public is necessary, but the private must not be abolished by it; and the individual must not be swallowed up by the concept of the social man."

Only in the individual, he says, can moral choice occur. And it is only the individual who can judge East and West. They cannot judge him, though they can destroy him. The personal narrative can conclude, then: "I had to be myself, choose and not be chosen."

We can now see not only that the reported events regularly appear with interpretations of them but also that the interpretations all resolve themselves into a single theme—that man's individuality, threatened with defeat by war and with dissolution by mass political ideologies, is the saving force for civilization, the sole source of morality and human values; thus it must not be surrendered.

Repeated frequently, through different images, in one aspect and then in another, this belief, or attitude, provides a thematic unity for Spender's personal narrative over and above the basic unity of autobiography, one man's personal history. Thus a single, repeated theme whose exposition occurs through its variations is an important aspect of the form of *World Within World.*

Still another aspect of form is explicitly considered in the last portion of these excerpts. Beginning in paragraph 18 Spender pauses to examine the mold in which he has cast the whole of his narrative. Three conventional forms could have served his purpose: he has used autobiography; he might have used the novel form, keeping the pattern of autobiography but avoiding "the immediacy of the writer who says: 'the hero is I' "; or he might have recast his personal history within "the anonymity of the psychological textbook," producing a case history. Autobiography, fiction, and impersonal textbook manner were all possibilities. Each would accommodate the bulk of his personal history. Each is a conventional form.

What, then, made him choose direct, personal autobiography? Both "fiction and clinically analytic writing extend our knowledge of human personality." Fiction he says, would be easier, and case history may be preferred by many readers. But both of these forms "also offer avenues of escape from the glaring light of consciousness of him who says: 'I am I.' " Each is a disguise which obscures or denies the identity and individuality of the writer. And what has been the theme unifying the whole of his personal narrative? The insistence that man's individuality is threatened with defeat, but remains the only source of morality and human values. Clearly, then, a conventional form which obscures individuality and moral responsibility would contradict the thematic core of the work, though it might accommodate the narrative of personal events and the interpretations of them. That fiction or case history provide easy forms into which modern authors may cast intensely individualistic narrative without assuming all responsibility for what they say is plainly to Spender another sign that man's individuality is threatened with defeat even by the forms in which he commonly communicates with others: these forms "offer avenues of escape from the glaring light of consciousness of him who says: 'I am I.' "

"I am I: hero of a potential autobiographic novel in which I give the hero and the other characters their real names and their real attributes: curve on a psychiatrist's chart which I paste on my wall: and in spite of this, in fact because of it, I insist that I am a citizen, that I have views and take sides and accept responsibilities, and even hold opinions about public affairs." Here, in Spender's powerful, direct assertion of his own individuality and responsibility, we have his answer to the question of the right form for his autobiography: form and theme inevitably merge in a fusion of personal and public interpretations of events in the life of Stephen Spender.

"I am a citizen," Spender says, "who revolts against the concept of himself as 'social man,' with a respectable, official outside life, and two secret selves—a fictitious hero and clinical case history." He both restates here his belief in the individual's importance and responsibilities and he rejects impersonal chronicle of the anonymous "social man"; the "fictitious hero" and "clinical case history" are subordinated to the I-am-I narrative. Autobiography, directly embodying the life of an individual man, is thus chosen pragmatically.

We have discovered a basis for the decision among conventional forms which Spender made at the outset of his narrative. That initial choice apparently was made instinctively, just as most decisions regarding written forms are probably instinctive. Or, if these decisions should not be termed *instinctive*, they at least seem to proceed from reasonings and impulses too obscure to examine effectively as they occur. But choice of written forms, once it has been made, *is* subject to analysis, although it is seldom that a writer will discuss the form within a piece of writing itself. Nowhere else in this book, in fact, has a writer done this. For this reason the selection provides a rare opportunity for us to observe directly the pragmatic nature of choice among forms of writing; or, better, to test pragmatically a choice made intuitively.

To test a choice among conventional forms, several questions may be asked. First, does this form best accommodate the intentions and purpose of the writing? We have discovered in Spender's work that the dominant theme of the individual's pre-eminence and responsibility requires direct autobiographical form for its best expression. Next, what is the relation between the over-all form chosen and the other elements of form? In Spender's work, we have discovered three other kinds of form: (1) simple chronological order producing sequential form, with a single subject, the author's life, unifying all the events; (2) regular pairing of reported events (concrete statement) with their private and (or) public significance (abstract statement); (3) repetition of a single idea through variations on it throughout the entire writing. None of these three other elements of form conflicts in any way with the conventional form of autobiography. In fact, they make autobiography the necessary form, for, given the theme that arises in (2) from the events recorded in (1), a theme that becomes dominant with (3), nothing but autobiography is appropriate.

If the testing of a choice of forms is to be a responsible action, a writer must be aware, as Spender is, of alternate forms and the possibilities and limitations inherent in each. In choosing autobiography Spender rejects psychological case history and novel-type fiction. Choice requires not only that we take one but also that we leave others, and choice is responsible only when we are aware of what we use, and what we reject, and why.

Finally, choice of forms must be tested against the whole of the writing, to see whether each part embodies and is embodied by the over-all form and all that that form implies. The images Spender represents in his record of events fulfill this test; they are illustrative of the total theme. His mental picture of London, for instance, is an individual's picture of London. The audience at the midday concert scarcely allows interruption of their private experience. On the other side, images of machine, distance, impersonality, and mechanical destructive power illustrate the threat to individuality. Throughout the excerpts the implications of autobiographical form, culminating in the celebration of the individual self's importance and responsibility, are embodied in the substance of the personal narrative.

Elements of personal narrative, concrete image accompanied by abstract statement, repetition of a single idea, and autobiography—all these forms are nonlogical. In being nonlogical (but not illogical) they are neither less responsible nor more reliable than logical forms of discourse. Nor is the writing in Spender's autobiography either more or less responsible for having structural elements which are nonlogical rather than a mixture of logical and nonlogical forms. The legitimacy of Spender's use of nonlogical forms rests on his sense of the individual's responsibility and on the solid foundation of experience which, though personal, is publicly understood and shared.

Responsibility is not built into any of the forms of writing. In the ten chapters of this book we have observed responsible use of forms of definition and classification, logical forms of reasoning and explaining, and some nonlogical forms. We have gained knowledge of some methods and forms which enable us, when we assume responsibility for what we say, to use formal written English well. Responsibility, as Spender demonstrates, is the individual's obligation.

APPENDIX A

The Function of the Outline

BY referring to outlines which appear within the chapters of this book we can see the advantages of outlining and understand some ways in which outlines fulfill their function.

OUTLINE I: For the essay "The Dust Cloud Hypothesis." [See p. 141]

Paragraphs 1-2 constitute a brief *introduction*, acquainting us with the subject of the essay, and informing us that the author will explain a theory of the origin and charactersitics of the solar system.

Paragraphs 3-9 provide the *background* of this theory, which both informs us of the factual basis on which the theory rests and recounts the development of the theory.

Paragraphs 10-16 *explain the origin of the solar system*, by means of a series of subsidiary explanations.

Paragraphs 17-28 *explain the characteristics of the solar system*, again by means of a series of subsidiary explanations.

Paragraphs 29-32 *examine other theories*, in terms of their adequacy in explaining the origin and characteristics of the solar system.

Paragraph 33 *assesses* the possibilities for the author's theory being correct.

OUTLINE II: For the essay "Logic and Lyric." [See p. 94]

J. V. Cunningham's essay "Logic and Lyric" explicitly takes a controversial position: that the notion of an opposition between logic and poetry is false. Cunningham's procedure in establishing this proposition is twofold. First, he makes clear the precise nature of his dispute with those critics who hold an opposing view. Then he proceeds to a logical argument to establish his own position. In effect, he proposes that if poetry which is generally recognized as good is logically organized, then it is false to say that logic and poetry are incompatible. He uses analyses of three poems to establish the factual truth of the if-clause of his proposed hypothesis; and he concludes that since the truth of the if-clause is established, the then-clause must follow and all contradictory positions must be false.

OUTLINE III: For the essay "The Types of Languages." [See p. 56]

I. Structural classification: formal processes.
   A. "The relative degree of synthesis or elaboration of the words of a language."
      1. "The isolating type."
      2. "The weakly synthetic type."
      3. "The fully synthetic type."
      4. "The polysynthetic type."
   B. "The degree to which the various parts of a word are welded together."
      1. The "isolating" type.
      2. The "agglutinative" type.
      3. The "inflective" type.
      4. The "symbolistic" type.
   C. "The extent to which the fundamental relational concepts of the language are expressed as such."
      1. "Pure relational languages."
      2. "Mixed relational languages."

II. Genetic classification: sources of change and differentiation.
   A. "Inherent changes."
      1. "Phonetic changes."
      2. "Changes in form."
      3. "Changes in vocabulary."
   B. "Changes due to contact with other linguistic communities." *Example:* "borrowing."

OUTLINE IV: For one paragraph (10) from "The Dust Cloud Hypothesis." [See p. 138]

1. If angular momentum remains constant within a rotating system, then if the rotation of the mass of a system when widely scattered

from its center is very slight, the rotation of the mass when concentrated at its center will be slow.

2. Angular momentum remains constant within a rotating system.
3. Thus, if the rotation of the mass of a system when widely scattered from its center is very slight, the rotation of that mass when concentrated at its center will be slow.
4. Moreover, the rotation of the mass of the solar system when widely scattered from its center (in the dust cloud) was very slight.
5. Thus, the rotation of that mass when concentrated at its center (in the sun) is slow.

OUTLINE V: For the writing of definitions. [See p. 22]

I. An adequate definition should answer as fully as needed three questions about the term-to-be-defined. These are:
What is it?
Where does it come from?
What is it good for?

II. These queries are answered by:
What is it?
A. FORMAL definition in the form of:
"It is something which . . . (give characteristic attribute)."
B. MATERIAL definition stating:
1. substance,
2. arrangement, and
3. varieties of the thing defined.

Where does it come from?
C. HISTORICAL definition giving:
1. development of the *word*,
2. origin of the *thing* in race or in individual, and
3. evolution, extent, cause, and so on, of the thing defined.

What is it good for?
D. FUNCTIONAL definition giving:
1. purpose of the thing defined,
2. method of using it to accomplish this purpose, and
3. value, measured by the desire for the thing itself or by the efficiency with which it attains its end.

EXAMPLE: The purpose of a clock is timekeeping and its value depends upon the efficiency with which it keeps time.

III. These questions and answers can be arranged in a multitude of ways.

The outline functions as a brief, systematic description of a longer piece of writing. It enables a writer to project his material and its organization before and during the full-scale composition, and to review the composition when it is completed; thus he is able to plan, modify, and check his own writing for its unity, its order and emphasis, its completeness, its responsibility and form. It enables a reader to see in reduced scope the substance and organization of a piece of writing; thus he is able to review conveniently what the writing deals with, to examine readily the relationships among its parts, and to evaluate the structure he discovers in the discourse.

Its brevity alone makes the outline convenient and helpful. To be able to see on a single page the substance and organization of a piece of writing, say, four to ten times the length of the outline, simplifies our planning or examination of the material and its form. Other names for the outline—sketch, blueprint, skeleton, framework—suggest the advantages of brevity. And brevity necessarily renders the outline more abstract, more impersonal, and more open to analysis of organization and scope than the full composition.

By means of Outline I, for example, we can easily grasp the organization of the 11-page essay "The Dust Cloud Hypothesis" and go even further in evaluating the effectiveness of that organization. Explanation, we see, is the author's central purpose; his series of specific explanations makes up the body of the essay, accounting for two-thirds of the paragraphs (10-32) of the whole. Explanations are preceded by introduction of the topic to be explained and by presentation of information which the reader will need if he is to understand the explanations. The explanations themselves are arranged so that we understand the dust cloud hypothesis; and having understood that, we are aware that any hypothesis about the origin and characteristics of the solar system must be able to *explain* aspects of the solar system in a similar way. We can see, further, that this criterion enables the author to evaluate other hypotheses as well as to assess the value of his own. Thus, we realize, the explanations at the center of the essay are arranged in an effective order, and the material preceding and following them has a direct bearing on them. We judge the organization, as it clearly appears in the outline, to be highly effective.

Its systematic nature, however, is perhaps the more directly helpful characteristic of the outline. If we recast the above outline, putting it into conventional outline form, we can see this value most clearly.

I. Introduction: identification of subject–the dust cloud hypothesis; statement of purpose–exposition of the hypothesis.

II. Background information.
   A. The facts which the hypothesis deals with.
   B. The development of the hypothesis.

III. Exposition of the dust cloud hypothesis.
   A. Capacity of the hypothesis to explain the origin of the solar system.
   B. Capacity of the hypothesis to explain the characteristics of the solar system.

IV. Comparison of the dust cloud hypothesis to other hypotheses in regard to their capacity for explaining the origin and characteristics of the solar system.

V. Conclusion: the relative superiority of the dust cloud hypothesis to other hypotheses, in regard to their capacity for explaining the origin and characteristics of the solar system.

Both this outline and the earlier one show the same divisions of Whipple's essay and the order in which they appear. But by assigning headings—numbers and letters—to each section, we indicate not only the relations of order, but also relations of co-ordination and subordination. In Part II the divisions labeled *A* and *B* merely separate conveniently the two parts of the section named earlier for paragraphs 3-9. In Part III, though, the co-ordinate topics of explanation (*A* and *B*) are subsumed under a broader heading—"Exposition of the dust cloud hypothesis." The headings *A* and *B* in Part III show the co-ordinate relation of these two topics of explanation, as well as the subordinate relation of these explanations to the exposition stage of the essay.

Similarly, Outline II can be recast into conventional form:

I. Identification of the issue: the controversy over the relation of logic and poetry, which is embodied in two opposing views:
   A. The view that logic and poetry are opposites (either contradictory or incompatible).
   B. The view that logic and poetry are not necessarily opposites (or contradictory or incompatible).

II. Argument to prove that the second position is correct (and, hence, the first position is not).
   A. If poetry which is generally recognized as good is logically organized, then it is false to say that there is an opposition (or incompatibility) between logic and poetry. [Hypothesis–major premise]
   B. Poetry which is generally recognized as good is logically organized. [Minor premise–to be verified]
   C. It is false, therefore, to say that there is an opposition between logic and poetry. [Valid conclusion of deductive argument]

Now, if we insert into this outline the additional topics in the essay "Logic and Lyric"—the analyses of the three poems—we show systematically not only their place in the order of the essay, but their co-ordinate relations to each other and their subordinate relations to the three main propositions of the logical argument:

II. Argument to prove . . .
   A. If poetry which is generally recognized . . .
   B. Poetry which is generally recognized as good is logically organized. [Minor premise–to be verified by demonstration following]
      1. Demonstration that "To His Coy Mistress" is logically organized.
      2. Demonstration that "Lament for Makaris" is logically organized.
      3. Demonstration that "Litany in Time of Plague" is logically organized.

Assignment of number and letter headings to topics for an essay, although it gives an abstract systematic structure to the outline, is not, however, a means of creating organization. Such an outline is no more than a means of keeping track of various trial organizations of material for an essay, as these various organizations occur to us. To some extent, use of these headings is like the writing down of a difficult problem in division in arithmetic: the lines and columns for various operations of long division merely help us keep our bearings as we proceed in solving the problem. One series of headings, capital letters, for instance, marks the sequence for topics of equal function: that is, these letters mark topics classifiable under a single heading. Sometimes these topics are the stages of the essay, like "Introduction," and so on, in the second version of Outline I. Or, as in Outline III, the topics marked by capital letters under the first part are of equal function in both the classification of languages and the progress of the essay. Each set of Arabic numbers in this outline (III) marks equal topics under the headings designated by the capital letters. Each series of headings, then, marks co-ordinate topics; and each additional series of headings (for example, Arabic numbers after capital letters) marks a subordinate series of topics. In brief, the conventional headings in an outline show us quickly for any topic its relations of sequence, co-ordination, and subordination to any other.

From the outlines presented, we can see that neither sentence nor topical outlines are inherently better. Outline III is made entirely without sentences. Although it is possible to pad out each topic into a sentence, the outline is no more complete for being expanded; as a matter of fact, the added length makes it cumbersome. Outline I in its first form (p. 189) has sentences for every topic, but in its recast form (p. 193) it has no sentences at all. Both forms are equally clear and usable. It is also possible to mix the two. Outline II, in its recast form (p. 193), mixes sentences and "topics," whereas its original form consisted of sentences making up a paragraph (p. 189). Again, both are clear and usable.

However, when the outline represents logical organization it must be consistently written in sentences, because the propositional nature of the logical forms is always expressed in sentences. But when the outline represents groupings for classification, sentences may be neither necessary nor desirable. And when the outline represents an arrangement that is neither logical nor classificatory, it is possible to use either topical (nonsentence) or sentence entries, or a mixture of the two. The decision, as in so many other matters in writing, is pragmatic; but it is not a matter of whim. For instance, co-ordinate topics can be recognized as such more readily when parallel grammatical structures are used consistently to express them. Outlines III and V are the clearest examples.

Outlines I, II, and III are outlines of specific pieces of writing and show both the contents and the order in which the contents appear. Outline IV, on the other hand, represents the contents of a paragraph, but not the order in which they appear; it is an outline giving the *logical* order of an explanation, whereas the paragraph it represents embodies an *expository* order which is different. When logical forms are used in writing, including the form of explanation, it is particularly important to distinguish between logical and expository order, since these orders may (and often do) differ. In explanation, for instance, the fact to be explained often appears first in a paragraph or essay, although it is the conclusion in the logical form of explanation. Outlines for logical and expository order each have valuable functions—the one for testing logical form, the other for planning order of writing—but they should not be considered interchangeable.

Outline V is not an outline of a specific piece of writing; rather, it is a "dummy" outline for a kind of writing—writing whose purpose is definition. Although it may be used to plan the order of materials for writing—the expository order—its function is primarily to guide the writer in completeness and method of definition.

Understanding the function of the outline is a valuable resource for responsible rhetoric.

APPENDIX B

The Nature of Report

A REPORT is a verbal account of an experience or set of experiences. Strictly considered, it is a series of true propositions describing the experience which are so selected and arranged as to translate the experience accurately—without distortion—into words. A report differs from an interpretation, an inference, or a judgment, in that its intention is limited to the conveying of information; upon the basis of information conveyed by the report, interpretations, inferences, and judgments may be made.

Although we can easily define the nature of report, there are many obstacles to the writing of pure report. The discussion of propositions in Chapter V shows that any proposition may be stated in a variety of sentences. But these sentences vary in what they convey in addition to factual information. The sentences "Eisenhower was victorious in the Presidential campaign of 1952" and "Eisenhower was elected President in 1952" both state the same proposition. The first, however, carries affective military overtones and communicates the writer's feeling toward the fact he is reporting. The second is more flat and objective. Choice of words, thus, in part determines the degree to which the sentence is a pure report.

Likewise, the structure and arrangement of sentences may convey attitudes beyond the propositional content. In Chapter VII we saw that Russell's sentence structure as well as his arrangement of sentences into paragraphs were so devised as to evoke in the reader responses sympathetic to Russell's own choice of the alternatives in his major premise. Most of the sentences, in content, in structure, and in arrangement, are not intended so much to inform the reader as to shape his attitude. When we strip a sentence, paragraph, or essay of all emotive overtones, all noninformative sentences, all words and devices to affect the reader's attitudes rather than his knowledge, we have only the propositional content—the substance of report.

Given the well-worn and familiar language, then, and the affective nature of many of the words and arrangements of words, a sustained, pure report is nearly impossible. We would need words antiseptically clean of affective overtones; we would need a means to express simultaneously simultaneous parts of an experience; we would need an arrangement of sentences which would prevent the beginning and the ending of a sentence, paragraph, or essay from being more emphatic than other parts, and so on. We would need an ideal report-language in which an ideal report-writer could communicate with an ideal report-reader.

In practical terms, though, there are several aspects of the report which we can bring under control. First, we can distinguish between report, inference, and judgment. If we write "Fluoridation of drinking water reduces dental caries," we are stating an inference—an inductive generalization—based on facts; we are not stating fact. (Obviously, the word *fact* has several meanings, one of which is applicable to what we have just called an inference. *Fact*, as the term is used here, refers to a state of affairs capable, at least in principle, of being observed.) If we write "Since fluoridation of drinking water reduces dental caries, community *X* should fluoridate its water supply," we have stated a judgment (phrased as a recommendation), based on an inference, which is in turn based on facts. However, if we write "In community *Y*, before the fluoridation of the water supply, 642 dental caries per thousand first-graders were found; five years after fluoridation of the water supply, there were 218 cases of dental caries per thousand first-graders," we come as close as practicable to factual statement. When our purpose is to report, it is essential that we distinguish and eliminate inference and judgment.

When we report on something we have read—a kind of experience—special care is required. For when the experience is cast in words already, the ready-made verbal segments of the total experience easily slip through our attempt to analyze them allowing us, say, to repeat an inference under the guise of a fact. It is especially demanding upon our attention to distinguish in our own writing, for example, between an inference and a report of an inference that appears in the written material we are reporting on. Because students must frequently use reports on reading, as in the writing of examinations and course papers, it is important for them to understand this distinction and to have practice in writing such reports.

The problems of writing a report suggest at once its strength and its limitation. The strength of the report lies in its ability to convey information plainly and without affective elements which tend to distort or conceal facts or shape an attitude toward them. When our intention is to convey facts by themselves, the report is our only resource. The limitation of the report is that it gives only facts. It leaves out much that we usually need for responsible writing and much that is often of greatest importance in general communication. It has, in short, a specialized function and is seldom the only element in an extended piece of writing.

Another problem of the report is one of selection: how many facts should be stated from the immense number usually available, and which ones should be selected and which rejected? Suppose, for instance, that we were assigned to write a report on the Army-Navy football game. Some comment on the structure, size, and facilities of the stadium might be relevant. But how much? It is conceivable that a long paper or even a book might be written just on the stadium. Some comment on the crowd might be relevant. Again, how much? Detailed description of each of 90,000 people attending, their clothing, their professions, or their reasons for attending would be taking things too far. Relevance is a problem even when we are commenting on the actions of the players on the playing field: each play involves separate and often multiple actions of twenty-two different men; different plays involve different actions; and every play occurs under a new set of circumstances.

Clearly, a report must have a specific limiting purpose. It is the writer's responsibility to define that purpose, making it plain to the reader either explicitly or implicitly, and then sustain that purpose throughout the entire report. Often the purpose of a report is defined by the end which the report is designed to serve. An engineer's report, for example, may be presented with a series of recommendations for improving the efficiency of an operation or for inaugurating a new process. The definition of purpose for a report serves a function similar to the hypothesis in explanation: it assists the writer in selecting information.

Both completeness and accuracy of a report are ultimately pragmatic issues in each separate situation which requires a report. In one case a footnote listing sources of information for a statement, or sources for further information on a topic, may serve as an adequate report. In another, a report may run into dozens of pages. For one audience entirely unfamiliar with the subject, a thorough, detailed, and lengthy account may be required. For another, somewhat familiar with the subject, much can be left out, condensed, or merely alluded to. In report writing, as in any other kind of writing, the pragmatic problems of intention, audience, occasion, and the like, can be solved only by assumption of individual responsibility.

APPENDIX C

Responsibility and Correct Acknowledgment

WHENEVER, in our writing, we draw directly on the writing of someone else, it is our responsibility to acknowledge that fact. The procedure of acknowledgment is conventional. That is, there are generally understood simplified techniques for showing indebtedness to other writing. As both writers and readers, we must understand these techniques and abide by them.

Responsibility for correct acknowledgment is undertaken in two ways. First, we need to show what we have borrowed, and in what form we are using it; second, we need to identify the source of the material we have borrowed.

Material drawn from another person's writing may be used in various ways, ranging from allusion or brief reference, to summary, to paraphrase, to quotation. There are conventions to simplify our indication of all these. In order to observe various ways of using outside material and the conventions for acknowledging them, let us assume that we have found the material which appears below in a book called *The New History;* on the title page of this book James Harvey Robinson is named as the author, and The Macmillan Company, in New York, is given as the publisher in 1912. The material appears on pages 17-20 of Robinson's book.

History is doubtless

> *An orchard bearing several trees*
> *And fruits of different tastes.*

It may please our fancy, gratify our serious or idle curiosity, test our memories, and, as Bolingbroke says, contribute to "a creditable kind of ignorance." But the one thing that it ought to do, and has not yet effectively done, is to help us to understand ourselves and our fellows and the problems and prospects of mankind. It is this most significant form of history's usefulness that has been most commonly neglected.

It is true that it has long been held that certain lessons could be derived from the past,—precedents for the statesman and the warrior, moral guidance and consoling instances of providential interference for the commonality. But there is a growing suspicion, which has reached conviction in the minds of most modern historians, that this type of usefulness is purely illusory. The present writer is anxious to avoid any risk of being regarded as an advocate of these supposed advantages of historical study. Their value rests on the assumption that conditions remain sufficiently uniform to give precedents a perpetual value, while, as a matter of fact, conditions, at least in our own time, are so rapidly altering that for the most part it would be dangerous indeed to attempt [page 17] to apply past experience to the solution of current problems. Moreover, we rarely have sufficient reliable information in regard to the supposed analogous situation in the past to enable us to apply it to present needs. Most of the appeals of inexpensive oratory to "what history teaches" belong to this class of assumed analogies which will not bear close scrutiny. When I speak of history enabling us to understand ourselves and the problems and prospects of mankind, I have something quite different in mind, which I will try to make plain by calling the reader's attention to the use that he makes of his own personal history.

We are almost entirely dependent upon our memory of our past thoughts and experiences for an understanding of the situation in which we find ourselves at any given moment. To take the nearest example, the reader will have to consult his own history to understand why his eyes are fixed upon this particular page. If he should fall into a sound sleep and be suddenly awakened, his memory might for the moment be paralyzed, and he would gaze in astonishment about the room, with no realization of his whereabouts. The fact that all the familiar objects about him presented themselves plainly to his view would not be sufficient to make him feel at home until his memory had come to his aid and enabled him to recall a certain portion of his past. The momentary suspension of memory's functions as one recovers from a fainting fit or emerges [page 18] from the effects of an anaesthetic is sometimes so distressing as to amount to a sort of intellectual agony. In its normal state the mind selects automatically, from the almost infinite mass of memories, just those things in our past which make us feel at home in the present. It works so easily and efficiently that we are unconscious of what it is doing for us and of how dependent we are upon it. It supplies so promptly and so precisely what we need from the past in order to make the present intelligible that we are beguiled into the mistaken notion that the present is self-explanatory and quite able to take care of itself, and that the past is largely dead and irrelevant, except when we have to make a conscious effort to recall some elusive fact.

What we call history is not so different from our more intimate personal memories as at first sight it seems to be; for very many of our recollections are not personal experiences at all, but include a multitude of things which we have been told or have read; and these play a very important part in our life. Should the reader of this page stop to reflect, he would perceive a long succession of historical antecedents leading up to his presence in a particular room, his ability to read the English language, his momentary freedom from pressing cares, and his inclination to center his attention upon a discussion of the nature and value of historical study. Were he not vaguely conscious of these historical antecedents, he would be in the bewildered condition [page 19] spoken of above. Some of the memories necessary to save him from his bewilderment are parts of his own experience, but many of them belong to the realm of history, namely to what he has been told or what he has read of the past.

I could have no hope that this line of argument would make the slightest impression upon the reader, were he confined either to the immediate impressions of the moment, or to his personal experiences. It gives one something of a shock, indeed, to consider what a very small part of our guiding convictions are in any way connected with our personal experience. The date of our own birth is quite as strictly historical a fact as that of Artaphernes or of Innocent III; we are forced to a helpless reliance upon the evidence of others for both events.

So it comes about that our personal recollections insensibly merge into history in the ordinary sense of the word. History, from this point of view, may be regarded as an artificial extension and broadening of our memories and may be used to overcome the natural bewilderment of all unfamiliar situations. . . . [page 20]

Let us begin with *quotation*—with the borrowing of the words of another person's writing. A quotation is indicated to the reader in either of two ways, depending on the length of the quotation. In either case the source of the material is immediately identified in a reference in parentheses, in a footnote, or in the introduction to the quoted passage in our paper. Short quotations are distinguished simply by quotation marks, as when we use Robinson's concluding statement that "History, from this point of view, may be regarded as an artificial extension and broadening of our memories and may be used to overcome the natural bewilderment of all unfamiliar situations."[1] Because quotation marks indicate that the material appearing between them is the writing of another, the other person's writing must be reproduced accurately. Every word, every mark of punctuation, irregular capitalization, even misspellings will appear as they appeared in the source. The only conventional alteration is the substitution of single for double quotation marks *within* the quotation, required obviously for clarity: "Most of the appeals of inexpensive oratory to 'what history teaches' belong to this class of assumed analogies which will not bear close scrutiny."[2]

Thus any omission or interruption of or addition to the quoted material must be indicated. "History," as Robinson defines it, "may be regarded as an artificial extension and broadening of our memories and may be used to overcome the natural bewilderment of all unfamiliar situations." Our own words, *as Robinson defines it,* occur outside conventional pairs of quotation marks and hence are recognized as ours, not Robinson's. The same technique of closing and reopening quotation marks allows us to omit material from the original statement, in this case Robinson's words *from this point of view.* If the context of our writing makes it undesirable to insert the words *as Robinson defines it* and if we still feel that *from this point of view* were better omitted, ellipsis marks (three period dots), by convention, indicate omission of words within quotation marks, thus: "History . . . may be regarded as an artificial extension and broadening of our memories. . . ." When the omission is at the end of a sentence, the points of ellipsis fall next to the period, making four dots in all. Finally, for convenience, the use of square brackets (not parentheses) shows by convention that material in the brackets is not part of the quotation. Insertions may be for alteration, explanation, correction, interpolation, comment, and the like. "History . . . may be regarded as an artificial extension and broadening of our memories [that is, to include knowledge of things not personally experienced

[1] James Harvey Robinson, *The New History* (New York, The Macmillan Company, 1912), p. 20.

[2] *Ibid.*, p. 18. (This convention comes from the Latin *ibidem* meaning "in the same place." In other words, the source is the same as the one cited in the note immediately preceding).

by an individual] and may be used to overcome the natural bewilderment of all unfamiliar situations."

Longer quotations—more than five typewritten lines, usually—are indicated by blocking the material *instead of* using quotation marks, thus:

> We are almost entirely dependent upon our memory of our past thoughts and experiences for an understanding of the situation in which we find ourselves at any given moment. To take the nearest example, the reader will have to consult his own history to understand why his eyes are fixed upon this particular page. If he should fall into a sound sleep and be suddenly awakened, his memory might for the moment be paralyzed, and he would gaze in astonishment about the room, with no realization of his whereabouts. [Even seeing familiar objects] would not be sufficient to make him feel at home until his memory had come to his aid and enabled him to recall a certain portion of the past. . . . In its normal state the mind selects automatically . . . just those things which make us feel at home in the present. [Its efficiency, promptness, and accuracy in selecting] what we need from the past in order to make the present intelligible . . . [beguiles us] into the mistaken notion that the present is self-explanatory. . . .[8]

Omissions and additions in long quotations are shown by the same conventions used in short quotations.

Drawing upon another person's statement, but expressing the substance of it in our own words, is known as *paraphrasing*. To paraphrase, essentially, is to restate. The purpose of restating may be to condense a longer expression (as we did just above, within the form of quotation), to express an idea in more familiar words, or merely to adjust the statement to our context, manner, and purpose in writing. In paraphrasing the reduced quotation above, we might say: Robinson argues that if we are to understand a particular personal situation, we shall most likely have to rely on personal memory. If memory fails, then, no matter how familiar the objects around us are, we fail to understand the situation. Normally, the mind performs its memory functions automatically, selecting "just those things in our past which make us feel at home in the present." Because memory is prompt and precise in helping make the present intelligible, we easily but mistakenly infer that the present is "self-

[8] *Ibid.*, pp. 18-19.

explanatory."[4] In restating we are still using another person's writing and acknowledge that fact by identifying the source in the usual manner; if we use some of his words, we must indicate that use appropriately. Aside from differences in length, the principal differences between the reduced quotation and the paraphrase of the same passage, both given above, is the relative degree to which Robinson's own words and sentences or our own are used. Each of these is a *summary* of Robinson's original paragraph.

We may also draw on the writing of someone else simply by referring to it, without summarizing it. *Reference* has a variety of uses. When we simply mention the fact that Robinson explains history by analogy with memory,[5] when we dispute his definition without taking time to quote or summarize, when we wish to point out that another theory of the nature of history contradicts Robinson's theory, or when we feel that for any reason a reader might wish to know the source of our information—whatever the reason, we refer or allude to the writing drawn upon by identifying the source of our information fully in a footnote or in the body of the paper.

These are, generally, the ways in which we can use material from other writers and the conventions by which we can show what we have borrowed (by use and placement of references) and the form in which we are using it (by use or nonuse of quotation marks or "blocking," often with direct statement of the form the material takes in our paper). Although these techniques are conventional, the use of them is pragmatic and leaves responsibility for that use always with the writer (and the reader). There is no intrinsic merit, for example, in either avoiding or using direct quotations; to only allude and never summarize might cause the reader difficulty. However, there is no defensible reason to disguise another person's ideas, and especially his words, by neglecting—either deliberately or through carelessness—to show that the material we present is not our own. The moral demands for honesty are codified in copyright laws, college policy, and instructor's specifications.

Forms for identifying sources of information vary. Publishing companies, encyclopedias, and periodicals for scholarly organizations, scientific information, and government offices often differ

[4] *Ibid.*
[5] *Ibid.*, pp. 17-20.

from each other in the forms they prescribe for documentation, and even within these groups there are differences. Here again convention is the rule: part of our obligation as writers (and readers) is to learn which forms are prescribed and to observe meticulously the rules set for their use.

In college composition courses the forms are usually stipulated in a handbook, style sheet, or specially prepared guide for documentation. The examples offered here are all drawn from material in this textbook. Their form represents conservative practice in order that they may illustrate the order and punctuation of the more thorough and inclusive methods of correct acknowledgment.

FOOTNOTES

[1] William James, "What Pragmatism Means," *Pragmatism* (New York, Longmans, Green and Co., Inc., 1907), pp. 43-66.

[2] Roy Dubisch, *Trigonometry* (New York, The Ronald Press Company, 1955), p. 5.

[3] "Cubism," *Collier's Encyclopedia,* Vol. VI.

[4] "Motive," *Dictionary of Psychology,* Howard C. Warren, ed., p. 171.

[5] "Cubism," *Collier's Encyclopedia.*

[6] From George H. Hildebrand's Introduction, "The Idea of Progress: An Historical Analysis," to Frederick J. Teggart, *The Idea of Progress: A Collection of Readings* (Berkeley, University of California Press, 1949), pp. 3-4, 29, 26.

[7] *Ibid.,* pp. 9-14.

[8] John B. Bury, *The Idea of Progress* (New York, The Macmillan Co., 1920).

[9] Julian Huxley, *Evolution in Action* (New York, Harper & Brothers, 1953), p. 74.

[10] Edward Sapir, "Language," *Encyclopedia of the Social Sciences,* IX (1933), 161-164.

[11] *Ibid.*

[12] Albert Einstein, Foreword to Philipp Frank, *Relativity—A Richer Truth* (Boston, The Beacon Press, 1950).

[13] J. V. Cunningham, "Logic and Lyric," *Modern Philology,* LI (August, 1953), 33-41.

[14] Sapir, "Language," p. 164.

[15] Carl G. Hempel and Paul Oppenheim, "The Logic of Explanation," reprinted in Herbert Feigl and May Brodbeck, eds., *Readings in the*

Philosophy of Science (New York, Appleton-Century-Crofts, Inc., 1953), pp. 319-352.

BIBLIOGRAPHY

BURY, James B. *The Idea of Progress* (New York, The Macmillan Company, 1920).

Collier's Encyclopedia, Vol. VI. Article, "Cubism."

CUNNINGHAM, J. V. "Logic and Lyric," *Modern Philology*, LI (August, 1953), 33-41.

Dictionary of Psychology, Howard C. Warren, ed. (Boston, Houghton Mifflin Co., 1934).

DUBISCH, Roy. *Trigonometry* (New York, The Ronald Press Company, 1955), p. 5.

EINSTEIN, Albert. Foreword to Philipp Frank, *Relativity—A Richer Truth* (Boston, The Beacon Press, 1950).

HEMPEL, Carl G., and Paul OPPENHEIM. "The Logic of Explanation," reprinted in Herbert Feigl and May Brodbeck, eds., *Readings in the Philosophy of Science* (New York: Appleton-Century-Crofts, Inc., 1953), pp. 319-52.

HILDEBRAND, George H. Introduction to Frederick J. Teggart, *The Idea of Progress: A Collection of Readings* (Berkeley, University of California Press, 1949).

HUXLEY, Julian. *Evolution in Action* (New York, Harper & Brothers, 1955).

JAMES, William. "What Pragmatism Means," *Pragmatism* (New York, Longmans, Green and Co., Inc., 1907), pp. 43-81.

SAPIR, Edward. "Language," *Encyclopedia of the Social Sciences*, Vol. IX (1933).